The 90th O. V. I. Colors, as brought from the war. Taken at Camp Dennison, O., June 1865. The center man is D. C. Goodwin; the one on his left is Jacob S. Cockerill; the one on his right is Andrew Irvin. The latter has been dead some years. The others are living in 1902.

# HISTORY OF THE
# 90TH OHIO
# VOLUNTEER INFANTRY

## IN THE
## WAR OF THE GREAT REBELLION
## IN THE
## UNITED STATES

### 1861 TO 1865

H. O. Harden

HERITAGE BOOKS
2025

# HERITAGE BOOKS

*AN IMPRINT OF HERITAGE BOOKS, INC.*

## Books, CDs, and more—Worldwide

For our listing of thousands of titles see our website
at
www.HeritageBooks.com

A Facsimile Reprint
Published 2025 by
HERITAGE BOOKS, INC.
Publishing Division
5810 Ruatan Street
Berwyn Heights, MD 20740

Originally published:
Stoutsville, Ohio
Press of Fairfield-Pickaway News
April 1902

International Standard Book Number
Paperbound: 978-0-7884-4147-9

## ONLY AN OLD TATTERED FLAG.

*❧ ❧ ❧*

Only an old tattered flag,
But still heaven never smiled upon banner so brightly before.
'Tis the emblem of freedom, the hope of our nation,
The flag of our country and it we adore.

Only a weather-stained piece of bunting,
Only a rag I hold to view,
But by it's power I conquered the lion,
And bound him with threads of the red, white and blue.

Only a remnant of that once mighty army,
Only a few now remaineth with you,
Only a few more years at most and that army
Will camp no more 'neath the red, white and blue.

From a photo by H. O. Harden, 1900.

The 90th O. V. I. Monument at Chickamauga, Ga. This marks the position of the regiment from the afternoon of Sept. 19, 1863, until its withdrawal from the field, Sept. 20, 1863. On the opposite page is the inscription on the bronze plate in the base of the Monument.

## INSCRIPTION ON THE 99th MONUMENT.

### ✌ ✌ ✌

This Regiment, Col. Charles H. Rippey commanding, became engaged on the 19th of September, 1863, about 12:30
P. M., in the south side of the Brock field, about 1200 yards
east of the Lafayette Road. The fight lasted about two hours
and was very hot. There was a cessation of firing for nearly
two hours, during which it replenished ammunition. About
4:30 P. M., there was an assault on the right flank of the
Brigade. The regiment changed front to the right, made a
successful charge and took some prisoners. It was then withdrawn by orders to the Rossville road.

September 20, 1863, from daylight till about 11 o'clock
A. M., it was in the second line, a short distance in the
rear of this position. At that time it relieved the regiment in
the first line, and occupied this position till about 5:30 P.
M., when it withdrew under fire, by orders, for Rossville.

Loss.— Killed, 7; wounded, 62; missing, 15; total, 84.

From a photo by H. O. Harden, 1900.

Position of the 90th O. V. I. at the battle of Chickamauga. The farthest monument is the 90th. The battery is the 1st Ohio. The scars in the pine tree, 6 feet from the ground, were made by Confederate shot.

# DEDICATION.

T HIS volume is dedicated to my comrades who died on the field of battle; in hospital and prison pens; to those who have died since the war; to those who are yet living; to our brave and loyal fathers, mothers, brothers, sisters, wives and sweethearts who so nobly stood by us and our flag during the great Civil War.

H. O. HARDEN,

Pres. 90th O. V. I. Association.

# OFFICERS

## 90TH O. V. I. ASSOCIATION—1901-2.

H. O. HARDEN, *President*....................Stoutsville, O.

THOMAS PARRISH, *Vice President*.................Stella, O.

JOHN W. TRITSCH, *Secretary-Treasurer*.........Logan, O.

CAPT. JOHN S. WITHERSPOON, *Chaplain* .........Creola, O.

MRS. S. M. YEOMAN, *Mother of the Regiment*..........
....................................Washington C. H., O.

### HONORARY MEMBERS.

MRS. A. R. KELLER.................... Lancaster, O.

MISS HELEN KELLER................. Lancaster, O.

REV. E. ROSE........................ New Lexington, O.

DAVID JENNINGS .................... Atlanta, O.

CAPT. U. R. BENDING (Confederate).... Hallsville, O.

DENNIS PIPER ...................... Lancaster. O.

M. J. DILGER........................ Colfax, O.

MRS. MARY FLOWERS................. Columbus O.

CAPT. FRANK P. MUHLENBERG, U. S. A. Galesburg. Mich.

CAPT. E. R. BLACK, wife, and daughter,
Helen ........................... Leistville, O.

CAPT. G. M. EISCHELBERGER........... Jeffersonville, O.

ADAM BROWN (died)................. Starr, O.

NATHAN WILCOX .................... Jeffersonville, O.

R. S. WILCOX........................ Hamden Junction, O.

GENERAL I. M. KIRBY................. Upper Sandusky, O.

DR. G. A. HARMON................... Lancaster, O.

MISS MAE MONTGOMERY.............. Logan, O.

J. E. TRITSCH....................... Logan, O.

GEORGE C. ANGLE.................... Fulton, Kan.

MRS. JENNIE OGLE.................... Washington C. H., O.

REV. DR. C. B. TAYLOR................ McArthur, O.

5

## LIST OF BATTLES IN WHICH THE REGIMENT WAS ENGAGED.

Perryville, Ky ................ Oct. 8, 1862.
Stone River, Tenn............. Dec. 31, 1862, Jan. 2, 1863.
Ringgold, Ga ................. 1863.
Tullahoma Campaign .......... Sept. 11, 1863.
Chickamauga, Ga ............. Sept. 19 and 20, 1863.
Resaca, Ga ................... May 14 and 15, 1864.
Kenesaw Mountain, Ga......... June 9–30, 1864.
Battle of Kenesaw Mountain..... June 27, 1864.
Nickajack Creek, Ga........... July 2–5, 1864.
Atlanta, Ga .................. July 22, 1864.
Jonesboro, Ga ................ August 31 to Sept. 1, 1864.
Franklin, Tenn ............... Nov. 30, 1864.
Nashville, Tenn .............. Dec. 15–16, 1864.
Asheville, N. C............... April 6, 1865.

Besides the smaller engagements of Wild Cat, Ky,; Burnt Hickory, Ga.; Bald Knob, Ga.; Columbia Tenn., and almost innumerable skirmishes.

6

# A TRIBUTE TO THE 90TH O. V. I.
### BY GENERAL I. M. KIRBY.

UPPER SANDUSKY, O., *December 26, 1901.*

*To the 90th O. V. I.:*

I congratulate the "old boys" of the 90th Ohio, that at this late day there is to be printed THEIR chapter in the history of our country. The historic era embraced in the years of 1861 and 1865 is more eventful, fraught with impending consequences more important to the well-being of our country, to the protection of humanity, the advancement of civilization, than that contained in all the combined years preceding, save the seven eventful years that gave our country existence. No men did more to make that history glorious than did the men of the gallant old 90th. You made history as you trudged along on the weary march under the scorching rays of a southern sun, or through the rain and sleet and snow of winter, poorly clad, shelterless at night, with three days' rations of hard tack and bacon in the haversack to last five days. You made history as you stood alone in the silent midnight watch of the lonely picket post. You made history when you faced all day long the deadly storm of shot and shell, and with rigid muscles and undaunted spirit met the charging bayonet. You made history as you lay in the cheerless hospital suffering uncomplainingly the torture of gaping wounds, the agony of burning fever without cooling drink or nourishing delicacy to soothe and strengthen the wasting body. You made history as you silently endured the horrors

7

of rebel prison pens, indignantly refusing all offers of clemency that would break your allegiance. Glorious boys! True to the last to country and flag!

When the marble shaft, commemorating the deeds of heroes shall have crumbled to dust, and the teeth of rust have eaten away the bronze tablet that tells of heroic deeds, YOUR history will be told to the listening ears of children.

With fervent wish that your remaining years may be full of comfort, I am, with kindest regards,

Your comrade,

I. M. KIRBY.

# INTRODUCTION.

*Dear Comrades:*

The history of the grand old 90th O. V. I. has been talked of for years, and at our re-union at Stoutsville last September those in attendance were so enthusiastic that action was taken, and by a unanimous vote the matter was left in my hands, with assurance of financial aid. I have worked the enterprise through the *Fairfield-Pickaway News,* the official organ of the 90th O. V. I. Association, of which I am the editor. I sent out return postal cards to all who do not take the paper, and to some who do. By this means, and by the assistance of many comrades, have succeeded in making it a success, and the history is a reality.

I have not asked financial aid, further than that subscribers pay for the book in advance. I assure you it was a difficult undertaking, after the lapse of forty years, to gather the material, and although I know it is not perfect, I believe it is as well done as possible by any one at this late date.

I have given the names of all who served in the regiment, with a brief note as to whether they were killed in battle; were mortally wounded; died of disease; were discharged for disability, and so far as possible, whether captured or wounded; and lastly, whether they were so fortunate as to serve their time, and were mustered out with the regiment, at Camp Harker, near Nashville, Tenn., June 13, 1865. These personal sketches had necessarily to be short.

As to the engravings, I have given war-time pictures, where they could be procured. I had intended to have a full page illustration for each, but so many of the boys did not respond for a book that I had to "cut the coat according to the cloth." I would have been glad to have given the picture of each subscriber, but that was out of the question, so have given those of the officers; especially those who were killed; some privates, to show how a "soldier boy" of 1861-5 looked; also some who have been very prominently connected with the publishing of this book; and the present officers of the 90th O. V. I. Association.

I give the names and postoffice addresses of all living members, so far as known.

A "roll of honor," containing the names of 234 of our dear comrades, who gave up their lives in defence of the flag; the place and date of death. This will recall to you sad memories.

The manner in which I have arranged the book I think the best. The history proper is in the form of a diary, interspersed with sketches and personal recollections of the boys.

I have attempted to give only the history of the regiment. For the history of the war and its causes I refer you to other historians.

I have been aided very much by our Secretary, John W. Tritsch, of Logan, O.

In writing the diary, I am indebted to Comrades John Chilcote, of Sego, O., and W. G. Mauk, now dead, for their diaries kept while in the service.

I am indebted to so many of the comrades that I cannot name them all, but cannot refrain from mentioning D. C. Goodwin, J. B. Rife, W. H. Strode, J. S. Cockerill, James Dobbins, Capt. William Felton,

Gen. I. M. Kirby, H. S. Brown—well, I must stop, but refer you to their sketches in the book. They speak for themselves, but I must mention Capt. F. P. Muhlenberg, who furnished me the original muster-in rolls.

I have verified dates as well as I could, and to some these may seem wrong, but I have placed the most reliance in records in writing, made at the time. No two persons saw the same thing alike.

I have put the book in a compact form, so as to bring the cost within the price. I could have written a thousand pages as well, and then not have told it all.

I now leave it for your perusal and criticism, but could you, or anyone else, have done better?

Now, comrades, I have done the best I could under the circumstances. I know you and your children will appreciate this little book, and that it will be read with interest long after its author and you have joined the comrades on the other shore.

God bless you all. God bless and protect the country for which you fought, and may "Old Glory" never be lowered from a flag-staff in dishonor.

Your comrade,

H. O. HARDEN.

Stoutsville, O., January, 1902.

# REGIMENTAL HISTORY.

The 90th Regiment, Ohio Volunteer Infantry, was made up of 10 companies: Companies A and F, in Pickaway county; Company B, in Vinton county; Companies C and K, in Fayette county; Companies D and I, in Fairfield county; Companies E and G, in Hocking county; Company H, in Perry county.

August 29, 1862, the regiment was mustered into the United States service, by Capt. Frank P. Muhlenberg (who is still living at Galesburg, Mich.), at Camp Circleville, Ohio. Its aggregate strength was 38 commissioned officers and 943 enlisted men, a total of 981 men and officers; 126 recruits were afterward assigned to the regiment, making a grand total of 1,107 men and officers. Of this number 236 were killed in battle, died of wounds and disease, while in the service. There were 468 men discharged from the service by reason of wounds and disease. There were mustered out June 13, 1865, 363 men who enlisted first, and with the 40 recruits mustered out at Victoria, Texas, the total mustered out was 403 out of 1,107, a loss of 64 per cent. About half of the men composing the regiment were 22 years of age; 16 per cent. 18 years and under. This is the age, on an average.

There are now (Jan. 1, 1902), living, as near as can be ascertained, 408. The longevity of so many is attributed to the fact that they were the flower of the land physically, and that since the war have lived temperate and moral lives, the most of the living members being good Christian men, with several ministers among the number. The youngest of the men are now nearly 60 years old, while the oldest members are near 75, and the oldest one, we think, is Jacob Ulm, of Company F, who is nearly 80, having enlisted at the age of 44. He attended our reunion last fall at Stoutsville, Ohio, and is still living at Circleville, Ohio.

There is some misunderstanding as to the date when the regiment was mustered. The companies were mustered prior to the mustering of the regiment, and on different dates, but the regiment, as a regiment, was mustered Friday, August 29, 1862.

Thirty-nine years — nearly forty — have elapsed since we assembled by companies at Camp Circleville, on the Evans farm, on the pike three miles southeast of Circleville, O., where quarters had been erected, or were being erected. Here all was hurry and excitement. Fathers, mothers, sisters, brothers, wives and sweethearts came to bid adieu to their loved ones, and, in many cases, here it was that they saw each other for the last time on earth. Can we, who are still living, ever forget those memorable scenes? They are printed on our memories with blood and tears, of hardships, privations and sorrow, and when we meet in our annual reunions is it any wonder that we display a more than ordinary friendship for each other? And what led to these sacrifices? Was it money? No. There were none but could have made from three to ten times the pay of a soldier at home. Then you ask, again, was it the love of war, strife and bloodshed? No. We were quiet, country lads, most of us, many of whom had never been fifty miles from home. It was the love of country which had been instilled in us, and we knew but one flag, one government and one people—no North, no South, no East, no West. It was patriotism, pure and undefiled.

On the 29th day of August, 1862, after the regiment had been mustered, or on the evening of that day, the regiment was formed in line and marched three miles to the railroad depot at Circleville. What a long march it seemed, with our overcoats, extra clothing, guns and accoutrements. We boarded the cars about 9 o'clock p. m., our destination being the front. As we reached Washington C. H. bonfires were burning; the people, especially the ladies, loaded us with pies, cakes and other good things to eat. The train pulled out and we were again on our way to the front, arriving at Cincinnati on the morning of August 30, and disembarked. Many were strung along on Front street, on cellar doors, some sleeping, some already homesick, some having fun, until later, when we were ferried across the Ohio river to Covington, Ky., where it reported to Maj. Gen. Wright. Breakfast was served the regiment here. At 10 o'clock a. m. the regiment took up the march for the K. C. depot, and on its way passed the home of Jesse R. Grant, father of Gen. U. S. Grant, stopped and gave three cheers for the old gentleman, then resumed the march to the depot. Here we boarded the cars, box cars at that, with orders to report to Gen. Nelson at Lexington, Ky. It was the intention to send us to Gen. Nelson as a reinforcement, but the battle of Richmond, Ky., had been fought and lost; Gen. Nelson wounded. We went no farther than Lexington, where Col. Ross reported to Gen. Wright, who had assumed command. He ordered Maj. S. N. Yeoman to take four companies and picket all approaches to the city of Lexington. This duty was faithfully performed until 3 o'clock p. m. of September 1, when the rumor of the advance of the rebel army from Richmond, Ky., under Gen. Kirby Smith became so strong that orders were issued to burn the army stores and prepare to move at once. By 7 o'clock p. m. the regiment was in line on the Versailles pike, detailed as guard for the wagon train, four companies in the rear under Maj. Yeoman, and six companies in advance under Cols. Ross and Rippey. When we started most of the men thought we were going out to have a fight, and were in high spirits. As we marched out to the pike, it being warm, the men cast their new government overcoats in a pile alongside of a hedge fence, intending to get them when they came back, but if any of them have been back since we have not heard of it.

At 4 o'clock next morning the army reached Versailles, a distance of 12 miles, and was in full retreat. On the evening of September 2 we arrived at Frankfort, the capital of Kentucky, crossed and guarded the bridge across the Kentucky river. Here we had plenty of river water.

September 3 we were again on the march, as also on the 4th. On the 5th we reached a camp in a grove, about four miles from Louisville, having marched 100 miles in 86 hours, with less than 16 hours' sleep. The men suffered terribly on this march from thirst and stifling dust. The fatigue was truly agonizing. This suffering was intensely aggravated by guarding wells and cisterns on the pike, which compelled the men to drink from stagnant pools. The army consisted mostly of raw troops, consequently they were unused to such hardships, and many sank beneath the terrible strain. At Shelbyville, a beautiful town, the thirst of the men was alleviated by the clear, cold spring water, kindly issued to each man by the citizens, as the column passed by. This march so completely broke down many of the men that they were never able for duty again. Drinking the filthy water gave them disease from which they never recovered. A stream of water ran by this camp, and its banks were soon lined with men washing and bathing their feet. Some, when they pulled off their socks, pulled their toe nails with them. Here we received our camp equipage, such as tents, cooking utensils, etc.

The regiment was assigned to Gen. Charles Cruft's brigade, Gen. Woodruff's division. It was afterwards Gen. Cruft's brigade; 5th division, Gen. W. S. Smith; 21st army corps, Gen. Thomas L. Crittenden.

Here we first met the 31st Ohio, and visited many old acquaintances.

Just at this time Gen. Bragg with his army had moved north from Chattanooga, Tenn., followed by Gen. D. C. Buell, on a parallel line, but Buell reached Louisville first, and began to fortify. At one time matters looked so badly that the citizens were ordered across the river.

From this camp we were taken on a grand review through the narrow, hot streets of Louisville, at a double quick pace. A hotter set of men was never seen. Hot at the general who ordered it, and hot from the sun's rays in the narrow streets. Many dropped unconscious; the cellar doors formed couches for the exhausted. This uncalled for march was more disastrous to the men than a hard-fought battle would have been, and it was done for the purpose of giving a general a chance to show off. Who was directly responsible for it we never knew.

From a photo taken about 1885.

COL. S. N. YEOMAN.

Col. Yeoman went out as Major, and remained with the Regiment until the close of the war.

FORT WAYNE, IND., March 12, 1894.

While we were camping near Louisville, Ky., from Sept. 5 to the 20, we all surely remember the great review that took place under Gen. Nelson.

We camped four miles from the city. The first lieutenant of Company C, Comrade Black the name, but he was red-headed by nature, and red-hot when we got back from the review.

Well, it is vivid to my memory, and always will be, the ordeal we passed through on that march, that hot afternoon, from four to eight-story buildings on each side of the street, with knapsacks, canteens and accoutrements weighing 60 pounds, with arms at shoulder for about one-half mile and double quick time.

The end came at last. When we got near the river the command "halt" was given. The 90th sprawled out in all forms. Every one of us was too weary, and some completely exhausted, to stand. The most of us lay on our backs, using our knapsacks for pillows. In that attitude we remained for nearly one hour, the quietest repose I ever had in this life, because I was never so tired before nor since, nor never will be, I sincrely trust.

I came to the conclusion then that those who survived that "Nelson Review" could endure all hardships in the future, let the war last five years—four miles to the city, four miles of parade in the city and four miles to camp after the great display of human endurance. No wonder Lieut. Black uttered those thrilling words that I'll never forget. When we reached the spot we left some five hours before the good lieutenant was completely used up. We all felt like fighting Gen. Nelson just then. Comrade Black's words are in my diary, taken down the same evening. They are: "God forbid that I shall ever have to go through hell again. Capt. Caddy, I know you are my friend, and you don't blame me what I say in regard to Gen. Nelson, but let come what will, I'll receive it

cheerfully, let it be fighting battles with the enemy, or
marching day after day on half rations, or death in
prison pen or hospital or on the battlefield, but by the
Eternal I'll never review again for Nelson, or the devil
or any of his kin.

(Nelson was shot shortly afterward by Gen. Jeff. C.
Davis.—Ed.)

The good lieutenant was freckle-faced, but when
we got to camp that evening he took his sword, stuck
it in the ground and then declared those thrilling
words, mentioned already in my letter.

Well, we could not see a freckle on his face. He
was red-hot all over, externally and internally. Wm.
Beecher, of Company D (now dead), told us an anec-
dote on Comrade Mumaugh.

On Sept. 20, 1862, we moved out in the suburbs of
the city, and began to fortify, and the next day Mumaugh began to crave for more to eat. He was always
hungry, day and night. Beecher took Mumaugh to
a bakery to appease his tremendous appetite, and pur-
chased seven loaves of bread for him. Beecher declared that Mumaugh ate six loaves, and the seventh
to the bulge.

S. D. Soliday,
Company D.

We lay in and around Louisville, Ky., until September 29, drilling, digging rifle pits, doing picket
duty, etc., when we moved down the river about three
miles and put up our tents in a potato patch. The
same day Gen. Nelson was shot by Gen. Jeff. C. Davis
in the Galt House, for an alleged insult by the former.

September 30 many of the boys went to the river
and washed up, came back and went out on picket
duty three miles out. Here we smoked our pipes—
we were just learning—and some got quite sick.

Gen. Bragg had abandoned the idea of capturing
the city and moved off south.

October 1st.— We started in pursuit of Bragg, and marched about five miles out on the Bardstown pike, where we camped for the night. Our supper consisted of hard-tack and muddy water, nevertheless we slept soundly.

2nd.— The men were aroused at daylight, made some coffee, drank it, and marched 12 miles toward Bardstown. It rained very hard. The rebels had torn up the bridge and we had to wade the stream. We then lay down and slept in the rain until morning.

3rd.— Marched eight miles in pursuit of Bragg. Were drawn up in line of battle. There was heavy cannonading in front of us. Passed through Mt. Washington.

4th.—Moved seven miles and camped for the night in a rebel camp. Here some of the boys captured some hogs and some honey, and had quite a feast. Water is very scarce.

5th.—Passed through Bardstown and went on picket two miles east of the town. Before we got to this town we stopped and got over into a graveyard where we saw the graves of several of our soldiers.

6th.—The regiment again on the march after Bragg. We marched east from Bardstown, across Rating creek, over the worst roads we ever saw, where we camped near Springfield, having marched 15 miles. Provisions are very scarce.

7th.—Started from camp near Springfield, passed through the town, marched through a very rough country, across the Danville, Ky., pike, through below Lebanon, and camped 21 miles from Danville. Had some skirmishing today. Provisions still very scarce. Our camp was on Rolling Fork.

8th.—This morning we started from our camp on Rolling Fork, marched seven miles toward Danville, and camped two miles from the battlefield of Perryville. The musketry of the battle was distinctly heard, but for some unaccountable reason the regiment was not allowed to take part in the engagement. It is very hot, and water scarce.

9th.—We moved east three or four miles to the west of Danville, near where the battle was fought yesterday. We rested very well and were much refreshed.

10th.—Ate breakfast, marched three miles, passed through Perryville and camped on the Danville road. It began to rain, and rained all night. Water plenty at this camp. Cannonading heard in front all day.

11th.—This morning it turned cold. Got marching orders, formed in line of battle, but did not have to march today. Drew three days' rations, and the men ate nearly all of it today.

12th.—Again ordered to march. Marched past Danville, and within four miles of Camp Dick Robinson to the left of the town, turned around and countermarched back to Danville, and went into camp.

13th.—Stayed in camp until evening. Had plenty to eat. In the evening marched back toward Camp Dick Robinson two miles, and went into camp. Got supper and lay down until 4 o'clock next morning.

14th.—Marched back to Danville, drew three days' rations, then moved seven miles toward Crab Orchard, near Stanford, in pursuit of Bragg. Stopped and got supper, lay down and slept until 10 o'clock p. m., when we got orders to be ready to march, and started at 2 o'clock a. m.

15th. — Marched 8 miles before daylight. .Stopped and got breakfast, and then moved 8 miles, over Copper Creek Mountain, through Mt. Vernon, and camped at the foot of a large hill, in the bushes.

### MY COMPLIMENTS TO THE 65TH O. V. I.

#### COLUMBUS GROVE, O.

MR. EDITOR ; — In compliance with the request of the boys to give experiences of the service, I will relate a reminiscence in which S. S. Rogers, of Co. E, and myself were the principal actors, while on the drive after Bragg, in Kentucky.

My story begins at the foot of Wild Cat mountain, where I had my first ague chill. The regiment was ordered to the Salt Works the next morning, to destroy them. The orders were that "all men not able to march forty miles and back, without rest, must go back to the wagon train, then in camp on Copper Creek, close at hand. Our good old Dr. Tipton gave me an excuse and two day's rations, and I went back, finding S. S. Rogers there on my arrival. He had nothing to eat but beans, coffee and salt. I divided up with him, and we went it three days on my two day's rations, and by that time we began to feel a vacancy in the region where our stomachs used to be.

In those days the 90th was called a green regiment, but we got just as hungry, if there was nothing to eat, as a regiment that was ripe and ready to pull. So Rogers and I and our appetites held a council of war, and the council resulted in an order for fresh meat to season our coffee and beans with. I detailed myself to hunt for a porker which I knew to be close at hand. There was an old rebel lived in the big house on the hill near by, and the house had a porch in front. Green recruit though I was, I had noticed a fine lot of porkers "roosting" under that porch.

Harker's brigade of Wood's division was camped all around that house, and the tug of war lay in the how to get one of those pigs under the porch. I finally went up near the porch, and began picking up some old boards, as if to make a fire, and by some means or other just at that time the hogs under the porch got scared, and started for the woods. I kept in sight of them with my kindlings until they got through the camp; then I dropped the wood and got ready for business. The pigs were driven up on the side of the mountain, and I got a fine one.

By some unexplainable coincidence Rogers was soon on hands with a mule and a couple of corn sacks, and we soon had our forage in camp.

We had unfortunately left head and hide on the spot, and some of the 65th Ohio coming along and observing the relics, reported the matter to the old rebel; he in turn reported to Col. Young, of the 65th Ohio; Col. Young sent out a guard to hunt for the hog, and the guard found the hog cooking in our camp kettle. Young wanted to take the hog, but Rogers said, "No, that is our meat, and when it is cooked we'll look after that part of the program."

"Who is we," asked Young.

"Rogers and I," said I.

"Then I have got you," said Young.

"And we've got the hog," said Rogers.

We were promptly marched to Harker's headquarters, where, for the first time, we came in contact with regular army officers. The General was standing in his tent door, the guard reported, and the General said, "Well, you have got a couple of hog thieves." Sitting down on a large stone in front of his tent, he turned to us and commanded "Attention!" When we failed to come to that position he repeated his command, when I simply said, "Talk away, we're listening." And when, in answer to his question we told him we belonged to the 90th Ohio, he said, "You green troops it appears to me, came out for no other purpose than to plunder and steal. What did you come out for, any way?"

"We came out to fight for our country," said I, "and we're not going to starve while doing it if we can find plenty of hogs."

"Don't you dare talk back to me," said he.

"Don't ask us questions if you don't want them answered," said we.

"They don't know anything; take them to the guard house," said he.

"We know a fat hog when we see it," we responded, as the guard took us out of his presence.

We were taken to the guard house and chucked in with ten or a dozen of the 65th. We lay around until about noon, getting acquainted with the boys, when we were marched back to the wagon train to look after our pork, which the teamsters had finished cooking.

Our good old friend, Col. Young, came over from headquarters and made it his business to propose to divide the pork for us. But we respectfully informed him that as we were paying for that hog, we'd do the dividng ourselves.

The wagon train moved that afternoon, and we laid our plans to get away from the guards. Our plan was to get a guard to go with us to the creek to wash. To get to the creek we had to pass through the wagon train. I was to make the break, and wait for Rogers at the top of the mountain. I got away all right, and waited for Rogers at the proper place, but he failed to put in his appearance. After waiting a long while I made up my mind to go back to Rogers at the foot of the mountain, for I knew he had not got away from the guard.

Just then the officer of the guard passed me, and in reply to my question as to whether he had lost anything or not, he said, "Yes, one of those infernal 90th prisoners has run off, and I am looking for him."

"Did he look anything like me?" I asked.

He looked me over and remarked that he guessed I was the chap. I told him I would be glad to ride back with him, and got on behind, and we went back to the foot of the mountain. He then reported me to Col. Young, and the latter ordered me bucked and gagged for twelve hours.

But I kicked on that, saying, "No, I will not be bucked and gagged. No man can live in that shape twelve hours and I won't die like a dog, with a root in my mouth."

"I have my orders," said the officer of the guard.

"And you have heard what I said to them," I replied.

He went to Young and got the order countermanded by agreeing to stand good for my safe keeping. His name was Lieut. Tonnahill, 65th Ohio.

In a few days we were court-martialed. Gen. Woods, of the 3rd division, was judge advocate. This being our first experience in this direction we were a little anxious as to the outcome, and we did not have long to wait. I have just to remark that a court-martial is a short horse and soon curried.

"Guilty, or not guilty?" they asked us.

"Don't know what you'd call it,' was the reply, "but we certainly killed the hog."

Then the old judge spoke up and said, "They are guilty. Stop four months' pay, and give them 40 days hard labor of 8 hours each day." And we got it. I will just say that when the proceedings were sent up to our good old Colonel, he poked them in the fire, and we got our pay just the same.

I do not care to detail the hardships we endured the three weeks we were under guard, but I look back on them as the hardest part of my army life. I have omitted the bitterest parts of the story because I do not care "to live it all over again," as we sometimes term it.

D. C. GOODWIN.

These men both served their time, proved good soldiers, and were mustered out with the regiment, Goodwin being color bearer. — Ed.

16th. — Got breakfast, marched 7 miles across Wild Cat Mountain to within 4 miles of Wild Cat, and stopped for the night. The road is blockaded with trees, cut by the enemy to retard our march. Some skirmishing on the route.

From a photo taken in middle life.

GEN. I. M. KIRBY.

1st Brigade, 1st Division, 4th Army Corps. Gen. Kirby first
served as Captain in the 15h O. V. I., having enlisted in the ranks
in April, 1861.

17th. — Marched 2 miles, crossed Rock Castle River, to Wild Cat, where the regiment was sent out on picket on top of a large hill, where four companies of Indiana troops repulsed one whole brigade of rebels. This was a cool day.

18th. — Visited the graves of the rebels at Wild Cat. Ordered in off of picket, marched all day without anything to eat. Camped where the brigade had a skirmish about 6 o'clock in the evening. The regiment surprised 1,200 of the enemy, and with a yell, swooped down on them, capturing 200 prisoners, and over 200 head of cattle. Three rebels were killed, and 8 wounded.

19th. — Remained in camp all day, where we had the fight yesterday.

20th. — Called up before daylight for a long march, without anything to eat. Marched 13 miles toward Cumberland Gap and back before sundown. The boys were about played out on reaching camp.

21st. — Remained in camp all day and rested. It is 65 miles to Cumberland Gap, and about the same distance to Lexington, Ky.

22nd. — Got orders to march toward the Gap again. The regiment was on this raid during the 22; 23, 24 and 25, when it marched back toward Somerset, to Mershone's Cross Roads, where the disabled had been left, and then to Rock Castle River and camped for the night. On this raid it destroyed the Goose Creek Salt Works, a valuable depot from which the rebels had long been drawing their supply of salt. Began to snow about dark and kept it up all night.

26th. — Snow six inches deep this morning. Started on the march at 7 o'clock, marched 17 miles and camped. Lay down in the snow and slept soundly.

This was a gloomy Sabbath day. Snow all melted before night, making it quite muddy. The march through this country was of great hardship. Many of the men were without shoes, and marching over the snow, left their foot-prints marked with blood. Some tied sacks around their feet, in place of shoes, otherwise they would have been barefooted, yet they did not murmur or complain.

### A STEER COW.

1862, about October 27th, the time of the big snow in the Wild Cat Mountains, Ky. Would like to know the name of the contractor who furnished beef for the brigade, as I wish to thank him for that roast pork and fine, big, corn pone that was in a grain sack, hanging on the limb of a tree at the side of the road. How considerate I was to leave the corn for the poor horses.

I cannot tell the color of Chilcote's cow, but James R. Vansickle's was a brindle steer. Jim and Ovid Coleman, one night, on picket, got a likely looking cow penned up in a fence corner, Jim patting Brindle on the back, "So, so, Brindle." Then passing his hand to the udder, when Brindle kicked, sending Jim about twenty feet to the rear. Getting up, Jim said, "Thunder, Ove, its a steer cow."

JONAS H. CHENOWETH, Co. H.

27th. — Very cold this morning. Got up and got breakfast and started for Somerset, Ky. Marched 17 miles through mud and snow shoe top deep. Camped 3 miles from Somerset.

28th.—Today was very nice and clear. The snow melted entirely away, and it was nice and warm. We stayed in camp, three miles from Somerset, and rested, without anything to eat until evening, when we drew rations.

29th.—This morning we started on our march again for Columbia, passing through Somerset, marched eight miles and camped on Fishing Creek, near the battlefield of Mill Springs, where Gen. Zollicoffer, the rebel general, was killed.

PEEKSKILL, N. Y.

The recent storms of clinging snows, in which a frosted foliage burdens the forests, and gives a really phenomenal appearance to the landscape, recall vividly to my mind one of the same character I encountered while wearing the blue away down in the wilds of Kentucky—wilds in fact differing from what they were in the days of Boone and Davy Crocket only in the absence of "bars," the coons and opossums were still there.

We had been down to Wild Cat, in the direction of Cumberland Gap, and while our command was pursuing a fleeing enemy, it became necessary to send to the rear many who had broken down under our daily forced marches. I remember one of those days on which we pursued the enemy seventeen miles and returned to sleep in the bivouac, called camp, that night.

At this time our brigade was to go out and destroy a salt works. Of those who were thought unfit to travel 38 miles before night and back the next day, I was one. A few hours after the brigade had gone those of us in the rear were ordered farther back, a distance of 15 miles. We were given two days in which to make the distance. Arriving then at a branching stream called Rolling Fork, I was put in charge of a detachment of 13 men and ordered to proceed to Somerset, a distance of 30 miles, where we would arrive about the time our brigade would be due at the same place.

It was near the end of October. The weather was mostly fair and dry, with an occasional day that held a chill in the air that would penetrate to one's bones. Remember, we had not been under a tent for a month.

Had traveled a-foot over four hundred miles at that time, had smelled the smoke of battle and heard the whizzing of shells, had lived on half rations, most of us were without overcoats, our only protection at night being one single blanket.

The first day's march was without incident, save that we met our Maj. Gen. Smith and his staff, and his directions were to take things moderately, as our brigade would not be at Somerset until five days later.

The second day was raw and chilly, the sun never once showing himself. At noon we stopped by the roadside to prepare our coffee and hard-tack for dinner. A hundred yards or so down the road a squad from a Kentucky regiment followed our example. Before our meal was quite prepared the 10th brigade of troops, belonging to our division, passed us. After the troops came their wagon train. It halted in front of us. At the time of the halt a major rode up and ordered me to move on with my squad. I explained our situation and he turned to leave us. Just as he turned his horse, a man was removing a musket from one of the wagons and managed to let the hammer of the gun catch in a rope that secured the wagon cover. The gun went off, the bullet whistled past the major's ear, and his instant impression was that one of my squad had shot at him. Then there was fun. The situation was really an alarming one, for the major became as fierce as a madman, uttering imprecations and threats, and riding about giving orders and making frantic efforts to find the culprit who dared fire at an officer. I felt the gravity of the situation, for I saw that the major in his anger was likely to do some one an injury, but to this day I distinctly recall how I only stood there and admired the tableaux he was presenting to us. He was on a good horse; for he was a Kentuckian. With one hand he kept the animal rearing now here, now there, his other hand gesticulated about his head, and between his own movements and the sweeping wind the red lining of his blue overcoat was all a flutter about his shoulders.

Talk about equestrian statues! Ah, Kodakers, that was a subject to have made your camera smile!

I finally undertook to explain the firing of the gun to the major. He would listen to nothing. "I'll see if you don't get out of this! Move on!" he exclaimed, turned his horse once more and rode to the group of Kentuckians below us. Then he jumped from his steed, uttered a fierce blessing upon the men, seized a ram-rod one of them was using as a "broiler" to roast a ration of bacon, and with the rod the major gave one of the men a good drubbing.

Well, we concluded we would move on, and as a result we bivouaced that night near the 10th brigade. They reaching camp first, gobbled up all the fence rails and loose firewood about, so we could find only a scant supply. We had likewise a scant supply of food, so our supper was soon prepared, and as it was dark before we made our halt, and we were very tired we soon disposed ourselves to rest. Our number had been increased by one, a straggler who had joined us from another company.

Reader, imagine a day's tramp through a chilling wind, a scant supper prepared by your own hands, a short supply of fire wood, a single worn blanket to wrap about you. I say imagine the discomfort of it. But you can't! And no one can describe it so you can imagine it.

Winding my blanket around me I leaned against a slender tree, as near the fire as I could get without scorching, and went to sleep. It is the brief forgetfulness in sleep that enables us to endure. I don't know how long I had slept, but I awoke and found I had rolled away from the tree, and was half covered with snow. That was a new experience, but I think I was only half awake, for I shook off the snow, crept back to my place, and repeated the same routine several times before morning.

In the morning the ground was hidden with six inches of soft snow.

I dread six inches of snow now because we have sidewalks — and an ordinance — but in our condition, and with our journey, it was simply too much to think of enduring. We waited before setting out on the march until the brigade ahead of us should break a path. While we waited word came to us that the major of the day before was a major under arrest that morning, the Kentuckian whom he had beaten having reported the occurrence to the general in command. We also received especial word that the rear guard of the brigade had instructions not to interfere with my squad. So we were at least free again to "go as we pleased"—but there is somehow a sort of understanding on the part of a soldier that "go as you please" does not mean to go home. Since we will not meet the major again, I will say that a few years ago I read an account in the New York papers of his getting into a fracas in Kentucky; and since then I have read an account of his death. Peace to him! He made a fine picture once in his time.

When we thought the roads had been well broken we set out on our march. They had indeed been well broken, churned, in fact, into a slush of snow and mud. Our march that day was barely more than five miles. I think the beauty of the forests was all that helped me over the journey. The great trees were bending beneath the masses that clung to them just as it has on two occasions here this winter, and every now and then a tremendous crash and roar would come out of the shadows, as some mighty branch gave way under the weight. The snow fall was a phenomenal one there, an old gray-haired darkey, whom we met, telling me that in all his life he had never before seen such a storm. In comparison with the discomforts the day before, this day was terrible. Our dinner consisted of parched corn. We overtook numerous stragglers from the brigade ahead of us, and some were not more than half clad, and might as well been without shoes. One poor fellow I saw, who coughed as

though each paroxysm might be his last, had pieces
of bagging tied about his feet in lieu of shoes. When
I met my regiment again, the boys told me that during
their forced marches through the snow some of them
left blood in their footprints. The snow disappeared
rapidly that day, but the night set in freezing cold.
We halted at dusk near a farm house, and spent the
night in comparative luxury, sleeping in hay in what
was actually called a barn, and although a mule was
unhaltered in a corner of the place, and our blankets
being wet were soon frozen stiff, we really slept comfortably on a pile of hay. The next morning I pur-
chased a big corn "pone" which made us a sumptuous
feast, and we resumed our march, once more ready
"to do or die."                    H. ANDERSON.

30th. — To-day we had a very hard march.
Marched 22 miles and carried our knapsacks all day.
We ate all our rations before night.

31st. — This morning we started again without anything to eat, except what we could pick up along the
way, and arrived in camp at Columbia after dark, where
we drew rations for two days, to last us four days.
Marched over twenty miles to-day, making the 31st
day of our march. We received mail to-day. It has
been nice weather. Warm during the day, but cold at
night. This ends one month of hard marching. The
regiment has now marched about 400 miles since leaving Lexington, Ky., and about 600 miles since leaving
home, two months ago. This surely is a great record
for raw troops.

November 1-2. — We lay in camp and washed our
clothes. Had plenty to eat. Drew some clothing, but
not much. This is a nice place, but we will have to
travel on. This is Sunday, or would be if we were
at home. Stayed here until 2 o'clock, got ready and

started on the march for Glasgow, Ky. Moved 8 miles and camped for the night. Here some of the boys got about 20 pounds of honey. It is said it was John Chilcote and Ras Cooper.

3rd. — Again started on the march and marched 15 miles and camped, passing through Edmonton, a small town 22 miles from Columbia.

4th. — This morning we started on the march again, marched to within 2 miles of Glasgow, Ky., halted and got dinner. Rested one hour and resumed our march, passing through Glasgow, and one mile beyond and went into camp.

5th. — This was a nice, clear day and we remained in camp all day, rested and washed and cleaned up ourselves. One of the boys traded a pair of old shoes for bread, and then sold the bread for 50 cents.

6th. — Cleaned up our tents this morning. Drew some clothing. The regiment had dress parade at 4 o'clock. Began raining at dark and rained all night.

7th. — This was a very bad day. It rained and snowed, and was very cold. Drew rations to-day to last four days.

8th. — Left Columbia this morning and started for Tennessee. Marched 18 miles and crossed two rivers. The bridges were burned and we had to wade them.

9th. — Started again, marched 8 miles and camped at Scottsville. We had preaching here to-day, the first time since we left Louisville.

10th. — Left camp and started for Gallatin, Tenn. Marched across the line between Kentucky and Tennessee, at noon. Ate dinner and marched 8 miles and camped for the night.

11th. — Resumed our march this morning, marched 19 miles to Gallatin, passed through town and went 4

HENRY O. HARDEN, CO. G.
President 90th O. V. I. Association, and Publisher
of this Book, 1900.

miles to the Cumberland river and went into camp about sundown.

12th. — Left our camp, crossed the Cumberland River on trestles, passed through Gallatin, and marched to the Nashville pike, about 7 miles, and camped.

13th. — Moved about 2 miles toward Nashville, cleaned off the ground and went into camp at Silver Springs. There was a new rail fence in front of the regiment, and it was not five minutes until there was not a rail left, but before we got our fires started, an order came from the General to carry the rails back and lay them up, which we did, but the next morning there was not a rail in sight.

14th. — To-day we lay in camp, washed and cleaned up, and cleaned up the street in front of the General's tent. Had company drill, and then went on picket, about a mile from camp.

15th. — Stayed on picket till night, then went to camp and got supper, went to bed, but did not sleep much, as we were too much crowded in our bunks. Got mail to-day,

LANCASTER, O., February 6, 1894.

If all the members of the 90th are as much interested in the letters written by the comrades, as I am, they await with anxiety, the arrival of the mail that brings them your valuable paper. I hope all will give some of their personal experience while in the service.

"The old Blue Hen," by Johnny Moore, reminds me of an adventure in that line.

If my memory serves me right, it was near Gallatin, Tenn. As soon as we went into camp for the night, a comrade and I started out to see if the people of Tennessee had anything better to eat than we had.

The first house we came to, was a Union man. (All the inhabitants were Union when the Yankee army was near.)

We wanted to buy some chickens, (honest now) and he asked us 50 cents apiece. We thought this price a little too high, and parleyed with him for some time. In our interview, we found his love for the Union was not as ardent as it should have been.

But we started out for something, and something we must have.

It was now dark and we must see the chickens before we would buy. He took us to the hen house and held up the light so we could take our choice. After careful inspection, we declined to buy, and bidding him good night, started for camp.

We did not go very far, when we stopped and held a council of war, and decided that 50 cents was too much to pay for chickens out of a salary of $13 per month, and we concluded to try a game of draw.

The house was a double cabin with a porch, or entry between them. The hen house was about 20 feet from the entry and a fence on the west and south joined up to it, so in coming from the rear, we had to climb the fence to get to the door of the hen house. A little risky, we thought, but I told him I would try. When I reached the rear of the building I stopped to listen and I heard him express his love for the Union and the Yankees, (over the left).

Climbing the fence, I entered the hen roost. I knew just where to reach for my rooster, got him by the legs, pulling him quickly down, with the other hand caught him by the neck, but not until he had given one squawk, which aroused the man, who came out, hissing his dog and cursing the Yankees.

It is useless to say I made tracks, holding the rooster by the neck. When I got a safe distance, I stopped to rest, when, lo and behold! my rooster was dead! Putting my foot on his head and pulling with all my might, off come his head.

That night, or should have said the next morning, for we cooked him nearly all night, and then we had tough chicken to eat. W. H. STRODE.

16th.—This is Sunday. We lay in camp all day. Went to a burying in the morning. There was to have been preaching at 2:30, but it rained so hard there was none. Grand dress parade in the evening.

17th.—This was a wet, drizzly day. Had to stand camp guard in the rain all day and all night. One of the boys, David Crist, of Company I, was buried to-day. It was so rainy that we had no drill.

18th.—One of the 31st Indiana boys was buried today. Very rainy, and our regiment had to go out on picket. Another rainy night.

19th.—Left camp at Silver Springs and moved towards Nashville, 10 miles. Left the pike one mile and camped for the night. A man in the 2nd Kentucky got into a fight and shot himself in the thigh and nearly killed the other man.

20th.—Left camp, moved half a mile and camped in the woods. Cleaned off the ground and pitched our tents.

21st.—Lay in camp. Cleaned off the ground and washed our clothes.

22nd.—Had company drill and dress parade. This was a nice, warm day.

23rd.—General inspection this morning of guns and clothes. About noon 100 men were ordered to guard a train to Mitchellville and back, a distance of 40 miles. The detail started, moved to Nashville, crossed the river and camped for the night. This detail started next morning at 5 o'clock and arrived at Mitchellville after dark, got supper and then loaded the wagons, ready to start back in the morning of the next day. It got back on the 26th. In the meantime the regiment had moved to within two miles of the city and camped in an open field.

27th.—Remained in camp today and drilled. This was a cloudy day and quite cold.

28th.—This was a cold day. Had company drill.

29th.—Still in camp near Nashville. Weather cold and windy.

30th.—This being the Sabbath, there was no drilling, but had inspection of arms this morning. Cold and rainy, with a very heavy storm.

December 1st.—We are still in camp. The weather is cold and cloudy. Considerable sickness.

2nd.—Still in the same camp. Cloudy and cold.

3rd.—This was a pleasant day, and the sun shone, making it quite warm. The regiment was called out on grand review today.

4th.—Another pleasant day overhead, but muddy under foot. The regiment had battalion drill today.

5th.—Cloudy this morning, and began snowing about daylight, and kept it up till evening. Consequently had no drilling.

6th.—A very bad, snowy day, and the weather cold. No drilling today.

7th.—This is Sunday, so there was general inspection of clothes and guns. Dress parade in the evening. A very cold day.

8th.—A nice, clear day, but cold. Our brigade went out on a foraging expedition today.

9th.—The boys got back from their foraging expedition of yesterday, and rested in camp, without any drill, except dress parade. Some of the boys received boxes of clothing, eatables, etc., from home, which were highly appreciated. Although the eatables were stale, yet they were from home.

10th.—This was a nice, warm, clear day. Had company drill in the morning.

11th.—The regiment went out on picket duty today. Weather nice and clear.

12th.—Regiment came in off picket duty. John Chilcote, from whose diary we have been quoting, says: "Brother Henry died at 5 o'clock this evening. It was a sad night to me." And next day he says: "We sent Henry to Nashville today to be sent home as soon as possible."

13th.—This was wash day. No drill, except dress parade. Henry Chilcote was taken to Nashville today to be sent to his home in Perry county, Ohio, for burial.

14th.—This is Sunday. We had general inspection in the morning, and preaching at 10 o'clock. Dress parade in the evening.

15th.—Company drill today. It commenced to rain at noon, and kept it up until midnight.

16th.—Company drill today. The wind is blowing, and it is quite cold, but the sun is shining. Still in the same camp.

17th.—The regiment went out to the front today on picket duty.

18th.—After the regiment came in off of picket and rested up we had dress parade.

19th.—Company drill today. This is a nice, warm day, and we enjoy it very much.

20th.—The division went out today on a scouting expedition, and the regiment did not get back until 11 o'clock at night.

21st.—General inspection this morning. We leveled off the camp ground and had dress parade.

22nd.—The division went out on a foraging expedition, and did not get back to camp until 10 o'clock at night. These foraging expeditions were to gather feed for the horses and mules, and provisions for the men.

23rd.—We had until 1 o'clock to wash up, then had a company drill and dress parade.

24th.—The regiment went out on picket duty again today.

25th.—This is Christmas, and what a contrast between *our* Christmas and those who are at home in good, comfortable houses, with plenty to eat and good beds to sleep in, and good nurses when sick. The regiment came in off picket and we afterward had dress parade.

We have been quoting from John Chilcote's diary, in connection with our personal knowledge, and that of others. Chilcote became sick and was sent to barracks No. 1, Nashville. The measles, mumps, chicken pox, smallpox, and about everything else had broken loose and taken hold of the boys, and the death rate was alarming. There are 102 of the 90th buried in the National cemetery at Nashville, including those who were killed. As there is a gap in Chilcote's diary, we now quote from W. G. Mauk's diary, for a while.

26th.—Our brigade received marching orders this morning. This proved to be the advance on the enemy at Stone River, or Murfreesboro. A large army was concentrated here, and moved out on different roads to meet the enemy. Gen. W. S. Rosecrans was the commander of the Union army, and Gen. Braxton Bragg of the Confederate army. Our division moved towards Murfreesboro and skirmished with the enemy's outposts. The regiment passed through Lavergn, which is half way between Nashville and Murfreesboro, on the 27th, and camped on Stewarts creek.

28th.—The army is still advancing on the enemy slowly, and a big battle is expected. What the outcome will be God only knows.

29th.—At 8 o'clock the forward movement was resumed, the regiments marching in divisions and in columns at half distance. We arrived near Murfreesboro, where we remained in position.

30th.—At 7 o'clock p. m. the division was massed in a cotton field, badly mixed, and in no condition for offensive movements. This was within one mile of Stone River.

31st.—The morning of the 31st found the regiment in line. After standing thus for some hours, hearing the din of battle in the rear, its turn came to be placed face to face with the enemy, where it fought as coolly as if it had been on a hundred battlefields. The enemy was, however, in too great numbers, and the 90th being without support, was compelled to fall back on the main force. At 12 o'clock m. the regiment was formed in line on the left of the pike and supported a battery the remainder of the day. The men having lost their blankets and knapsacks, suffered terribly that night from the cold.

January 1, 1863.—The second day of the battle the regiment was in line all day, but most of the fighting was done by artillery. On the eve of January 1 the regiment, with the 31st Indiana, was ordered to charge across an open field. They obeyed, and drove the enemy from its position.

1st.—The day was quiet on both sides, the two armies resting for a death grapple, which was to take place the next day.

2nd.—On the morning of the 2nd the regiment occupied a position on which 58 pieces of artillery had been massed which sent Gen. Breckenridge's rebel corps howling back over Stone River. At 5 o'clock p. m. Gen. Palmer ordered the 90th Ohio and the 31st Indiana to move across an open field. They obeyed, and charged the rebel position still on the national side of Stone River, and with but little loss became masters of it.

The best account we have ever seen of this part of the battle is given in an article in the Chicago Inter-Ocean, and which we give, although its author is unknown to us. The boys of the 90th will recognize the graphic scene described, as they were a part of it. Here is the article, as far as it relates to that memorable charge and counter-charge, turning the tide of battle and the defeat of the first day into a grand Union victory.

"Breckinridge's charge at Stone River on the 2d of January, 1863, has been described by hundreds of officers and military historians, and yet not one gives a picture of the battle on that day as I saw it. Nothing that appears in the official reports of Rosecrans, Crittenden or Palmer, or Bragg, or Breckinridge, shakes the impression or blurs the picture that holds possession of my mind. I read acquiescently the reports as to the situation on the morning of the 2d of January as to the position of the troops, as to what Rosecrans saw and surmised as to what new dispositions were made to meet the expected onslaught, as to what Maj. Mendenhall did in concentrating artillery, as to what happened before the rebels reached the river, and what followed. But another picture comes up in my mind.

W. D. Hudson,
1st Lieut. Co. I.

Capt. S. D. Widener,
Co. E.—1863.

Capt. Robert D. Caddy.

Co. C. Killed Sept. 20, 1863,
in the battle of Chicka-
mauga, Ga.

Capt. A. R. Keller.

From a war-time photo. Capt.
Keller was the President of
the 90th O. V. I. at the time
of his death.

"We were in Palmer's division and our brigade occupied a point of high ground that seemed to extend out tantalizing toward the enemy. We had spent the greater part of New Year's day and night in throwing up breastworks, and shortly after noon, on the 2d, we were lounging in line, arms stacked behind the works, gossiping over hardtack without coffee. There had been a good deal of noise, of course, but artillery firing didn't count with the boys, and just at that time there was a lull. It was so quiet that we distinctly heard the tramp of marching men, and, looking to our right, we saw a full division of our own troops massed in close battle order moving toward us. They came within a few hundred yards, and settled down like a great flock of blackbirds. Then another division settled down in the same way, a little to our left and rear.

"We noticed that there was no talking among the men, that orders were given in low tones, and that the brigades were unaccompanied by batteries. We noticed also that there was a gathering of general officers in our rear, and that there was no firing along the line. There was so little noise and confusion that we heard Col. Granville Moody, sitting on his horse some little distance from us, say, 'May God have mercy on those poor men.' Looking then to the front we saw in the distance great orderly masses of gray pressing forward. On they came, line after line, until there were five lines visible, and then, while we stood gawking in amazement, there came down upon us a hail of bullets, knocking splinters of stone from our breastworks and splinters of wood from our guns, still stacked.

"We dropped to the ground, crept to the gun-stacks, took our rifles, and fell into line along the breastworks. On the instant it seemed to me the heavy masses of men in blue on our left and right spread out like great fans and came into line of battle. Away in the distance to the left we saw our advance brigades crumble to pieces and the men come trailing back. At a signal, sixty pieces of artillery massed near us opened on the advancing Confederate column. We were in the midst of teriffic battle before we realized it.

"We could see then that there had been careful preparation for this attack. We knew that long line of belching cannon was not there by accident. We knew that the divisions that had come over so quietly to us had been sent by some one who anticipated the attack, but to us the storm came like the sudden bursting of a hurricane. Minute after minute passed and still the sixty canon roared and the ground in front of us was half hidden by smoke. Then suddenly all was still again, and looking forward we saw charging columns meet with a crash. We saw thin lines of our own men in blue plunge down into the smoky indistinctness of the conflict. Still we crouched with tense nerves, until the major general commanding the division said hoarsely, 'Go.' Then it seemed to me that the whole army swept forward.

"When I read the accounts of the battle I know that this is not true, but the vision comes up of all the army in sight sweeping forward at a full run; of fleeing men in gray, of captured flags and artillery, until in the dusk we came squarely upon the intrenched lines of the rebel army and were recalled. Then I remember the elation with which the brigadier and major general spoke to us and with what a quick, elastic step we returned to our old intrenchments.

"The picture, as I see it, is that of the magnificent advance of Breckinridge's corps; the silent gathering of our own divisions to meet the attack; the mysterious, awesome silence that came just before the Confederates opened fire; the sheet of flame that came from the line of cannon, the magnificent countercharge of the Union troops, and the retreat of Breckinridge's men, shattered and broken. In no official report, in no letter of any correspondent is the battle described as I saw it, and no historian gives an adequate idea of the tremendous activities of those three hours in which victory came to the Union army."

THE MEN SAVED THE GUN.

TIFFIN, OHIO, January 29, 1902.

*Comrade Harden:*

In the official reports of our Regiment's engagement at Stone River, note that one of our commissioned officers, aided by several "men," drew off one of the abandoned brass field pieces. You will find the officer's name in the report, but *not* those of the *men.* I want to *vindicate history,* if not myself, by saying that I was *one* of the *men* — can't think now, of the name of another of Co. D Boy, who shared in the rescue. As I think of it, now, I seemed possessed of *double, mule strength,* and we marvel when we consider the *inducements* we had to move on, about that time. Any way, we saved the handsome, brass guns, but when we had landed the trophy on *our ground,* we experienced "that tired feeling," which suggested that we "go way back and sit down!"

This is our pleasant recollection of Stone River. Among our unpleasant recollections of that day, is the *strong impression* that when we fired our parting salute, before turning our backs on the Cowan House, somebody was hurt in that great crowd that rushed down on our then weak and abandoned lines. They shot to kill, and when I was detailed to assist in burying our regimental dead, we saw something of their deadly aim. They had both time and opportunity to study *ours.* Just what they found as fruits of our "careless shooting," we can't tell, and it is well.

S. C. GOSS, Co. D.

THE BATTLE OF STONE RIVER.

We give the account of the battle of Stone River, as written by Lieut. Col. G. C. Kniffen, of General Crittenden's staff, who commanded the corps of which the 90th was a part, the account being the best and most accurate we can get, or have seen.

"On the 26th of December, 1862, General W. S.
Rosecrans, who on the 20th of October had succeeded
General D. C. Buell in command of the Army of the
Cumberland, set out from Nashville, Tenn., with that
army with the purpose of attacking the Confederate
forces under General Braxton Bragg, then concentrated in the neighborhood of Murfreesboro, Tenn.,
on Stone River.

"The three corps into which the army was organized moved by the following routes: General Crittenden by the Murfreesboro turnpike, arriving within
two miles of Murfreesboro on the night of December
29th; General Thomas's corps by the Franklin and
Wilkinson turnpikes, thence by cross roads to the Murfreesboro pike, arriving a few hours later; General
McCook's corps, marching by the Nolensville pike to
Triune, and bivouacking at Overall's creek on the same
night. The forward movement had not been accom-
plished without some sharp fighting. The advance of
Crittenden had a spirited action at Lavergn, and again
at the Stewart's Creek bridge. McCook fought at
Nolensville, and the cavalry, under General Stanley,
found the march a continuous skirmish; but the Confederate advance pickets had fallen back upon the main
line, where they rejoined their division.

The armies were about equally matched. Bragg's
effective strength was about 37,712, and Rosecrans'
43,400.

Rosecrans' left wing, under Crittenden, bivouacked
on the night of December 29th, within seven hundred
yards of the Confederate lines in front of Murfreesboro. His orders were to go into Murfreesboro, and
he was inclined to obey them."

We wish our readers to bear in mind, Crittenden's
corps, Palmer's division and Cruft's brigade, and by
reference to the map, can readily see the position of the
90th regiment. — Ed.

"Riding forward, he found the two advance divisions arranged in line of battle, and, against the re-
monstrance of General Wood, ordered a forward movement. Palmer united with Wood, however, in protest,

on the ground that an advance at night over unknown ground, in the face of a force of unknown strength, was too hazardous to be undertaken.

".General Crittenden finally suspended the execution of the order an hour, and soon after it was countermanded by General Rosecrans, who came up to Crittenden's headquarters at the toll-house on the Nashville pike.

"Crittenden's line of battle was the base of a triangle, of which Stone River on his left, and the line of a dense cedar thicket on his right formed the other two sides. General Wood's division occupied the left, with his flank resting on the river, General Palmer's the right, while General Van Cleve was in reserve near a ford of Stone River. Of Thomas' two divisions, Negley formed on the right of Palmer, with his right on the Wilkinson pike, while Rousseau was in reserve.

"The soldiers lay down on the wet ground without fires, under a drenching rain. The slumbers of the commanding general were disturbed at half-past three on the morning of the 30th by a call from General McCook, who had just come up, and who was instructed to rest the left of his corps upon Negley's right. Of his divisions, Sheridan, therefore, preceded by Stanley's cavalry, moved on the Wilkinson pike, closely followed by R. W. Johnson and Davis. Skirmishing into position, the line was formed by resting the left of Sheridan's division on the Wilkinson pike, Davis taking position on his right, and Johnson in reserve.

"The general course of the Nashville and Murfreesboro pike, and the railroad where they crossed the line of battle, is southeast. On the left of the turnpike, and opposite the toll-house, was a grove of trees of about four acres in extent, crowning a slight elevation known as the "Round Forest," in which Wagner's brigade was posted. The line of battle trending irregularly southward, facing east and accommodating itself to the character of the ground, was much nearer the Confederate line in front of McCook than on the left, where the flanks of the contending armies were separated by Stone River. At 4 o'clock General Mc-

Cook reported the alignment of the right wing, together with the fact that two divisions of Polk's corps
and two of Hardee's were in his front, extending far
to his right out on the Salem pike.  General Rosecrans
objected to the direction of McCook's line, and said it
should face strongly south, and that Johnson's division,
in column of regiments at half distance, should be held
in reserve in rear of Davis' right at close musket range;
but he left the arrangement of his right wing with
the corps commander, who had been over the ground.
The right wing, generally occupying a wooded ridge
with open ground in front, was further protected from
surprise by an outlook over a narrow cultivated valley,
widening from left to right from 200 to 500 yards,
beyond which, in a dense cedar thicket, the enemy's
lines were dimly visible.  Confidence in the strength
and staying qualities of his troops, and reluctance to
yield a favorable position without a struggle, together
with the fact that the retirement of his line must be
executed in the night, induced McCook to make the
fatal mistake of leaving his position unchanged.

"The plan of battle was as follows:  General Mc-
Cook was to occupy the most advantageous position,
refusing his right as much as practicable and necessary
to secure it; to receive the attack of the enemy, or, if
that did not come, to attack sufficiently to hold all
forces in his front.  General Thomas and General
Palmer were to open with skirmishing and engage the
enemy's center and left as far as the river.  Crittenden was to cross Van Cleve's division at the lower ford
and to advance on Breckinridge.  Wood's division was
to cross by brigades at the upper ford, and, moving
on Van Cleve's right, was to carry everything before
it to Murfreesboro.  This move was intended to dis-
lodge Breckinridge, and to gain the high ground east
of Stone River, so that Wood's batteries could enfilade
the heavy body of troops massed in front of Negley
and Palmer.  The center and left, using Negley's right
as a pivot, were to swing around through Murfreesboro and take the force confronting McCook in rear,
driving it into the country toward Salem.  The suc-

cessful execution of General Rosecrans' design depended not more upon the spirit and gallantry of the assaulting column that upon the courage and obstinacy with which the position held by the right wing should be maintained. Having explained this fact to General McCook, the commanding general asked him if, with a full knowledge of the ground, he could, if attacked, hold his position three hours, — again alluding to his dissatisfaction with the direction which his line assumed, but, as before, leavng that to the corps commander, — to which McCook replied, "I think I can."

"Swift witnesses had borne to the ears of General Bragg the movements of General Rosecrans. He had in his army about the same proportion of raw troops to veterans as General Rosecrans, and the armies were equally well armed. By a singular coincidence Bragg had formed a plan identical with that of his antagonist. If both could have been carried out simultaneously the spectacle would have been presented of two armies turning upon an axis from left to right. Lt. General Hardee was put in command of the Confederate left wing, consisting of McCown's and Cleburne's divisions, and received orders to attack at daylight. Hardee's attack was to be taken up by Polk with the division of Cheatham and Withers, in succession to the right flank, the move to be made by a constant wheel to the right, on Polk's right flank as a pivot. — The object of General Bragg was by an early and impetuous attack to force the Union army back upon Stone River, and, if practicable, by the aid of the cavalry, to cut it off from the base of operations and supplies by the Nashville pike.

"As has been shown, the Union and Confederate lines were much nearer together on the Union right than on the left. In point of fact, the distance to be marched by Van Cleve to strike Breckinridge's right, crossing Stone River by the lower ford, was a mile and a half. To carry out the order of General Bragg to charge General Rosecrans' right, the Confederate left wing, doubled, with McCown in the first line and Cleburn in support, had only to follow at double-quick the advance of the skirmish line a few hundred paces, to find themselves in close conflict with McCook.

"The Confederate movement began at daybreak. General Hardee moved his two divisions with the precision that characterized that able commander. Mc-Cown, deflecting to the west, as he advanced to the attack left an opening between his right and Withers' left, into which Cleburne's division fell, and together the two divisions charged upon R. W. Johnson and Davis, while yet the men of those divisions were preparing breakfast. There was no surprise. The first movement in their front was observed by the Union skirmish line, but that first movement was a rush as of a tornado. The skirmishers fell back steadily, fighting upon the main line, but the main line was overborne by the fury of the assault. Far to the right, overlapping R. W. Johnson, the Confederate line came sweeping on like the resistless tide, driving artillerists from their guns and infantry from their encampments. Slowly the extreme right fell back, at first contesting every inch of ground. In Kirk's brigade 500 men were killed or wounded in a few minutes. Willich lost nearly as many. Goodspeed's battery, on Willich's right, lost three guns. The swing of Bragg's left flank toward the right brought McCown's brigade upon the right of Davis' division. Leaving the detachments in R. W. Johnson's division to the attention of two of his brigades and Wheeler's cavalry. McCown turned McNair to the right, where Cleburne was already heavily engaged. Driving Davis' skirmishers before him, Cleburne advanced with difficulty in line of battle, bearing to the right over rough ground cut up with numerous fences and thickets, and came upon the main line at a distance of three-fourths of a mile from his place of bivouac. It was not yet daylight when he began his march, and he struck the Union line at 6 o'clock. General Davis now charged the front of Col. Post's brigade nearly perpendicular to the rear. Pinney's battery was moved to the right, and the 59th Illinois assigned to its support. One-fourth of a mile to the right of Post, Baldwin's brigade, with

Color Bearer DAVID C. GOODWIN, Co. E.

Severely wounded at the battle of Chickamauga, Ga., Sept. 19, 1863, being the ninth color guard to fall on the first day. He served as Color Sergeant without promotion.

Simonson's battery on its right, took position behind a
rail fence on the margin of a wood. Carlin's, Woodruff's, and Sill's brigades were on the main line of
battle. Against this force, about 7,000 strong, without works of any kind, Hardee hurled the seven brigades commanded by Manigault, Loomis, Polk, Bush-
rod Johnson, Wood, Liddell and McNair — 10,000
men. The engagement which followed was one of the
fiercest of the day. Baldwin was the first to give way.
After half an hour's spirited resistance, finding the
left of McCown's division in pursuit of the remnants
of Willich's and Kirk's brigades, advancing far beyond his right, Baldwin withdrew to the edge of the
woods in rear of the front line, and tried to make a
stand, but was driven back. The salient angle formed
by the junction of Post's brigade with Carlin's, which
at this time formed the right of the extreme Union line
of battle, was in the mean time fiercely assailed. In
front of Post, the Confederates under McCown, in
command of McNair's brigade of his own division,
and Liddell of Cleburne's division, received a decided
repulse; and Cleburne was for a time equally unsuccessful in pushing back the main Union line. Three
successive assaults were made upon this position. In
the second, Vaughan's and Maney's brigades of Cheatham's division relieved Loomis' and Manigault's. In
the third attack Post's brigade was enveloped by
Hardee's left, which sweeping toward his rear, made
withdrawal a necessity. Sill had been killed in the
first assault. Schaefer's Union brigade was brought
forward to the support of the front line. The dying
order from General Sill to charge, was obeyed, and
Loomis was driven back to his first position. Manigault advanced at about 8 o'clock and attacked directly
in his front, but meeting with the same reception, was
compelled to retire. A second attack resulted like the
first. Maney's brigade now came up and advanced in
line with Manigault's supported by Vaughan's. Turner's Confederate battery took position near the brick
kiln and opened fire, under cover of which Manigault

made an unsuccessful dash upon Houghtaling's Union battery. Colonel Roberts was killed, and Colonel Bradley of the 52nd Illinois, succeeded to the command of the brigade. Having completed the formation of his line, Hardee gave the order for a general advance, and that portion of the right wing, which, up to this time had resisted every assault made upon it, retreated in perfect order toward the left and rear, with empty cartridge boxes, but with courage undaunted. Schaefer's brigade, being entirely out of ammunition, obeyed Sheridan's orders to fix bayonets and await the charge. Roberts' brigade, having a few cartridges left, fell back, resisting the enemy. With the country to the right and rear overrun by McCown's infantry and Wheeler's cavalry in pursuit of R. W. Johnson's routed division, one-half of which were either killed, wounded, or captured, and with a strong, determined enemy pressing them upon front and flank, Davis and Sheridan now found themselves menaced by another powerful auxiliary to defeat. Their ammunition was nearly exhausted, and there was none nearer than the Nashville pike in rear of Crittenden. On the other hand, McCown, in his report, refers to the necessity of replenishing his ammunition at this juncture, Liddell's brigade having exhausted forty rounds per man.

"Carlin's brigade retired and reformed on the Murfreesboro pike. Woodruff held out some time longer, but finally followed Carlin toward the left, taking all the artillery with him, with the exception of one gun from Pinney's battery. Captain Pinney, dangerously wounded, was left upon the field. The withdrawal of the artillery was a matter of greater difficulty. Nearly all the horses having been killed, the attempt was made to withdraw the pieces by the use of prolonges. Lieut. Taliaferro, commanding a section of Hescock's battery, was killed, and his sergeant brought off his two guns by hand. The ground was, however, too rough, and the road to safety too long, and in consequence the six guns of Houghtaling's battery were abandoned. Dragging the remaining pieces of artillery with them, Sheridan's division at 11 o'clock emerged from the

cedars on Palmer's right, passing Rousseau on his way
to the front.  Cheatham's Confederates advanced in
line of battle over the ground vacated by the Union
right wing, and came up with Stewart's brigade hotly
engaged with Negley, while Cleburne and McCown,
sweeping toward the Nashville pike driving hundreds
of fugitives before them, encountered a new line improvised by Rosecrans to meet the emergency.

"Thus far the plan of battle formed by Bragg, had
been carried out in strict conformity with its require
ments.  It now remained for Withers and Cheatham
to drive the Union center back upon the Union left.
The retirement of Sheridan's division precipitated the
entire command of Cheatham and a portion of Wither's
upon Negley's two brigades and two brigades of Rousseau, on the left of the Wilkinson pike, taking them in
front, left flank and rear.  The roar of artillery and
the sharp rattle of musketry had aroused these brigades
early, and they stood in line for hours, in momentary
expectation of an attack upon their front.  This, it is
possible, would have been repulsed; but when it came
in such a questionable shape, preceded by a cloud of retreating troops, but one course appeared to present
itself to the commander, and that was to fall back.
Nevertheless, he faced Colonel T. R. Stanley's brigade to the right, and ordered Col. John F. Miller to
hold his position to the last extremity.  Miller arranged his brigade in convex order, with Schultz's
battery on his right and Ellsworth's battery on the left.
Simultaneously with Cheatham's advance upon his
right, Stewart's and Anderson's brigades attacked
Miller in front.  Miller's lines were barely formed
when a heavy musketry and artillery fire opened upon
his men, who met the charge with a well directed fire.
On his right was Stanley, and the rapid discharge of
Schultz's and Ellsworth's guns told with terrible precision upon the ranks of the advancing Confederates
who soon halted, but did not abate their fire.  The
29th and 30th Mississippi, of Anderson's brigade, made
a dash upon Schultz's battery, but were hurled back
behind the friendly cover of a stone wall, where Stewart

passed them in his charge upon Miller. A bayonet charge was met by the 21st Ohio, and repulsed with great gallantry. The fighting at this point was terrific. All along the front the dead and wounded lay in heaps, and over their bodies came the assaulting host, seemingly strong and brave as when the first charge was made in the morning. But the inevitable result of a successful flank movement, by which the ammunition trains had been captured, came to Negley's strong fighting brigade as it had come to those of Sheridan and Davis. Ammunition was nearly exhausted, and it could only be replenished in rear of Crittenden, whose lines still stood intact. Negley ordered Stanley to retire, which he did in perfect order; and Miller's brigade, after holding its position until the ammunition on the persons of the killed and wounded was all used, slowly fell back to reform in Palmer's rear.

"Rosecrans, having arranged his plan of battle, had risen early to superintend its execution. Crittenden, whose headquarters were a few paces distant, mounted at 6 A. M., and with his staff rode to an eminence, where Rosecrans, surrounded by his staff-officers, was listening to the opening guns on the right. The plan of Bragg was instantly divined, but no apprehension of danger was felt. Suddenly the woods on the right in rear of Negley appeared to be alive with men wandering aimlessly in the direction of the rear. The roar of artillery grew more distinct, mingled with the continuous volleys of musketry. The rear of a line of battle always presents a pitiable spectacle of a horde of skulkers, men who, when tried in the fierce flame of battle, find, often to their own disgust, that they are lacking in the element of courage. But the spectacle of whole regiments of soldiers flying in panic to the rear was a sight never seen by the Army of the Cumberland except on that occasion. Captain Otis, from his position on the extreme right, dispatched a messenger, who arrived breathless, to inform General Rosecrans that the right wing was in rapid retreat. The astounding intelligence was confirmed a moment later by a staff-officer from McCook, calling for re-enforcements.

"Tell General McCook," said Rosecrans, "to contest every inch of ground. If he holds them we will swing into Murfreesboro and cut them off." Then Rousseau with his reserves was sent into the fight, and Van Cleve, who, in the execution of the initial movement on the left, had crossed Stone River at 6 A. M., at the lower ford, and was marching in close column up the hill beyond the river, was arrested by an order to return and take position on the pike facing toward the woods on the right. A few moments later this gallant division came dashing across the fields, with water dripping from their clothing, to take a hand in the fray. Harker's brigade was withdrawn from the left and sent in on Rousseau's right, and Maston's Pioneers, relieved at the ford by Price's brigade, were posted on Harker's right. The remaining brigades of Van Cleve's division formed on the extreme right, and thus an improvised line half a mile in extent presented a new and unexpected front to the approaching enemy. It was a trying position to those men to stand in line while the panic-stricken soldiers of McCook's beaten regiments flying in terror through the woods, rushed past them. The Union lines could not fire, for their comrades were between them and the enemy. Rosecrans seemed ubiquitous. All these dispositions had been made under his personal supervision. While riding rapidly to the front, Col. Garesche, his chief-of-staff, was killed by his side by a cannon-ball. Finding Sheridan coming out of the cedars into which Rousseau had just entered, Rosecrans directed Sheridan to the ammunition train, with orders to fill his cartridge-boxes and march to the support of Hazen's brigade, now hotly engaged on the edge of the Round Forest. The left was now exposed to attack by Breckinridge, and riding rapidly to the ford, Rosecrans inquired who was in command. "I am, sir," said Colonel Price. "Will you hold this ford?" "I will try, sir." "Will you hold this ford?" "I will die right here." "Will you hold this ford?" for the third time thundered the general. "Yes, sir," said the Colonel. "That will do," and away he galloped to Palmer who was contending against long odds for the possession of the Round Forest.

"At half past 10 o'clock Rousseau's reserve division, shorn of one brigade, under command of Major General Lovell H. Rousseau, was ordered into action on the right of General Negley. The two brigades commanded by Colonels John Beatty and B. F. Scribner, known as the 17th and 9th of the old army of the Ohio, were the same that only three months before had hurled back the strong fighting brigades of Hardee on the bloody slopes of Chaplin Hills at Perrysville. The regular brigade, composed of five battalions of the 15th, 16th, 18th and 19th United States Infantry, commanded by Col. Oliver L. Shepherd, under perfect discipline, was placed on the extreme right. The line was formed in a dense cedar thicket, through which Cleburne's and McCown's victorious columns were advancing, sweeping everything before them. On the left the roar of battle in Negley's front showed that all was not lost, and to his right Col. John Beatty's brigade was formed. Scribner was held in reserve. The shock of battle fell heaviest upon the regulars; over one-third of the command fell either killed or wounded. Major Slemmer, of Fort Pickens fame, was wounded early. Steadily, as if on drill, the trained battalions fired by file, mowing down the advancing Confederate lines. Guenther's battery could not long check the fury of the charge that bore down upon the flanks and was fast enveloping the entire command.

"Lt. Col. Kell, the commander of the 2nd Ohio was killed; Col. Forman, the boy Colonel of the 15th Kentucky, and Major Carpenter of the 19th Infantry, fell mortally wounded. There was no resource but to retreat upon support. At this moment Negley's division, with empty cartridge boxes, fell back, and Rousseau, finding his flanks exposed, after a heroic fight of over two hours, fell back slowly and stubbornly to the open field, where his flanks were more secure. Captain Morton, with the Pioneers and the Chicago Board of Trade battery, pushed into the cedars, and disappeared from view on their way to the front simultaneously with Harker. The general course of the tide of the stragglers toward the rear struck the Nashville pike at the point where Van Cleve stood impatiently awaiting the order to advance. All along the line men were falling, struck by the bullets of the enemy, who soon appeared at the edge of the woods on Morton's flank. At the order to charge, given by General Rosecrans in person, Van Cleve's division sprang forward, reserving their fire for close quarters. It was the crisis in the battle. If this line should be broken all would be lost. Steadily the line moved forward, sending a shower of bullets to the front.

"The brigades of Stanley and Miller having fallen back, as previously described, and the entire strength of Cheatham and the brigades of Mithus and Cleburn having come upon Rousseau, the latter had fallen back into the open field, where he found Van Cleve. Loomis' and Guenther's batteries, double shotted with canister, were posted on a ridge, and as the Confederate line advanced, opened upon it with terrific force. Men fell all along the line, but it moved straight ahead. The field was covered with dead and wounded men. The deep bass of the artillery was mingled with the higher notes of the minie-rifles, while in the brief pauses could be distinguished the quickly spoken orders of the commanding officers and the groans of the wounded. It was the full orchestra of battle. But there is a limit to human endurance. The Confederate brigades, now melted to three-fourths of their original strength, wavered and fell back; again and again they re-formed in the woods and advanced to the charge, only to meet with a bloody repulse. All along the line from Harker's right to Wood's left the space gradually narrowed between the contending hosts. The weak had gone to the rear; there was no room now for any but brave men, and no time for new dispositions; every man who had a stomach for fighting was engaged on the front line. From a right angle the Confederates left had been pressed back by Van Cleve and Harker and the Pio-

neers to an angle of 45 degrees. This advance brought
Van Cleve within view of Rousseau, who at once requested him to form on his right.

"General Harker, entering the woods on the left of
Van Cleve, passed to his right, and now closed up on
his flank. The enemy had fallen back, stubbornly fighting, and made a stand on the left of Cheatham. Brave
old Van Cleve, his white hair streaming in the wind,
the blood flowing from a wound in his foot, rode gallantly along the line where Harker was stiffly holding
his position, with the right "in the air." Bidding him
hold fast to every inch of ground, he rode on to Swallow's battery, which was working with great rapidity.
He then passed to the left, where Gen. Samuel Beatty's
brigade were firing with their minie-rifles at a line of
men which seemed to be always on the point of advancing.

"The advance of Bragg's left wing had brought it
into a position at right angles with the original line.
The entire strength of the center, and most of the left,
was concentrated upon the angle formed by Rousseau
and the right of Palmer's division. Chalmer's Confederate brigade, which up to 10 o'clock had lain concealed in the rifle pits on the right of Wither's line,
arose at the order, and under a terific fire, dashed forward across an open field upon Palmer's front. Finding that the time had come for a decisive blow, General
Bragg now directed General Breckinridge to send two
brigades to the left to re-enforce Polk. General Pe-
gram, who, with the cavalry, was posted on the Lebanon pike in advance of Breckinridge's right, had observed Van Cleve's movement and notified General
Breckinridge that a heavy column of infantry and artillery had crossed Stone River and was advancing
along the river bank upon his position occupied by
Hanson's brigade. Interpreting this as the initial
movement in a plan which was intended to strike his
division, Breckinridge declined to obey Bragg's order,
which in his report he terms a "suggestion." At ten
minutes after ten he replied, "The enemy is undoubt-
edly advancing upon me." Soon after he wrote to

JOHN D. NICELY.
1st Lieut. Co. D.

MAJ. GEORGE ANGLE.
1864.
Killed in action near Atlanta,
Ga., July 2, 1864.

SURGEON R. H. TIPTON.
1862.

CAPT. J. S. McDOWELL.
Co. B.— 1862.

Bragg, "The Lebanon road is unprotected, and I have no troops to fill out my line to it." At half-past eleven, upon Bragg ordering him to move forward and attack the Union left, Breckinridge replied, "I am obeying your order, but my left is now engaged with the enemy, and if I advance my whole line farther forward and still retain communicaton with my left, it will take me clear away from the Lebanon road and expose my right and that road to a heavy force of the enemy advancing from Black's." The withdrawal of Van Cleve appears to have passed unnoticed by Breckinridge, and was undiscovered until too late to accomplish any good by complying with Bragg's order. Thus, by simply thrusting forward the left flank of his army and at once withdrawing it, General Rosecrans had held four Confederate brigades inactive at a time when their presence in support of Chalmers might have administered the *coup de grace* to the center of the Union line.

"The movement of Crittenden's left and center divisions upon Bragg's right wing having been arested, Wood's division was in position to cross at the upper ford. Wayne's brigade was at the river bank. Hascall was in reserve some distance to the rear of the opening between Wagner's right and Hazen's left. The withdrawal of Negley from Palmer's right precipitated the attack of Donelson's and Chalmer's brigades against the right, and Adams and Jackson against the left. Chalmer's attack was made in great fury. His men had been confined, without fires, in their rifle-pits for forty-eight hours, and when finally the order came at ten o'clock to "up and at 'em,"they came forward like a pack of hounds in full cry. Cruft recoiled from the attack in the open field between the Round Forest and the wood in which Negley was engaged, and falling back, met the charge at the time that Negley moved to the rear. Now Cruft's right was in the air and exposed to attack by Donelson following Negley. Cruft repulsed Chalmer's in his front, but Donelson's brigade, pouring to his rear threatened to envelop him. Grose, from his postion reserve, faced to the right, and soon after to the rear, and bore back the charging columns, enabling Cruft to withdraw.

Cruft's brigade was composed of the 90th Ohio, 31st Indiana, 1st and 2nd Ky. — Ed.

"When Chalmer's assault first fell upon Palmer's right, Hazen faced his two right regiments, the 6th Ky. and 9th Ind., to the rear, where the impetus of Chalmers' assault on Cruft had borne him, at the same time retiring the two left regiments, the 41st Ohio and 110th Illinois, some fifty yards to the left of the pike and engaged to the front, the 40th Indiana having fallen back. A burnt brick house ( Cowan's ) in the immediate front of the Round Forest afforded cover for the enemy, and in the steady, persistent effort to force back the front of Hazen's line the action became terrific. All of Hascall's brigade, and two regiments of Wagner's being engaged on the right of the 6th Kentucky, and Wagner's remaining regiments being in position at the ford some distance to the left, the assault on the left was borne by Hazen, whose brigade was thought by Polk to be the extreme left of the Union line. Upon this point, as on a pivot, the entire army oscillated from front to rear for hours. Hazen's horse fell, shot square in the forehead. Word came that the ammunition of the 41st Ohio was nearly exhausted. "Fix bayonets and hold your ground!" was the order. To the 110th Illinos, who had no bayonets, and whose cartridges were expended, the order was given to club their muskets. but to hold the ground. The 9th Ind. now dashed across the line of fire, from a battery in front, to the left, to relieve the 41st Ohio. Cannon-balls tore through their ranks, but they were rapidly closed up, and the men took their place in the front line, the 41st retiring with thinned ranks, but in excellent order, to re-fill their empty cartridge boxes. An ominous silence succeeded, soon followed by the charge of Donelson's fresh Confederate brigade and the remains of Chalmer's. The time had been occupied in the readjustment of Palmer's line. The 24th Ohio commanded by Col. Fred Jones, and the 36th Indiana, shorn of half its strength in the previous assault, were

sent to Hazen's support. Parsons' battery was posted
on the left. The 3rd Kentucky, led by McKee, dashed
forward and took position on the right of the 9th Indiana across the pike. The terrible slaughter in the regiment attests its courage.

"While Hazen and Wagner were thus gallantly de-
fending the left of the line from 9 o'clock in the morning until 2 in the afternoon, the fight raged not less
furiously on their immediate right. Here a line was
formed, composed of two brigades of Palmer's division
and Hascall of Wood's, filled out by the remains of
Sheridan's and Negley's divisions, who, after they
had replenished their ammunition, formed behind the
railroad embankment at right angles with Hazen's
brigade, which alone retained its position upon the
original line. Farther to the right was Rousseau, with
Van Cleve, Harker, and Morton on his right. At the
supreme moment the chances of victory were evenly
balanced. The undaunted soldiers of the left and center had swept past the crowd of fugitives from the right
wing, and now in strong array they stood like a rock-
bound coast beating back the tide which threatened to
engulf the rear.

"Along this line rode Rosecrans; Thomas, calm, in-
flexible, from whose gaze skulkers shrank abashed;
Crittenden, cheerful and full of hope, complimenting
his men as he rode along the lines; Rousseau, whose
impetuosity no disaster could quell; Palmer, with a
stock of cool courage and presence of mind equal to
any emergency; Wood, suffering from a wound in his
heel, stayed in the saddle, but had lost that jocularity
which usually characterized him. "Good-bye, General,
we'll all meet at the hatter's, as one coon said to another
when the dogs were after them," he had said to
Crittenden early in the action. "Are we doing it about
right, now, General?" asked Morton as he glanced
along the blazing line of muskets to where the Chicago
battery was hard at work. "All right, fire low," said
Rosecrans as he dashed by. Colonel Grose, always in
his place, had command of the Ammen brigade, of
Shiloh memory, which, with Hazen's and Cruft's bri-

gades, had driven the right of Beauregard's victorious
army off that field. After the formation of this line at
noon, it never receded; the right swung around until,
at 2 o'clock, considerable of the lost ground had been
retaken. The artillery, more than fifty guns, was
massed in the open ground behind the angles in the line
( 28 Union guns had been captured ), where they
poured iron missiles continuously upon the Confederate
line. They could not fire amiss. The fire from Cox's
battery was directed upon Hanson's brigade across the
river, whence Cobb, with Napoleons, returned the com-
pliment with zeal and precision. Schaefer's brigade,
having received a new stock of cartridges, formed on
Palmer's right, where later its commander received his
death wound, the last of Sheridan's commanders to
fall during the day. At 4 o'clock it became evident to
the Confederate commander that the only hope of success lay in a charge upon the Union left, which, by its
overpowering weight, should carry everything before
it. The movement of Cleburne to the left in support
of McCown had deprived him of reserves; but Breckinridge had two brigades unemployed on the right, and
these were peremptorily ordered across the river to
support General Polk.

"The charge of Adams and Jackson, and the subse-
quent attack of Preston's and Palmer's brigades have
been described. The errors made by General Polk in
making an attack with the two brigades that first arrived upon the field, instead of waiting the arrival of
General Breckinridge with the remaining brigades,
was so palpable as to render an excuse for failure necessary. This was easily found in the tardy execution
of Bragg's order by Beckinridge, and resulted in sharp
criticism of the latter. The Union 3rd Kentucky, now
nearly annihilated, was relieved by the 58th Indiana.
The 6th Ohio took position on the right of the 26th
Ohio, with its right advanced so that its line of fire
would sweep the front of the regiments on the left.
The 97th Ohio and 100th Illinois came up and still
strengthened the position. They had not long to wait
for the Confederate attack. These dispositions had

hardly been made when a long line of infantry emerged
from behind the hill. Adams' and Jackson's brigades
were on the right, and Donelson's and Chalmers' badly
cut up but stout of heart, were on the left. On they
came in splendid style, full six thousand strong. Estep's case-shot tore through their ranks, but the gaps
closed up. Parsons sent volley after volley of grape-
shot against them, and the 6th and the 26th Ohio, taking up the refrain, added the sharp rattle of minie-
rifles to the unearthly din. Still the line pressed forward, firing as they came, until met by a simultaneous
and destructive volley of musketry. They staggered,
but quickly re-formed and re-enforced by Preston and
the Confederate Palmer, advanced again to the charge.
The battle had hushed on the extreme right, and the
gallantry of this advance is indescribable. The right
was even with the left of the Union line, and the left
stretched far past the point of woods from which Negley had retired. It was such a charge as this that at
Shiloh broke the strong lines of W. H. L. Wallace
and Hurlbut, and enveloped Prentiss. The Confederates had no sooner moved into the open field from the
cover of the river bank than they were received with a
blast from the artillery. Men plucked the cotton from
the bolls at their feet and stuffed it in their ears. Huge
gaps were torn in the Confederate line at every discharge. The Confederate line staggered forward half
the distance across the fields, when the Union infantry
lines added minie-balls to the fury of the storm. Then
the Confederates wavered and fell back, and the first
day's fight was over.

"New Year's was a day of fair weather. During
the night Rosecrans retired his left to a more advantageous position, the left resting on Stone River at
the lower ford, where Van Cleve had crossed on the
previous morning, the line of battle extending to
Stoke's battery, posted on a knoll on Rosecrans' right.
Walker's and Starkweather's brigades having come up,
the former bivouacked in close column in reserve in
rear of McCook's left, and the latter posted on Sheridan's left, next morning relieved Van Cleve's division,

now commanded by Colonel Beatty, which crossed the river and took position on the margin of a woodland that covered a gentle slope extending from the river to an open field in its front.

"Across this field the Lebanon road running nearly at right angles with Beatty's line, was nearly in sight. In his front and right, an elevation still held by Hanson's brigade of Breckinridge's division was crowned by Cobb's battery of artillery. On the left and rear, Grose's brigade of Palmer's division occupied a knoll in support of Livingston's battery on the following day.

"The Confederate line, formed by Polk and Breckinridge on the right and Hardee on the left, extended from the point of Stone River where Chalmer's brigade had bivouacked since the 25th, in a direction almost at right angles with its original line.

"At dawn on January 1st, the right flank of General Polk was advanced to occupy the ground vacated by the Union army on the west bank of the river. Neither commander deemed it advisable to attack, but each was watchful of every movement of the other. The picket lines on either side were thrust forward within sight of the main lines of the opposing force, on the alert to notify their commander of any movement in their front. Weaker in numbers, but more compact, and decidedly stronger in morals, each awaited the order to advance and close in final struggle.

"General Bragg confidently expected to find the Union troops gone from his front on the morning of January 2nd. His cavalry had reported the pike full of troops and wagons moving towards Nashville, but the force east of Stone River soon attracted his attention. Reconoissance by staff-officers revealed Beatty's line, enfilading Polk in his new position. It was evident that Polk must be withdrawn or Beatty dislodged. Bragg chose the latter alternative, and Breckinridge, against his earnest protest, was directed to concentrate his division and assault Beatty. Ten Napoleon guns were added to his command, and the cavalry was ordered to cover his right. The line was formed by placing Hanson's brigade of Kentuckians, who had thus far borne no part in the engagement, on the extreme left, supported by Adam's brigade, now commanded by Col. Gibson. The Confederate Palmer's brigade, commanded by Gen. Pillow, took the right of the line, with Preston in reserve. The artillery was ordered to follow the attack and go into position on the summit of the slope when Beatty should be driven from it. The total strength of the asaulting column was estimated by Bragg at six thousand men. His cavalry took no part in the action.

"In the assault that followed a brief cannonade, Hanson's left was thrown forward close to the river bank, with orders to fire once, then charge with the bayonet. On the right of Beatty was Col. S. W. Price's brigade, and the charge made by Hanson's 6th Ky., was met by Price's 8th Ky., followed by Hanson and Pillow in successive strokes from right to left of Beatty's lines. Overborne by numerical strength, the Union brigades of Price and Fyffe were forced back upon Grider, in reserve, the right of whose brigade was rapidly being turned by Hanson, threatening to cut the division off from the river. The space between the river bank and the ridge occupied by Grose, now presented a scene of the wildest confusion. The pursuit led the Confederate column to the right of Grose, and Lieut. Livingston opened upon it with artillery, but he was quickly ordered across the river. Crittenden, turning to his chief-of-artillery, said, "Mendenhall, you must cover my men with your guns." Never was there a more effective response to such a request; the batteries of Swallow, Parsons, Estep, Stokes, Stevens, Standart, Bradley, and Livingston dashed forward, wheeled into position, and opened fire. In all, fifty-eight pieces of artillery played upon the enemy. Not less than one hundred shots per minute were fired. As the mass of men swarmed down the slope they were mowed down by the score. Confederates were pinioned to the earth by falling branches. For a few minutes the brave fellows held their ground, hoping to advance, but the west bank bristled with bayonets.

"Hanson was mortally wounded, and his brigade
lost over four hundred men; the loss in the division was
1410.   There was no thought now of attacking Grose,
but one general impulse to get out of the jaws of death.
The Union infantry was soon ordered to charge.   Col.
John F. Miller with his brigade and two regiments of
Stanley's was the first to  cross the river, on the extreme left.   He was quickly followed on the right by
Davis and Morton and by Hazen in the center.   Beatty
quickly reformed his division and recrossed the river
and joined in the pursuit.   The artillery ceased firing,
and the Union line with loud cheers dashed forward,
firing volley after volley upon the fugitives who rallied
behind Robertson's battery and Anderson's brigade in
the narrow skirt of timber from which they had
emerged to the assault.   The Union line advanced and
took possession of the ground from which Beatty had
been driven an hour before, and both armies bivouacked
upon the battle-field. General Spears, with a brigade
guarding a much-needed supply train, came up and took
position on the right, relieving Rousseau on the following morning.

"General Bragg had been promptly notified by General Joe Wheeler of the arrival of this re-enforcement
to his antagonist, and says in his report: 'Common
prudence and the safety of my army, upon which the
safety of our cause depends, left no doubt on my mind
as to the necessity of my withdrawal from so  unequal
a contest.

"Bragg acknowledged a loss of over 10,000 men,
over 9,000 of whom were killed or wounded, — nearly
25 per cent of the total force engaged.   The loss in the
Union army was, in killed, 1,533; wounded, 7245=
8778; and in prisoners, 3489.   Total 10,734.

"Apprehending the possible success of a flank movement against his left, General Bragg had caused all
tents and baggage to be loaded on wagons and sent to
the rear.   On the night of the 3rd he began his retreat,
and continued it south of Elk River, whence he was
ordered  back  to  Tallahoma,  Tenn.,  by  General
Johnston.

From a recent photo.

CAPT. WILLIAM FELTON, CO. A.

Capt. Felton is now (1902) living in Columbus, O.

## OUR REGIMENT'S FIELD HOSPITAL AT STONE RIVER.

While it was the fate of some other regiments to do more actual battling than the 90th, the history proves that it was always alive to its position and duties, always prompt and faithful to its orders, aiming in every instance in camp, march, or field, to do everything that might be required of a regiment, and to this end its faithful officers carefully watched over the welfare of its men, and the completeness of its equipments.

As illustrative of these truths, I recall circumstances that led me across the Stone River battlefield, about two weeks after the engagement. I spent the night in Murfreesboro, sleeping in a store that had been a temporary hospital, and on a counter upon which I was told that a wounded soldier had died the previous night with vermin in his wounds. I mention this incident to show how deficient the medical staff of the army was in needed surgical supplies and attendants, and to indicate by contrast how far ahead the 90th was in its provisions for emergencies.

The next morning I crossed Stone River, and walked across the battlefield, almost over the route taken by our regiment, even looking inside of the brick house that was an object of interest to our boys during the fierce struggle. Arriving 'at the rear of the field, I came to a large, square hospital tent; and my heart gave a bound as I read upon the flag above it: "90 O. V. I." About the hospital were some smaller tents for the diet work and the attendants.

A corporal of the 6th Ohio, wounded in that battle, and taken to our hospital, thus refers to it in a story in Harper's Magazine of 1863:

"There was scarcely more than an hour of sunshine left on that Wednesday, the fearful first day at Stone River, when the driver assisted me out of the ambulance and gave me in charge of the attend-

5 90 O V I

ants at the field hospital of the 90th Ohio. The
large, square-made hospital tent was already becoming crowded, some of its inmates evidently newcom-
ers, like myself. At the further end one of the surgeons was busily at work bandaging a ghastly wound
in the arm of a poor wretch, the sleeve of whose
blouse, cut away at the shoulder and all matted and
stiff with gore, was lying on the ground beside him.
One of the attendants, with both sleeves rolled up
to the elbows, had just set down a basin of water
and was assisting the surgeon in securing the bandage.
Another of the wounded sat on the ground, a little
behind the group, waiting with mute patience for
his turn to come next. Close by, and down upon
one knee, was the chaplain, with a memorandum
book and pencil, taking the sufferers' names, with
the commands to which they severally belonged, and
the home address of the friends of each. Not in
vain, I thought, was even this last care, for it could
scarcely be very long before sad occasion to improve
it would be given by some of our number.

"The surgeon was soon ready for me, and proceeded to examine the wound with evident care and
interest. * * *

"In kind, skillful, tenderest hands, reader, though
strangers all, I felt that I was among friends at once.
Perhaps, though, you cannot have portion in the gratitude that wells up in my soul while I recall their un-
wearied ministrations, you will yet share in my confidence as I end here the story on my part in the
ranks at Stone River."

I think that nothing in all its arduous campaign-
ing gave me more pride in "ours" than this illustration of the readiness of the 90th to be and do the
utmost that was possible for a regiment. Later, I
was identified with some of the hospital work of
our eastern army, and I came to realize nearly all
it meant for a regiment to be prepared to care for
its men when the enemy's bullets put them out of
service. After all these years there comes to me a

thrill of satisfaction with every recollection of that 90th Regiment O. V. I. field hospital at Stone River.

CORPORAL H. ANDERSON, Co. I.

### CONNECTED WITH GEN. PALMER'S STAFF.

"It was after the battle of Stone River, and before going to Camp Cripple Creek, while temporarily camped in the timber, with a farm house near by, in whose yard Gen. Palmer was kindly ( ? ) asked to make his headquarters. Jacob Bibler and James Rittenhouse caught a pig, and were in the act of skinning it. Percival Stuter and I were gathering 'broom sage' for our bed, but came up as the slaughtering was going on, and looking on wishfully, when an orderly, John by name, came riding up and took all four of us to headquarters. Stuter and I proved an alibi, while the other two had every circumstance against them. We were dismissed to our quarters, while they were put under guard. They bore the disgrace ( ? ) of being guarded in camp, while the very next day we bore the fatigue of guarding a wagon train up to Nashville, walking back to camp the second and third days afterward, about thirty miles. When our division commander came to be "Senator John M. Palmer," of Illinois, I wrote to him for a favor, reminding him of my connection with his staff, which he still remembered. He was prompt to grant my request, and ever since I have a cabinet photo of our venerable "Pap" Palmer. It is more than likely the General got the hog.

S. C. Goss, Co. D.

### SNAP SHOT PICTURES TAKEN AFTER MORE THAN THIRTY YEARS.

When a boy we amused ourselves by setting on end a row of brick and then pushing over one at the end, which, by turns, caused the whole line to be prostrate. Here's something like it: When on our forced march from Lexington to Louisville, in

September, '62, we "tuckered out" under our load,
and Captain (then first lieutenant) Sutphen came to
our relief by carrying our gun. Next came Major
Yeoman, on his sorrel horse, and relieved the lieutenant by carrying the gun; then came some unknown comrade, who feigned to be the OWNER of
the gun, and said he'd "take it now," and did. Then
we had no gun to carry, until we came to camp
in the timber, near Louisville. Then, from that on,
we had!

Who took our gun; and whose was the last brick
to fall? Honest, now, and no arrests or court martial
shall follow. Our next view was taken at Stone
River, in the edge of the cedars, before the brick
(Cowan) house.

We stopped behind a tree, a rod or so from the
fence, when our regiment took position, relieving the
2nd Kentucky Regiment, intending, by our more advantageous point of view (?) to silence the rebel
cannon, playing on us in front! Capt. Perry said
some words, and we moved forward, and laid down
behind the fence. Rebels seemed to take advantage
of the fact of my being down, like the rest, with
my face to the ground, and fired more vigorously
now. Captain vehemently commanded: "Why ———
——— don't you shoot?" I couldn't see anything, and
Rosencranz had said in General order: "Don't shoot
till you see something"; and I didn't. At last we
saw something. It seems to me now as if the rebels
were six or eight lines deep as they moved down on
us. It was the first shot I ever made at a human
being, and it seemed like firing at the broad side of
a Pennsylvania barn. I can't tell how far away they
were at the time, but, putting several things together,
I concluded that my shot must have done terrible execution in those advancing lines. While the enemy
was rallying from the effects of my shot, our regiment withdrew, without one of our boys being shot
in the back, a thing which could hardly have happened if those Johnnies had not been in great trepi-
dation — from my volley. The evil which came out

of it, to our side, was that several of our company —
including Capt. Perry and Mahlon Harps — were so
deafened by the noise of my gun, and so shrouded in
the smoke of it, as to either not hear the command
to fall back, or else failed to find their way out of
the smoke, and were, accordingly, taken prisoners.
We apologize, at this late day, for the disaster which
our heroism brought these comrades. When we came
to consider the situation, the rebels seemed to be
faither away when we fired, although they were all
the while moving in our direction. As we think of
it now, every tree seemed to have a Confederate behind it, and we wonder how that, between two armies,
those trees ever escaped alive!

Our next view follows close on the one preceding:
We came up to the 31st Indiana, who were being
formed, or held in line, with difficulty. General Cruft
himself at their head, like a true hero, by word and
action, giving inspiration to the boys. We remember distinctly his words and more earnest appearance:
"Now, men, for God's sake, remember you are from
my own native state"!

They doubtless remembered it, but, like ourselves,
they carried that sweet memory hastily out of those
woods, and over that open country, to our new position, whose memory to us to day, is sweeter than that
of the Cedars.

The picture which we now give is located in the
edge of that timber and on the open ground beyond.
Noah Lutz belonged to my "mess," just then, and
we were making observations about its being "an in-
glorious morning," when, in our retrograde movement, we fell in with — Lieuts. Rains and Crow, who
hitched us to one of our abandoned brass cannon,
and together we hauled the thing rearward, and turned
it over to those who presently put it to use again.
This is the second instance where we appear as an
important factor in turning the tide of battle, and
saving our army from defeat and capture!

In his report the Colonel (Ross) mentioned only
the commissioned officers as deserving special mention

for meritorious conduct. But then Ross wasn't to blame, for "no one sees a battle," and at the time, he didn't see us, and we were too modest to let him know we did it!

If Lutz wasn't the man, we are mistaken. Others were there, but they were not officers, but simply "men," and so we can't remember their names!

We have more pictures, but we must draw the curtain and say good-night.

S. C. Goss, Co. D.

SHERIDAN, Mo., March 31, 1901.

*Friend and Comrade Harden*:

You appear to have made quite a stir among the "dry bones." They appear from all directions. Among others, I see the names of J. C. Shaw and William Switzer, Company G. Why! Bless my body! I have not seen Shaw since he and Switzer stopped to camp on a field, the last afternoon of the Chickamauga battle, when we were changing our lines in somewhat of a hurry, just after General Tom Wood had made room for Longstreet, in the Union lines.

And Lafe Gaston, Kerr, O., I think the highest point he ever touched, was on the Stone River battlefield, a. m., December 31, 1862, when the right of our army was being thrashed like a school boy, and when our regiment changed position to the rear, and to the cedar woods. On the field between the lines lay a wounded comrade, exposed to a galling fire from both lines, raised partly up on hands and knees, was begging for some one to come and rescue him from the hands of the rebels. Gaston cast his cartridge box and gun on the ground, rushed between the lines and rescued the poor fellow, carried him through our lines and laid him on the ground, and when Lt. Witherspoon remarked to Gaston that he might carry the wounded man back to the hospital if he wished, Gaston requested that some one else take him, as for himself he wanted to stay in the battle. Let's hear from the next. I wonder if this would not ornament a short history.

Were I a poet, I would try my hand right here. But let it go. I can't poetize. But I always cultivated Gaston's acquaintance after that. I do not know but that some time I may need him.

I hereby enclose a remittance for the History of the Regiment which you propose publishing.

We looked forward in those early years of '61 and '5. But now we are more inclined to be reminiscent, and then we will see how our backward view at this distance will correspond.

It will be worth the money.

Wishing you and all the Boys Good Luck and lots of it. CAPT. JAS. K. JONES.

## REMINISCENCES.

### BY SYLVESTER RADER.

While camped in the open field, near Nashville, Tenn., in 1862, the ambulance came around, gathering up the sick, among whom was myself. We were taken to Hospital No. 1, Nashville, and dumped. Here we found three of the 90th Boys, four of us in all. I am the only one that lived to get away. The boys were: William Downs, John Westenberger, and a young man from Co. I, whose name I do not recollect. I saw Downs and the Co. I man die. John Westenberger died in the night while I was asleep. No one knew he was dead, until morning. Finding men dead in their bunks in the morning occurred several times while I was there.

I heard Dr. Duff, the assitant surgeon, curse a sick man, accusing him of "playing off," and call him names that were a disgrace to his mother, and in less than a week that same man was in the dead house. Here I heard sick men complaining of being hungry, who were unable to walk the length of the room, yet,the government was furnishing plenty of provisions for us, but the hospital steward, whose name I think was Snelgrove, was selling our provisions to a citizen grocery-man near by, and blowing in the money for drinks, theaters, and on the inhabitants of "Smoky Row." He was detected, courtmartialed and sent to a military prison for two years. The Boys were going to lynch him the night before he got his sentence, but the authorities heard of it and hustled him off to prison early in the evening. Talk about absence of humanity, when a man will starve his sick comrades.

After the Stone River battle we received thirty wounded men, and I spent many hours pouring cold water on their wounds to keep down inflamation. Had they known the virtue of a small amount of carbolic acid, added to the water, thousands of men would be living to-day, who are under the sod.

I wish to speak of two incidents of our march from Lexington to Louisville. The Yankee trick we played on the Johnnies by hauling saw logs along, representing artillery; and the 90th being drawn up in line of battle on the south side of the pike to lock horns with the Johnnies.

---

On the 4th the enemy was nowhere to be seen, and the day was spent in burying the dead of the regiment, who were found stripped of all their clothing, except their drawers. Those seriously wounded were found with their wounds undressed.

The regiment lost in this battle 137 men killed, wounded, captured and missing. Six officers were wounded: Capt. M. B. Rowe, Lt. L. W. Reahard, Lt. Geo. W. Welsh, Lt. T. E. Baker, Lt. J. N. Selby, Capt. Thomas Rains, Capt. Alva Perry and Lt. J. F. Cook were captured. The names of the killed, wounded and captured, will be found in the regular roster, in another part of this work.

Col. Isaac N. Ross, who led the regiment in this battle, and who proved himself a brave and efficient officer, was immediately after sent to the rear in serious health. He afterward resigned, and Lt. Col. C. H. Rippy promoted to Colonel, and Maj. S. N. Yeoman to Lt. Colonel.

The dead were buried on the west side of the railroad and pike, in a low piece of ground, but were taken up and afterward interred in the Stone River National Cemetery near by. There are 34 of the 90th Boys sleeping the sleep of death in this cemetry, which is kept in fine style by the government they died to save. We quote from an article appearing in the *Fairfield-Pickaway News,* some ten years ago:

"The writer was over a great part of this battlefield in the latter part of 1864, and it was no uncommon thing to find the remains of men in the thick cedars, who had been covered with a little earth where they lay, heads and feet exposed as the dirt had washed off. Many of the fields where so much blood was shed, and where cannons thundered death and destruction on those memorable days, were planted in corn and cotton and men peacefully following the plow. Old Fortress Rosecrans is the best preserved fortification we have seen. Except the natural erosion, most of it is about as it was at the close of the war. The fortress is about half a mile north of Murfreesboro, and is about one mile long by half a mile wide, with the pike, railroad and Stone River running through it.

This was a memorable time, the men lying in mud and snow, suffered terribly from cold and exposure."

Bragg evacuated Murfreesboro and took up position at Tullahoma, Tenn., farther south on the L. & N. railroad. We lay at or near Murfreesboro, burying the dead and resting up, until January 7, 1863, when we moved on to Cripple Creek, about 6 miles farther, and went into camp. Here the regiment performed picket duty, drilled, etc., for some time.

Here is a blank in the diaries, which we are unable to get from any one, but the daily routine was camp and picket duty. We now come to where John Chilcote's diary gives us some information. We quote from it. Feb. 9th — Having been discharged from the hospital, we started on our way to join the regiment at Camp Cripple Creek. Passed through Lavergn and camped 20 miles from Nashville.

8th. — Started again, marched over the battlefield of Stone River, through the town of Murfreesboro and 2 miles beyond and camped.

9th. — Started again this morning and got to the regiment at Cripple Creek in the evening, and went on picket at night.

10th. — Was a rainy day. Were relieved and went to camp.

11th. — This is a very warm, nice day. Went down to the creek and washed some clothes. The regiment had dress parade this evening.

12th. — Cloudy and raining. It has been a very disagreeable day. Our camp is very muddy and disagreeable.

13th. — Turned cold. Went on picket to-day Traded for some corn bread out on the picket-line. It tasted good, and was a change from hard-tack.

14th. — The regiment drew two day's rations to-day. It began raining in the evening and rained all night.

15th. — Still cloudy, but did not rain much. Very muddy in camp. Our regiment drew some clothing to-day. I got a blouse.

16th. — The regiment worked on the intrenchments to-day in the rain and mud. It was very disagreeable work, but we had to do it.

17th. — The regiment went on picket to-day. We had a rainy time of it. Rained all day and night.

18th. — The regiment came in off of picket duty, ·˙w two day's rations.

19th. — Cleared off about 9 o'clock. Stood guard in another man's place.

20th. — This was a very nice day. Got breakfast and did a big washing. Everything quiet in camp.

ADJ. DAN. S. KINGERY.
Killed at Chickamauga, Ga.,
Sept. 20, 1863.

THOMAS PARISH, CO. D.
"The Old Blacksmith." Taken
at Cripple Creek, Tenn., 1863.

SERGT. S. C. GOSS.
Co. D.
From a war-time photo.

LT. J. L. HATFIELD.
Co. B.
From a war-time photo.

21st. — Began to rain about noon, but we had to go on picket, all the same. It seems it can rain down in this country any time. It makes it very disagreeable for us who are living in tents and have to stand out on duty.

22nd. — This is a cold, cloudy day. Wrote a letter while out on picket, and another after I came in. We have to put in the time, some how, to keep from getting homesick.

23rd. — Company's H and E went out foraging to-day for mule feed. We also concluded we wanted some feed for ourselves, and finding some hogs, killed four of them while the wagons were being loaded.

24th. — Stayed in camp and rested from our foraging trip yesterday, and enjoyed eating some of our fresh pork. It tasted very good.

25th. — Ordered to be ready to go on picket at 7 o'clock, to relieve those on duty so they could go to camp and draw their pay. It began raining, as usual, when we got there.

26th. — Came in off picket, drew three day's rations, and got orders to go on a foraging expedition to-morrow. We may get some more fresh pork, or something else good to eat.

27th. — After scouring the country for forage, started back for camp, arriving about 3 o'clock.

28th. — The regiment cleaned up guns and accoutrements for inspection. Also policed our quarters. It was so wet we had a hard time of it. Drew five day's rations. The regiment was paid off to-day. It was a busy day, and we were mustered for our next two months' pay.

March 1, 1863. — This is Sunday. Went on picket.

It was a beautiful day. The regiment got mail to-day, which the boys highly appreciated.

2nd. — This was another nice day. Nothing out of the general routine.

3rd. — This was a cold, cloudy day. The regiment worked on the fortifications to-day.

4th. — A nice day, but cold. There was nothing to-day, beyond the regular duties.

5th. — Cannonading all day, in the direction of the rebel army. Quite cold in the evening. Some of the men were on picket.

6th. — Began raining this morning. The forage wagons went to Murfreesboro, and a part of the regiment went as guards.

7th. — Worked on a road in front of headquarters, in mud up to our knees. There was cannonading in front all day.

8th. — This is another Sunday, and a cold, wet, drizzly day. Received mail to-day.

9th. — Went on picket, but were ordered back to get ready to move. Took down our tents, but did not move, but went back to the picket line.

10th. — It rained all day. Came in off picket and went to work putting up our tents again.

11th. — Order to move countermanded. A nice warm day, and the mud dried up.

12th. — Drew five days' rations to-day.

13th. This was our picket day again. A woman came to our post with some eggs, and sold them at 40 cents a dozen.

14th. — After coming in off picket, policed our quarters and cleaned up the camp.

15th. — There was general inspection this morning, and grand review in the evening.

16th. Policed camp in the forenoon, and in the afternoon had regimental and company drill.

17th. Our picket day again. It comes quite often. General Cruft and staff visited our lines to-day.

18th. — Came in off picket, took down our tents to "air them," then had battalion and brigade drill, and dress parade. Then put up our tents.

19th. — Had battalion drill in the forenoon, and brigade drill and dress parade in the afternoon.

20th. — This forenoon was wash day for many of the boys. In the afternoon we had brigade drill.

21st. — Picket day again. Also got mail. This was a nice day.

22nd. — Chaplain W. C. Holliday preached to-day, after which we had a brigade drill and dress parade. It might have done more good to have had the preaching afterwards.

23rd. — Company H went out on picket to relieve one of the 31st Indiana companies, in place of a company of the 1st Kentucky, which is out on Pilot Knob on guard.

24th. — Cleaned up our guns and accoutrements, and were inspected by the brigade inspectors; then went out to drill, but it rained and we did not drill.

25th. — Went out on picket. It was quite cold, but we were not allowed to have fires. Got mail again to-day.

26th. — Company drill in the forenoon, and in the afternoon battalion drill and dress parade.

27th. — Policed our quarters: John Haines, of Co. D, died to-day, and was buried same day.

28th. — No drilling to-day, as it was a wet day.

29th. — Went on picket again to-day, and although it was cold, we were not allowed to have fires.

30th. — Battalion drill and dress parade to-day.

31st. — Battalion drill again to-day.  Dress parade in the evening.

April 1st. — Had company drill in the forenoon, and battalion drill in the afternoon.  In the evening we got orders to pack up and be ready to move at a moment's warning.

2nd. — Started about 1 o'clock this morning, with two day's rations in our havresacks, in pursuit of the Rebels, towards Woodbury.  Got there about daylight.  The Rebels heard of our coming and left before we could head them off.  We captured 30 prisoners and all of their provisions and many mules.  We then turned about and marched back to our old camp, marching in all, about 30 miles, reaching camp about sundown.

3rd. — Went on picket, and had a nice day of it. Found a guinea's nest with five eggs in it.

4th. — Drew five days' rations, and policed our quarters.  Many of the boys amused themselves by pitching horse-shoes.  Others did their washing.

5th. — Relieved the 31st Indiana on picket, they going out on a scout.  Milked Chilcote's cow again.

6th. — Remained on picket in place of the two companies out on Pilot Knob.

7th. — Came in off picket, signed the pay-roll, and took down our tents again.

8th. — Did not get paid off to-day.  Drew two days' rations of beef.  In the evening had dress parade.

9th. — Drew four months' pay, which was $52 each, for the privates.

10th. — Had inspection in order to find the number of able-bodied men in the regiment.  Had dress parade in the evening.

11th. — Went on picket. At night there came a heavy thundershower, which lasted nearly all night.

12th. — John Chilcote milked the old lady's cow again, this morning. He was afraid the cow might go dry, if not attended to regularly. Went to camp and got ready to march, but did not move.

13th. — This was a very warm morning. Some of our men were detailed to go on picket, some on guard at headquarters.

14th. — Took down our tents again, to "air them," but about noon it began to rain and we put them up again.

15th. — A drizzly day, and we are on picket again. Rained all day.

16th. — Cleared off and was a nice day. Had dress parade in the evening.

17th. — Everything quiet in camp, and nothing worthy of note occurred.

18th. — Still quiet in camp. Chilcote says he was detailed to help fix up the surgeon's tent, but "played off" sick.

19th. — This was our picket day again, and was a damp, drizzly day.

20th. — General Rousseau's division marched through here to-day on its way to the front.

21st. — Most of the boys were detailed to work in camp. Dress parade in the evening.

22nd. — Dress parade, as usual. Not much going on. Some are working about camp.

23rd. Chilcote says he and Bradford Lott worked nearly all day, putting up a "pup" tent. When we went out we had large tents which would accommodate a number of men. These tents were hauled in wagons, and when the wagon train did not get up, we had to

sleep on the ground without any covering. In order
that we might save the mules, and have shelter for ourselves, at all times, these tents were dispensed with,
so far as the privates were concerned, and a square
piece of heavy muslin or duck, about 5 feet square,
with buttons on one edge, and button holes on the
other, were issued to the men. If the men divided off,
which they did, two or three messing together, and
each with a piece of "pup" tent, as they were called,
a shelter could soon be made by buttoning two pieces
together and putting up a ridge pole and staking the
edges to the ground, making a shed like the comb of a
house roof. The third piece was used to shut up one
end, or if a fourth piece, both ends. By this arrangement the men carried their own tents, and the teams
were used for other purposes.

24th. — On picket again. It is a nice warm day,
and the people are planting corn close to us.

25th. — Were to have been inspected by the brigade
inspector, but were not.

26th. — This is Sunday. Had preaching at 4
o'clock by Corporal James J. Holliday, of Co. H.
Dress parade after preaching.

27th. — On picket again to-day. Rained all night,
and was very disagreeable.

28th. — Cleared off and was a very nice day. The
regiment had dress parade in the evening.

29th. — Received orders this morning to pack up,
have two days' rations in our havresacks, and be ready
to move any moment, but did not move.

30th. — Mustered for our next pay. Had brigade
drill and dress parade.

May 1st. — Chilcote says he is on picket again, but

moved from his old post, down to the woods. Does
not say whether he took the cow along or not.

2nd. — Came in off picket, washed up, and cleaned
up our quarters. Battalion drill and dress parade
in the afternoon.

3rd. — We had inspection in the forenoon, and
general review in the afternoon.

4th. — Regimental drill and dress parade to day.

5th. — Very quiet in camp. Some of the boys are
out on picket.

6th. — Got mail to-day. It began raining this
morning and rained all day.

7th. — A damp, drizzly day. We drew rations
to-day.

8th. — Company drill in the forenoon, and brigade
drill in the afternoon.

9th. — The camp quiet, as usual.

10th. — General review this evening. Lieut. Geo.
Richey returned to the regiment to-day, from a furlough home.

11th. — A very warm day, and everything quiet.

12th. — The regiment had battalion drill to-day.
General Palmer moved his quarters to this place, to-
day. He is our division commander.

13th. — Nothing unusual to-day. It rained, but
that is no unusual occurrence.

14th. — Had brigade drill. Everything very quiet
in camp.

15th. — We began doing picket duty to-day, by
detail, that is so many from each company, each day.

16th. — This is Saturday, and wash-day. We had
dress parade in the evening.

17th.— This is Sunday. Had inspection this morning, and review in the evening.  A Kentucky chaplain preached to our regiment at 10 o'clock.

18th. — The men are putting in the time drilling, except those on picket.

19th. — Brigade drill to-day.  Squad and company drill were going on almost every day, in addition to battalion and brigade drills.

20th. — Started on a scout at daylight.  Went about four miles, and as we found no enemy, came back to camp, and drilled in the evening.

21st. — All quiet, except drill.  A nice warm day.

22nd. — The mail was distributed to-day.  Had brigade drill.

23rd. — Did not drill to-day, but did our washing, policed our quarters, and had dress parade in the evening.

24th. — General inspection and grand review.

25th. — Nothing unusual.  Details made for picket, guard duty, etc.

26th. — This was a very hot day.  We had battalion drill in the evening.

27th. — We got mail again, to-day.  A detail worked on a well.

28th. — Company and battalion drill.

29th. — A fine banner was brought to our regiment to-day.  A detail went to Murfreesboro.

30th. — Inspection at 1 o'clock.  No drill on account of rain.

31st. — General review to-day.  The fine banner was presented to the regiment to-day, while on review. This banner is one of the two tattered remnants seen at the annual reunions of the regiment.

June 1st. — Brigade drill to-day.

2nd. — Rainy, as usual, but as it is warm does not make us feel so disagreeable.

3rd. — Received orders this evening to pack up and be ready to move at any time.

4th. — A detail was made to go to Murfreesboro, with a wagon train.

5th. — Division drill this evening. There was a man hung at Murfreesboro to-day, for murdering one of our soldiers last summer.

6th. — Nothing more than usual in camp to-day.

7th. — We had division drill again to-day.

8th. — Weather very nice and warm. Division drill.

9th. — Drilling is all that is going to-day.

10th. — This was a wet day. Had drill in the evening.

11th. — Still rainy. Battalion drill this evening.

12th. — One of the 31st Indiana boys was buried to-day. The 31st is in our brigade.

13th. — A 2nd Kentucky man was buried to-day. He purposely shot himself last night.

14th. — Company drill and inspection.

15th. — Drilling is now the order of the day.

16th. — Chilcote says he was on picket, and sold two pounds of coffee to a woman for a silver dollar.

17th. — Drill and dress parade.

18th. — Not much doing, as it is a rainy day.

19th. — There are 15 regiments of cavalry reported near this place. Our regiment was held in camp as a reserve to re-enforce the pickets, in case they were attacked.

20th. — This is Saturday. Did our washing and cleaned up our quarters.

21st. — Our guns and clothing were inspected this

morning. In the evening we had review and dress parade.

22nd. — Rebels reported near here, in considerable numbers.

23rd. — To-day a man from the 1st Kentucky was shot for "bounty jumping" and desertion. The brigade was drawn up on the parade ground, and the man marched out, blindfolded, when a detail of men whose guns had been, part of them loaded with ball, and part with blank cartridges, fired at him, standing, when he dropped dead. This created more gloom that a hundred natural deaths, or deaths in battle.

24th. — Ordered to be ready to march at 7 o'clock this morning, but did not leave until 10 o'clock. Marched out through Bradyville toward Dug Hollow, through the rain.

25th. — Started on our march again. It rained very hard all the forenoon. Camped about noon. The cavalry brought in some Johnnies this evening.

26th. — A very bad, rainy day. Stayed in camp at Olive, or Hollow Springs, waiting for our wagon train to come up.

27th. — About noon we started and marched 7 or 8 miles and camped.

28th. — Marched to within two miles of Manchester, Tenn., and camped on Duck River, a nice stream. We camped in Breckinridge's old camp, where he camped after the battle of Stone River. Got some mail to-day.

29th. — Remained in camp until late in the evening, when we moved through Manchester and camped in another Rebel camp.

30th. — Remained in camp at Manchester. We cleaned up an old church for a hospital.

July 1st. — This was a very hot day. Marched out toward Tullahoma, six or seven miles and camped for the night. We traveled all the way through the woods.

2nd. — Moved about five miles and camped. Got some potatoes and beef, and had a very good supper. Got plenty of huckleberries.

3rd. — Moved to within one mile of Elk River; and as the water was so high we could not cross, we moved back about a mile and camped.

4th. — Lay in camp to-day. Got some potatoes and chickens, but not issued by the commissary, and had very good living.

5th. — Still in camp. Still rainy. Drew three day's rations this morning. Had inspection to-day.

6th. — Still in the same camp. A detail of 30 men went out to gather berries.

7th. — Got word this evening that Vicksburg had surrendered to General Grant.

8th. — Got orders this morning to move back to Manchester, and started at half past 6 o'clock, marched through mud and water all the way. Crossed streams by wading them all.

9th. — Stayed in camp at Manchester, and fixed up to stay awhile.

10th. — The day was spent in fixing up our camp again.

11th. — Received mail again. Cleaned up the camp.

12th. — Dress parade to-day. It rained this evening for a change.

13th. — A detail went out to gather berries. Some of the boys got dinner at a house, also apples. They were about 3 miles out from camp.

14th. — The men are on half rations, and a very small half at that.

15th. — Nothing unusual to-day. A detail dug a ditch in front of the Colonel's quarters.

16th. — Still on half rations, and a great deal of grumbling about it.

17th. — Some of the boys gathered blackberries, and Chilcote says he made some pies.

18th. — A very warm day. Had dress parade.

19th. — Had review to-day, at 5 o'clock .

20th. — Drew rations to-day, and are feeling better.

21st. — A detail was made to go out about three miles to help haul railroad ties.

22nd. — The wagons went out this morning, with a detail, for forage. They went to the foot of the Cumberland Mountains, got the forage, but did not get back.

23rd. — The forage train got back about 8 o'clock. While out the boys got apples, potatoes, chickens, pork, etc., but bought them, of course.

24th. — Signed the pay-rolls to-day, to be paid off to-morrow.

25th. — Did not get our pay to-day. Very warm.

26th. — No drill, so we have pretty good times. Dress parade. Morgan reported captured in Ohio.

27th. — Still in the old camp, and nothing of importance going on.

28th. — Dress parade. Some country people came in to-day, with wagons, with eatables to sell.

29th. — We were paid four months' pay to-day. The Colonel gave an order to some of the boys to get whiskey at the Commissary, and some of them got full and had quite a time.

30th. — Everything quiet. Except the details for picket, the boys have not much to do.

31st. — We had a very hard rain yesterday, and it was cool and nice last night. Colonel Rippey's wife is here. She came yesterday, on a visit.

August 1st. — Inspection and dress parade.

2nd. — This is Sunday, and a very nice day. Inspection this morning and review in the evening, and after that a funeral was preached in our regiment.

3rd. — Dress parade this evening. Colonel Rippey's wife was present.

4th. — Captain N. F. Hitchcock started home to-day, on a leave of absence.

5th. — Dress parade, as usual. Everything seems quiet.

6th. — Went with a detail on picket this morning. Plenty of trade with the citizens, on the picket line. Got some pies.

7th. — Back in camp. All quiet.

8th. — On picket again. Nothing going on in camp more than usual. Got some cucumbers at 25 cents a dozen.

9th. — Review this morning. Made some biscuits to-day.

10th. — All quiet. Went out a mile and a half to guard cattle. Got some roasting ears and peaches.

11th. — Still on guard. Have plenty of green corn. It is one year to-day since I volunteered. — We are quoting from John Chilcote's diary. — Ed.

LOGAN, O., February 14, 1894.

*Comrade Harden:*

I have been a reader of the history of the 90th O. V. I., of which I was an honored member. I enlisted August 2d, 1862, and was assigned to Co. I, and as the history has already stated, was in camp at Circleville, and my first experience was to get left when we got to Covington, Ky. It was understood that we would lay there over night, and I got permission to go up the river to Dayton, Ky., as I was somewhat, at that time interested in a young lady, and of course, I wanted to bid her good bye. I went up, and about 9 o'clock that night I was sent for by R. R. Pierce and Wm. Mason. After bidding the lady good bye, we started for Covington, but the regiment had left for Lexington, so we had to remain until Sunday morning, then took the train with the 99th, and got as far as Paris, where we had to stay over night. Monday morning we got on another train and got to the regiment just in time to start on that memorable march to Louisville.

I might give my entire experience as a soldier, but it would take too long, but will start in at Nashville. December 26, 1862, we started for the front but made slow progress on account of rain and the rebels in our front, but on the 31st day of December we got a good taste of what war is. It is useless to give you anything concerning that, as it has all been told, but will make mention that we lost two killed on that morning. One was Wm. Mason and the other Clay Leist, both good soldiers, and for Clay he was not only a good soldier but also a good Christian in every sense of the word. That brings in a notice in *Circleville Union*, of November 4, 1864, of the death of Sergt. Amos Leist of Co. F, killed in action at Kennesaw Mountain. After the battle of Stone River we were detailed to go back to Nashville with a supply train. When we got to Nashville a wagon drove up with pies for sale, which went fast. There was a basket full that the old man and his wife were reserving, and in order to make them safe, sat on the basket. But it was no use, when we had no money but an empty stomach, there was some way to get it filled. So, when the old man pulled out the other basket, lo, and behold! it was empty, — must have lost them.

From a recent photo.

Color Bearer J. S. COCKERILL, Co. C.

He planted the first colors on the Confederate works at Nashville, Tenn.

CAPT. ALVAH PERRY.
LIEUT. GEO. W. WELSH.          LIEUT. J. M. SUTPHEN.

From Stone River we went to Camp Cripple Creek, where we were quite a while and had, what I thought, a good time, in our own way. We were there until about the last of June, and started on the march.

I took sick and was left at Manchester, and was taken to Tullahoma, where it was thought by every one, I would die, but I was not ready for that, but had a close shave. From there I was dragged around from one hospital to another, until I wound up at Camp Dennison, where I got able to be around, and in November, 1863, I was transferred to the Invalids Corps. That ended me with the 90th, but I was with them through all the war in mind and soul. I was sent to Cincinnati, then to Washington, D. C., where I did duty until the war closed. Was in Washington during the closing of the war, the assassination of Lincoln, review of the armies, Early's raid on the city, and all the excitement of the war; was discharged after the regiment was mustered out.

So this is about all I will say of my history with the Grand old 90th, whose surviving members I am at all times glad to meet. While I was not with the boys, I was with them in spirit just as though I had been with them in the field, and if any of the old boys come around, the latch string hangs on the outside for any of them. I must close. Hope this will interest some one.

I have been very much interested in the letters written by the boys. Hope they will continue.

Yours in F. C. L.

J. W. Strentz.

Late Sergt. Co. I, 90th O. V. I.

12th. — Everything quiet, as usual.

13th. — My partner and I made some first-rate peach pies to-day. Our sutler, Sam Campbell, started for home this morning.

14th. — A very hot day until about two o'clock, when it rained.

15th. — We drew rations to-day.

16th. — Left camp at Manchester, Tenn., for parts unknown to us. Had a rough time of it, for it rained for about four hours as hard as it could pour down. We marched 15 miles.

17th. — Got out at daylight and went back 9 miles to help the wagons out of the mud, and then started on the march. Did not get up with the brigade to-day.

18th. — Started at daylight, but did not come up with the brigade until night.

19th. — Moved out at daylight for Dunlap, Tenn., 18 miles from where we camped, and arrived there about 5 o'clock in the evening. Went down the mountains.

20th. — Remained in camp to-day. Got a lot of peaches and sold a lot of them for $1.25. This is the county seat of Sequatchie county, Tenn., 46 miles from Manchester.

21st. — Lay in camp to-day, and rested.

22nd. — Remained in camp. Skirmishing reported near Chattanooga, Tenn.

23rd. — A great many stragglers from the country, came in to take the oath of allegiance. Dress parade this evening.

24th. — Got mail to-day, the first since we left Manchester. Expected orders to move, but did not get them.

25th. — A detail of 40 men was made to go out 5 miles and fix up a road up the mountains.

26th. — This was a nice day. E. M. Cooper, J. W. Smittley and T. Spicer of Co. H, came up to-day.

27th. — Captain Hitchcock came back to-day; from leave of absence, home.

28th. — Nothing going on worthy of note.

29th. — Still in camp at Dunlap. No sign of a move.

30th. — Had preaching this morning in the grove.

31st. — Drew 5 days rations. Got orders at night to be ready to march very early, if not before daylight. We were mustered this morning for our next two months' pay.

September 1st. Started on the march towards Jasper, Tenn. Marched about 23 miles. It was a hard march, so dry and dusty.

2nd. — Lay in camp to-day. Saw and explored a large cave near. It was a grand sight.

3rd. — Moved out of camp this morning and marched to the Tennessee River and went into camp a few hours, then went down to the edge of the river.

4th. — Waited until 2 o'clock before we could cross the river. Crossed over on some rafts, halted and remained for the day. Here we met the 31st Ohio. This place is called Shellmound.

5th. — Lay in camp at Shellmound, where we crossed the river, until 2 o'clock in the afternoon, then marched 8 miles nearer Chattanooga, Tenn. We camped in Georgia.

6th. — Marched 7 miles and camped again close to the 31st Ohio. We are still in Georgia, 16 miles from Chattanooga. Had preaching this evening.

7th. — Remained in camp near Trenton. Our regiment went out about 3 miles on a scout, but did not see any rebels. Got orders to move at 3 o'clock in the morning.

8th. — Left camp at Trenton, at 3 o'clock this morning, moved 4 miles and camped. A part of the regiment, three companies, went out on picket to-night.

9th. — Moved again this morning, moved past Chattanooga, which the rebels have evacuated, and camped in an old rebel camp.

10th. — Moved out in pursuit of the rebels. Came up with them about noon and skirmished with them all the evening. They made a dash on the skirmish line and took about 50 prisoners. We then went into camp for the night.

11th. — Marched on again in pursuit of the rebels. Began skirmishing with them about noon, and kept it up until we got to Ringgold, Ga., where we camped.

12th. — Still following up the enemy and skirmishing with them. We got to Lee & Gordon's Mills, on the Chickamauga River, where we camped for the night.

13th. — Our brigade went out on a reconnoisance. Our regiment had a skirmish and killed two rebels. None of our boys got hurt. Camped again at Lee & Gordon's Mills.

14th. — Lay in camp at Lee & Gordon's Mills to guard the wagon train. Skirmishing out in front of us. Rations getting very scacce.

15th. — Moved about 4 miles to-day and went into camp.

16th. — Lay in camp to-day, 11 miles from Lafayette, Ga., until late in the evening. We then went on picket. Heard cannonading and skirmishing all day.

17th. — Remained on picket until evening. We then moved back toward Lee & Gordon's Mills, about 12 miles, and camped for the night.

18th. — Lay in camp until evening. We then marched towards Lee & Gordon's Mills. Did not go into camp till late in the night. Had hard fighting here to-day. The past few days were spent by both our army and the enemy, in maneuvering for position, and in consolidating the troops for a final struggle on the banks of the Chickamauga River, for the final possession of Chattanooga, now held by the Union army.

19th. — This was the first day of the great battle of Chickamauga, Ga. We moved out from Lee & Gordon's Mills, on the Lafayette road, toward Chattanooga, some distance; then obliqued to the right in the woods, and got into the fight about 10 o'clock, and fought all day. Our brigade was in the hottest of the battle. A large number were killed and wounded. Among the wounded was Colorbearer D. C. Goodwin, who was severely wounded in the neck and shoulder by the explosion of a shell from the enemy's guns. He was carried to the rear, and thought to be mortally wounded, but is living yet. He was wounded near a scrub oak, just as he was passing the colors under a limb; and when at the battle ground in 1895, he found the tree and cut a limb from it.

Of this day's battle, Captain Felton says: "On the 19th we were ordered to move with the brigade, by the left flank to the support of Gen. Thomas. The line of battle passed quickly over a cornfield and through a strip of timber, and on emerging from it, discovered the enemy at close range, in the act of completing their movement of turning and enveloping Gen. Thomas' right flank. This line was established at 1 o'clock P. M. and notwithstanding the repeated efforts of the enemy, was held until 2:30 P. M. when the supply of ammunition being exhausted, Colonel Rippey received orders to retire his regiment to a strip of timber 150 yards to the rear. In his new position Colonel Rippey made application for, and obtained a section of Battery B, 1st Ohio Artillery, and with it, held the enemy in check until a supply of ammunition was obtained. It now became evident, from the advancing roar of musketry upon the front and right, that the position was again being flanked. To meet this new movement the regiment made a right half-wheel, about faced, and and was in a position to meet the impending charge of the enemy. To save the right it was plain, that a counter charge must be made. Gen. Turchin gave the order, and the 90th Ohio led the charge in gallant style, causing the enemy to retreat in confusion. The rebels were followed some 400 yards when Gen. Turchin called out, "Boys, we go far enough, we know not what is on our right, or what is on our left." The 90th Ohio was then ordered to the support of Gen. Johnson's division, now being hard pressed.

"In the evening the regiment took position a little to the rear and left of the position occupied during the day, and erected works from old logs, and held this position until the defeat of the army on the evening of the 20th. At these works a brave officer, a noble gentleman and a patriotic soldier was killed — Adjutant Daniel N. Kingery, of McArthur, Ohio. During the battle of the 20th, the breastworks caught fire on the outside, but the fire was extinguished, and the works saved by officers and men leaping the works and beating out the fire with their hands and sticks. The enemy concentrated their fire on these brave men, but not a single one was hit while so exposed. These men were a part of Co. A, and were commanded by a 2nd Lieutenant, modesty forbids the mention of his name. They were ordered to this work by Colonel Rippey, who commanded the regiment. The enemy again pressed the right flank of the position and succeeded in turning it, which compelled the abandonment of the works.

"Retreating under fire across the strip of woods and the Kelley field to the Dry Valley road, which connects with the Rossville road near that place, the command was again placed in position on a high ridge running parallel with the Dry Valley road. From this position the regiment was ordered to Rossville, near Chattanooga, which it reached at 10 P. M. and bivouacked in line of battle.

"The loss of the regiment on the 19th and 20th, was 3 officers killed: Adjutant Daniel Kingery, Captain Robert D. Caddy, and Lt. N. A. Patterson who was mortally wounded; and 83 men killed, wounded and captured."

The army fell back to Chatanooga and entrenched itself. Here the regiment remained in defence until October 24, receiving and returning assaults of the enemy on Lookout Mountain and Missionary Ridge. At this time for a period of nearly thirty days, all the troops at Chattanooga were on short rations and had to subsist on a few crackers, a little coffee, and corn stolen from the mules and parched.

We here give an account of the capture and imprisonment of one of the boys who was captured Sunday evening, September 20, written by himself, and which is a fair sample of the experiences of the others. It is as follows:

CROSSENVILLE, O., OCTOBER 15, 1893.

"I was captured at Chickamauga, Sunday evening, September 20, 1863. The next day after the battle we were taken to Dalton, Ga., where we were marched up, one at a time, stripped and searched, and then put on a train and sent to Atlanta, Ga., and put in the "bull pen" for the night, after which the jug was passed around to the guards. When dusk came we were ordered to lie down on the ground and lay there until morning. The boys would forget and get up in the night, and then the bullets would whistle among us. The next morning we were marched out, and left 9 of our old comrades dead or severely wounded by the guards' fire.

We boarded the train for Raleigh, N. C. The women cursed us and called us everything they could think of. One woman waved a rebel flag over us. Jesse Grubs, of the 65th Ohio, tore it off and swore no rebel flag should wave over him. We left Raleigh

for Richmond, Va., went via of Petersburg. It was
night when we went through Petersburg, but we
could see terrible works there along the road. We went
from Richmond to Libby Prison, where we stayed a
while, and then were sent to Castle Thunder. We were
in the two places about three months. Col. Strait was
with us. From here they moved us to Danville, Va.
Rations got very short and the boys got awfully dis-
heartened and began to plan some way of escape and
dug tunnels, and did nearly escape, but were caught.
Then times were harder than ever. We could hardly
subsist on what we got. They only allowed us a little
water. Sometimes they would cut the rations off for
three days for digging, and when we would give him
over to them, they would give us rations. The small-
pox broke out among us, and the boys died by the
dozen. It raged for a long time. In the morning they
would call for the dead, and we had to carry them out.
We would rush around to get to carry one out just to
get some fresh air. They kept bloodhounds there to
catch the boys who would get out, and sometimes they
would catch and kill them.

"The rations consisted of a little corn bread, once
a day, and a little rice, once in a while. The meal for
the corn bread was not sifted, and was stirred up with
a shovel and then dried.

"I was there 8 months. A squad was sent through
the lines and exchanged. I was one of them. Out of
our regiment was John C. Shaw, John K. Hill, Philip
M. Brunner, Dr. O'Hanlon, Joseph Wyatt. Out of
that squad I was the only one who got back to the
regiment. I reached the regiment near Resaca, Ga."

JOHN SWITZER, Co. G.

We think there is a mistake as to Hill being a member of the 90th, as we cannot find his name on the
rolls. — ED.

We now go back to September 3, 1863, and quote
from S. D. Soliday's diary. — ED.

From a recent photo.

JOHN W. TRITSCH, CO. E.
Sec'y 90th O. V. I. Association.

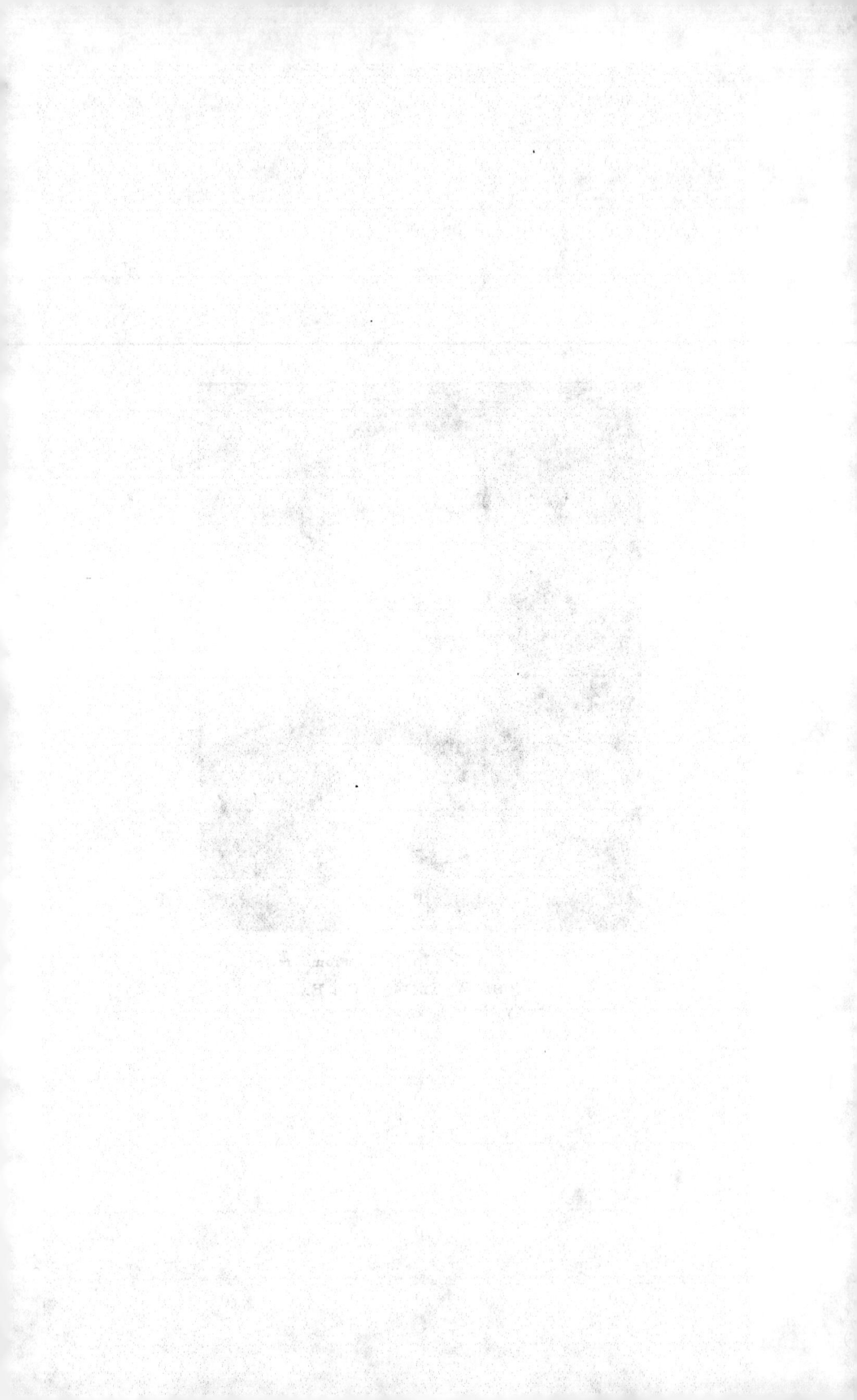

September 3rd. — Marched through Jasper, Tenn., the band playing "Yankee Doodle." We took the town by storm. Groceries, drug stores, etc., had to suffer. I got five bottle of Jaynes' Alterative and several books. I used all the medicine. I was healthy; never was sick while in the service; never was away from the company or regiment. Where the command was, I was present. I was contented and at home.

6th. — Sunday. Got within four miles of Trenton, Ga. Here we met the 17th Ohio for the first time.

15th. — Moved down to Pea Vine church on picket. Had goose for supper.

16th. — Relieved from picket. We were in a dangerous place, but did not know it while there, if we did kill geese, with the rebels not far off.

This must have been about the time Joe Rife and Isaac George captured the sheep. The story is so good we must tell it, and it is true, too, for George and Rife both acknowledge it.

As the regiment was marching across a field, about this time, or, perhaps, the next day, a flock of sheep — George says it was a patch of sheep — was discovered. George, after them, cornered them in a fence corner,, when the sheep began jumping over. George caught one by the hind legs as it went over the fence, and caught another between his legs. In this condition he was discovered by one of the boys who offered to lend assistance, but George said: "No, this is Company F's sheep." Just then Joe Rife of Company F, came on the scene and helped Isaac George out. Rife says the sheep George had by the hind legs was jerking him forward, and the one he had between his legs was jerking him backward. Rife

7 90 O V I

can go through the motions exactly, and if you don't think so, attend a reunion when he is present. But Rife says Co. F had mutton, and plenty of it, too.

September 19th. — This is the first day of the battle of Chickamauga. While our regiment was fighting in the clearing, John Emick, John C. Strayer, Elijah Howard, and Jacob McDaniel of Co. D, were wounded. (John C. Strayer died from the effects of this wound December 16, 1863.—ED.) Afterwards we were driven back into the woods, and at intervals we would drive the enemy a few hundred yards, then they would drive us. The last time we were ordered to fall back. A great many guns were left on the field by our dead and wounded. I thought it prudent to smash them around the trees and make them useless to the enemy. Sergt. S. A. Parsons, of my company, said: "Soliday, what are you doing?" I answered that the d—d rebels can not use those guns on us. Every time Parsons sees me, he says: "I never saw a person so mad and impatient as you were on that Sunday afternoon. Growled like a lion."

20th. — The second day of the battle, and never to be forgotten, Sergt. S. C. Cross was wounded in the hand. While we were supporting the battery, we were lying on our bellies. I went so far as to make a hole in the ground for my nose. I should have liked to creep in a hole my self just then. One of the cannoniers was horrible mutilated by a premature discharge of a gun. The suffering among the boys was most intense throughout the day for want of water, fighting for two days without water, was fearful. On Sunday evening, on our retreat to Rossville, we came to a small stream of water issuing from Missionary Ridge. Well, we drank water sand

and anything that got into our cups. I know I drank two quarts of water and sand, the best water, I thought, I ever drank in my life.

## CHICKAMAUGA.

### BY W. G. MAUK, OF CO. E.

( Written soon after the War closed.)

Through the plains of Chickamauga, where verdure
 ever grows,
Copiously and peacefully a gentle river flows.
At a very noted spring, the river has its source;
Whence its waters issue and flow a northern course.

The warriors often speak, the poets likewise sing
Of the times they slaked their thirst at the limped
 Crawfish spring.
For those who drink there once and bathe their fevered
 brain,
Would fain return there oft to quaff and bathe again.

Along that peaceful river the savage made his home,
And for its cooling waters the wild herds used to roam.
The weary traveler pauses upon its flowery brink,
And seeks a cool retreat where he may rest and drink.

The Chickamauga river, its vale and noted spring,
Are names that dear and sacred will to our memory
 cling.
The mother drops a tear; the maiden heaves a moan;
The widow heaves a sigh, and sits bereft alone.

For heroes, dear and true, who there so nobly stood,
And for their country's cause poured out their precious
 blood.

Heroes! from dear embrace went forth their homes to
    save,
And fell upon the plains and filled the soldier's grave.

On the 20th of September, the holy Sabbath day,
Two hostile armies met and fought a bloody fray.
The Rebel General Bragg, with his belligerant bands,
Attacked a force of Union troops under General Ros-
    ecrans.

On that awful morning the sun rose bright and clear,
And all was hushed and quiet — no din disturbed our
    ear.
But, 'ere the sun had o'er the trees poured forth his
    golden light,
Columns of "blue and gray" were stirring where they
    had passed the night.

In a dense and dreary wood of stately pine and oak,
Through the broad spread branches up curled the slug-
    gish smoke,
From campfires far extended by every log and nook,
As the soldiers all in silence of their scanty meals
    partook.

No ominous sound was heard to cause alarm or fear,
And one could half believe no deadly foe lurked near.
But such was not the case.  Within a gunshot lay,
Concealed, the Rebel forces preparing for the fray.

When Old Sol had risen high and poured a scorching
    flood
Upon the soldiers' heads who, all waiting, stood,
The enemy advanced in columns long and gray,
And pounced upon the Federal lines like a lion on his
    prey.

"To arms! to arms!" the cry burst forth; "be steady,
    true and brave,"
"You'll share a conqueror's fame this day, or fill a
    hero's grave."
The foe, in force, approach us near, but we will make
    them feel
The force of Northern arguments in Northern lead
    and steel."

Each soldier grasped his piece and in heroic pride
Stood firm as adamant, to check the sweeping tide.
When the Rebel legions rushed with hideous cheer
    and yell,
They met a sheet of fire and hail, and in confusion fell.

But, backed by columns long and deep, they onward
    madly rushed,
And to the cannon's fiery mouth their mangled col-
    umns pushed,
Hand-to-hand the conflict raged, and still more fierce-
    ly grew,
The belching cannons roared more loud, and thicker
    missiles flew.

From north to south in thunder tones the battle fiercely
    raged,
As all the forces on the plains became at once en-
    gaged.
With deafening roar the forests rang and groans arose
    on high.
While clouds of smoke enshroud the scene and fill a
    burning sky.

Tho' hours thus the battle raged without a turn of tide,
Before a single change occurred the conflict to decide.

A desperate effort being made, the foe was forced to
yield,
And with one loud prolonged huzza, the Federals won
the field.

The din of battle then was hushed, the cannons ceased
to roar,
The tramp of horsemen died away, and all was still
once more,
Except the piteous cries and groans of those, who
in their gore
Lay sweltering 'neath the scorching sun, where some
were doomed to rise no more.

Rebel trains were rolling in from east and south be-
times,
Which brought, in haste, fresh troops to fill their
broken lines.
Again the battle raged that day more fiercely than
before,
More bloody were the charges, more loud the cannon's roar.

For a time the Federals stood as lines of sharpened
steel,
Although the Rebs, three to one, with whom they had
to deal.
The Union forces held them long, but, alas! were
forced to yield,
And overwhelmed by outnumbered host, in tears, gave
up the field.

### WHERE IS THE 90TH?

Comrade Joseph T. Barron calls our attention to the time of the evening of the last day's battle at Chickamauga, when leaving the field. General Cruft rode along the line and called out, "My God, where is the 90th?" and when he rode up, how the boys cheered him, and the whole army took it up. The Johnnies fell back and left us without firing a gun. This incident probably had much to do in saving Gen. Thomas' army.

### A LETTER FROM CHICKAMAUGA.

We are not in the habit of publishing our private correspondence, especially from our lady friends, but we can not refrain from printing the one below, as showing the hospitality of the Southern people, and written on the bloody battlefield of Chickamauga. We know it will interest our old soldier comrades. We appreciate the letter very highly, and hope the lady will not take offense. We more more than admire her faith in the preservation of her little ones, and is a good and impressive lesson, and we trust her prayer has been answered. If we ever visit Chickamauga again, and we may, we shall certainly call to see this hospitable family, as well as others whose acquaintance we have made in our several trips there.

The picture referred to, was the old Brotherton house. If any of our people wish to see that picture, we will be pleased to have them call.

Lytle, Ga., Dec. 17, 1900.

Mr. H. O. Harden,

*Kind Sir and Lady:*

I will try to drop you a few lines in answer to the little groupe and log cabin, with many thanks I give you for it, so now I ask you and the beautiful lady to come again, but we do not live in the little log hut now. We live on the Alexander road just a mile from

the Alexander bridge, but if you ever come back to the
Old Park I ask you to call and see us.  We will treat
you with all kindness we can.  The little girl says
she will look now for Santa Claus to bring her an
Album to put her pictures in.  She knew the lady as
soon as she saw her.  I thank you very much for them
both; thank you for thinking that much of the little
crowd of dirty ones.  The little girl received a few
papers from Stoutsville, O., and I knew in reason it
must to come from you.  The little ones are well, only
bad colds, and anxiously looking for Xmas to come.
I trust the good Lord to spare them all to me to enjoy
a happy Xmas, and me with them.

So I will close for the first.  Hope we will hear
from you and the kind lady that was with you.  So
good-by for all the little ones to you.

Mrs. R. L. McDaniel,<br>
*Mother of the little ones.*

September 21st, 1863.  Threw up breastworks to-
day and remained in them until dark, and then fell
back to Chattanooga.

22nd.—Commenced building breastworks, and
worked all day without the enemy coming near enough
to bother us.  We burned several houses to get them
out of the way.

23rd.—Still fortifying, and expecting an attack
at any time.

24th.—Our pickets were attacked at night, but the
enemy lost several men in the attack.

5th.—Still in our breastworks.  A brigade went
out to see what the enemy were doing, and had some
heavy skirmishing.

26th.—Our pickets were attacked about daylight
this morning and driven nearly back to the breastworks, when they were reinforced and drove the
rebels back to their old position.

CAPT. J. B. ORMAN.
R. Q. M.—1863.

CAPT. J. S. WITHERSPOON.
Co. I.—1863.

CAPT. JAMES K. JONES.
"Kim Jones."—1864.

D. C. GOODWIN.
Co. E.—1862.

27th.—Still fortifying and getting ready for an attack.

28th.—In the field in front of Chattanooga, watching the enemy.

29th.—All quiet, and the boys are fixing up their tents.

30th.—Drew five days' rations to-day, about enough to last one day. It commenced to rain this evening.

October 1st, 1863.—Still raining. Our boys worked all day on the fortifications.

2nd.—Still fortifying. Worked on Fort Palmer to-day. We could see the rebels all day. They occupy Missionary Ridge and the valley between us and the ridge, across to Lookout Mountain; the Mountain and the river below us, their right resting on the river above us at the north end of Missionary Ridge; their left on the river below us, forming a semi-circle around us, with the Tennessee river at our backs, and the Cumberland mountains beyond. What provisions we did get, were hauled over the mountains, from Stevenson, Ala., a distance of 60 miles.

3rd.—Not much news, but plenty of work.

4th.—This is Sunday, but we work all the same as any other day. It is just two weeks since we left the battlefield of Chickamauga. What a change, and what experiences since we passed through this town the 9th day of last month.

5th.—The enemy began shelling us about noon and kept it up until night, doing no harm, the shells passing over us.

6th.—Everything quiet, each army watching the other.

7th.—Began to rain last night, and to-day is a wet,

disagreeable day. We are on what is said to half rations, but it is a very small half.

8th.—Some clothing was issued to the men to-day.

9th.—The left wing of our regiment worked on the breastworks to-day.

10th.—Still on short rations, and there is considerable grumbling.

11th.—All quiet. Some of the boys visited the 31st Ohio to-day.

12th.—Company H, went out on picket. Nothing of importance occurred to-day.

13th.—This election day, and the Ohio regiments held their election for state officers, giving Brough a big lift. It being election day, of course it rained.

14th.—Rain! Rain! !

15th.—And still it rains. A detail was sent out today to cut wood. It is very disagreeable; scarce of wood, short on grub, and scant of clothing, and having to work in the mud and rain. Still we do it, not for pay, but that our flag may float over every state in the Union, and treason be buried beneath our sufferings.

16th.—Drew full rations of bread, but only half of sugar and coffee. There was no forage for the mules and horses, and those that did not die, became so poor and were too weak to have drawn the wagons and artillery, in case of retreat. All of our provisions were hauled by wagons from Stevenson and Bridgeport, over a circuitous route up the Sequatchie valley and over Waldron's Ridge, a distance of 60 miles. A train of several hundred wagons was captured and burned by the enemy. I paid $1.00 for three ears of corn, then parched it, and I and my mess ate it for supper, one evening.—ED.

17th.—Worked on the fortifications to-day.

18th.—Still cooped up in Chattanooga.

19th.—This was a nice warm day, for a change, nothing unusual.

20th.—Everything quiet, and still in camp.

21st.—The same old thing—mud and starvation.

22nd.—Went out on picket with Co. G. This was out toward Missionary Ridge, near where the electric railway now runs. We traded with the Johnnies, meeting them half way between the lines.—ED.

23rd.—Rained nearly all day.

24th.—Colonel C. H. Ripley resigned, and Lt. Colonel S. N. Yeoman assumed command of the regiment.

Got orders to move. We left about 9 o'clock at night, and were ordered to leave our tents stand and fires burning, as the army was in a critical position, and the object was to get out without the rebels knowing that any troops had been taken away. We silently and cautiously left our camp, crossed the Tennessee river, and "took to the woods." It was dark, and we groped our way through brush, through the mountains on the north side of the river, and at daylight ran the gauntlet of the rebel sharp-shooters posted at the narrows near Lookout Mountain. The reason for this line of march was the enemy was in possession of Lookout Mountain, and the river for some distance below, and it was not healthy to march so close to the river. ED.

25th.—The regiment moved on in the direction of Bridgeport, Ala., 26 miles below Chattanooga, along the crest of Waldron's Ridge, a spur of the Cumberland Mountains, until evening, when we camped for the night.

26th.—Marched back about six miles, a part of us, to help get the wagons out of the mud, and then turned and marched until night, camping on the mountain overlooking the Sequatchie valley.

27th.—Moved on again and reached the foot of the mountain in the direction of Jasper, Tenn. Camped in the Sequatchie valley. While the detail was back helping out the wagons, the regiment moved on, crossing the Tennessee River at Shellmound, Oct. 25th, on a pontoon bridge. Here we gathered material for tents, having left ours at Chattanooga, expecting to stay awhile. Shellmound was a station on the railroad and half a mile or so from the great Nickajack Cave. From this cave the rebels secured saltpetre in great quantities, which was boiled outside in great iron kettles, and used in the manufacture of powder to shoot us fellows. The whole valley at this point seems to be composed of shells, hence the name. We remained in camp at this place several days, doing picket duty, and fixing up tents.

31st.—The pontoon bridge across the river at Shellmound was taken up.

November 1, 1863.—Still at Shellmound. This is Sunday. Got orders this evening to be ready to move.

2nd.—Did not move to-day, as ordered, but remained here.

3rd.—Started this morning for Bridgeport, Ala., and got there in the afternoon. The boys went to work at once fixing up tents. We are here for the purpose of guarding two railroad bridges across the Tennessee river, while being rebuilt, and also to guard the stores at this place, as this is as far as the railroad is in running order.

4th.—A part of the regiment went out on the

mountain to blockade the road. While here a part of the regiment was sent up on top of a spur of the mountain, about three miles, to guard an old Presbyterian minister and his family, who were loyal; also to protect some rebel deserters who had left and come home. The old minister had a piano, and a handsome daughter who played on it. The boys said she could play euchre, too. Here was the nucleus of a college, a frame building about the size of one of our country school houses, and was started by this minister and a man by the name of Gordon. It was afterward General J. B. Gordon, of the Confederate Army.—ED.

5th, 6th, 7th and 8th.—Worked at our tents, which we understood were to be and were our winter quarters. On the eighth we drew full rations.

9th.—We commenced throwing up breastworks in front of the regiment. The works were built more to give the men exercise than anything else.

10th, 11th, 12th and 13th.—We spent in putting the finishing touches on our tents, reading and writing letters.

14th.—Began to rain. General Sherman's army from Mississippi is passing through here, on its way to Chattanooga to re-enforce Gen. Grant. The men look tired, but they tramp, tramp on.

15th.—This is Sunday. Had inspection this morning, and review in the afternoon.

16th, 17th and 18th.—Were spent in working on the breastworks, doing picket duty, etc.

19th.—To-day we were paid three months' pay.

20th.—Cloudy, and rained some.

21st.—Still raining. A detail was made to fix up the road at the river bank on the Bridgeport side, where the pontoon bridge is laid.

22nd.—This is Sunday. Had inspection and got mail.

23rd, 24th, 25th—the time was spent in regular camp routine, picket duty, etc.

26th.—This is Thursday, and the day set apart in Ohio, and the Union, as Thanksgiving Day. We kept it, too, and did no duty except picket duty.

27th.—This was a quiet day in camp.

28th.—Wet and disagreeable. A detail ditched a pond at the right of the regiment.

29th.—Got orders this morning to have three days' rations in our haversacks and be ready to start at two o'clock for Nashville with a lot of prisoners captured at Missionary Ridge, but they did not arrive, and we did not go.

30th.—Same orders to-day. The prisoners arrived about two o'clock, and our regiment took them on the island and guarded them during the night. And a sorry lot they were. Ragged, nearly bare-footed, and no tents, and the ground frozen hard. They managed to keep from freezing by building fires of logs and wood, of which there was plenty. They were sick of the job they had undertaken, and when asked how many men Bragg had left, one of them replied, "Well, about another killing."—Ed.

December 1st.—Still guarding the prisoners. Remained here all day, and drew rations for the prisoners. About 3,000 in this lot, and were sent north, in all, 6,100. The battles of Lookout Mountain, Chattanooga and Missionary Ridge were fought November 23-27.—Ed.

LANCASTER, O., August 5, 1894.

DEAR COMRADE : — While we lay at Bridgeport, Ala., I, with a company of 16 others were detailed as teamsters to take an ammunition train through to Chattanooga. As the enemy was in possession of a part of the river road, we went via of Jasper and Whitesides, guarded by a small detachment of cavalry.

We arrived near the town of Chattanooga, just as Hooker was opening the battle of Lookout Mountain, and leaving our teams in a sheltered place, we ascended Cameron Hill, from which we witnessed the great battle above the clouds.

When the fighting commenced on the north end of Mission Ridge, we were ordered up through the town, to a sheltered place in rear of Orchard Knob. We witnissed the Army of the Cumberland charge the works and take the Knob. From our position we saw the storming of Mission Ridge, and we became so excited that we forgot we had wagons loaded with ammunition. It was one of the grandest sights I ever witnessed. After the fight we reported to our command at Bridgeport.

I remember an incident of the battle of Chickamauga. About 4 o'clock on Sunday afternoon, I was detailed to go into the gap and assist in carrying off the wounded. We got them in the ambulances, and the way we went for Stevenson, Ala., was a caution. At Shellmound we stopped for a little rest. When I examined I found I had one dead man, whose name we learned from some papers on his person, to be Wilson, of an Illinois regiment. When we left the field of Chickamauga, that Sunday afternoon, it looked as if the devil had brooken loose, and was in control of the whole field.

I do not think General Rosecrans was fairly treated, in being relieved. If they had furnished him the men that they afterwards furnished General Grant, things would have been different. We all have a warm spot in our hearts for "Old Rosy."

S. E. WRIGHT, Co. I.

2nd. — Took our prisoners across the river to Bridgeport about 2 o'clock P. M., and put them on cars, (box cars), and ran to Stevenson, Ala.

3rd. — Started at 3 o'clock this morning for Nashville, and arrived there about dark. Took the prisoners to the barracks. Here we met some of the 90th boys on their way up to the regiment.

4th. — Remained at the barracks till evening, then went out near the state prison and went into camp.

5th. — Lay in camp. The balance of the regiment came up this evening with more prisoners. — All of the regiment was not on one train, and this explains seeming confliction of dates. — Ed.

6th. — Lay in camp, with orders to move at 3 o'clock in the morning.

7th. — Started back to Bridgeport, Ala., at 3 o'clock this morning, and arrived there about 8 o'clock in the evening. Part of the regiment did not leave until the 8th. They were delayed on account of a wreck, and did not get back until the 11th.

8th, 9th and 10th. — Lay in camp, drew rations, and read our mail.

11th. — The balance of the regiment got back from Nashville to-day.

12th, 13th and 14th. — Lay quiet in camp. Not much doing.

15th. — A detail was sent out to clear the road we blockaded when we first came here.

16th. — A detail from the regiment was sent out on a foraging expedition.

17th. — This was a cold, windy day.

18th, 19th. — Still cold. Nothing going on in camp more than usual.

From a recent photo.

THOMAS PARRISH, CO. B.
"The Old Blacksmith."

20th. — This is Sunday. Inspection as usual, on Sunday.

21st. — A detail was made to-day to go to Jasper, Tenn., as guard at General Stoneman's headquarters, over in the Sequatchie Valley.

22nd, 23rd and 24th. — Lay quiet in camp.

25th. — This is Christmas. How many changes since our last Christmas, when we lay near Nashville, starting the next day for Murfreesboro, where was fought the battle of Stone River. .Since that great battle we participated in the battle of Chickamauga. How many of our comrades have been killed, wounded, and have died! Where will we be next Christmas, and what will be the changes? We shall see.

26th and 27th. — Cold and rainy. Nothing of importance to record.

28th. — Lay in camp. Did not rain to-day.

29th. — Late in the evening went out after some rebels who were driving our cavalry back toward Stevenson.

30th. — Camped about 8 miles from Bridgeport. — This, we believe, is where the joke on Col. Yeoman originated: "Attention! 90th, I think I heard a gun!" The Colonel enjoyed the joke as much as any one, and used to laugh about it when he met us in our reunions after the war. — ED.

31st. — Raining. Started back to camp about noon, and got a good drenching from the rain. About night it turned cold.

January 1st, 1864. — This was a bitter, cold day, the coldest we have had this winter. — Our people who were in the North, remember the "Cold New Years." This was the day. — ED.

2nd. — Received our mail to-day. Still cold.

8 90 O V I

3rd. — Moderated and began to rain in the evening.

4th and 5th. — All quiet.  It has turned cold again.

6th. — This was another cold day.  A detail was made to haul sawdust from the Government mill across the river, to put in front of the Colonel's quarters.

7th. — Turned warmer and snowed some. — The boys had lots of fun at this time.  The woods were full of racoons, and they caught quite a number of them and dressed and cooked them. — ED.

8th. — Some of the boys went hunting.  They killed five rabbits.

9th. — We were inspected to-day, by Captain Fairbanks.

10th. — Nothing new in camp, only a few "grapevine" dispatches.  No war news.

11th. — The regiment drew rations to-day.

12th, 13th. — Cloudy but not cold.  Received mail again.

14th. — Drew 10 days' rations.  Nice weather for the time of year.

15th. — James Moravy, of Co. D, was buried to-day.  A funeral sermon was preached.  It was a good one, but short.

16th. — No war news to be had here.  Still warm.

17th. — This is Sunday.  Preaching at the chapel.  Most of the boys are on picket duty.

18th to 23rd. — Nothing only the regular routine of camp duty.

24th. — Inspection in the morning, and dress parade in the evening.  Got mail again.

25th. — Dress parade this evening.  Ordered to be ready to march at 7 o'clock in the morning.  We are to go up on the Georgia and East Tennessee R. R.

26th. — Left our camp at Bridgeport, Ala., and started on the march. Marched until 1 o'clock and went into camp at Whitesides. — W. G. Mauk calls it "Possumtail."

27th. — Resumed our march in the direction of Chattanooga, Tenn. Marched about 10 miles and went into camp in Lookout Valley.

28th. — Moved at 7 o'clock, crossed the point of Lookout Mountain, and camped in the Chattanooga Valley.

29th. — Left camp this morning, passed through Chattanooga, over Missionary Ridge, near Bragg's old headquarters, crossed Chickamauga Creek, near Graysville, and camped on "Scrub-bank Ridge."

30th. — Remained in our camp of last night until evening. We then got orders to take down our tents and put them up in regular order.

31st. — Policed our camp and had dress parade.

February 1, 1864. — Still in our camp.

2nd. — Still remain in camp. Quite cold and blustery.

3rd. — Broke camp, moved 2 miles and went into camp at Tyner's Station, 10 miles east of Chattanooga.

4th. — Worked hard putting up our tents, and at night got orders to move at 8 o'clock in the morning.

5th. — Moved on toward Knoxville, Tenn., this morning, marched 6 miles and went into camp at Ooltewah, Tenn., on the railroad.

6th. — Still in camp. No mail since we left Bridgeport.

7th. — Preaching at the church to-day, at 11 o'clock, and at 3 P. M. Our chaplain preached in the morning, and the chaplain of the 31st Ind., in the evening. Three companies of the 90th camped at Julian's Gap, about a mile east.

8th. — Nice weather. No mail, so no news.

9th, 10th, 11th and 12th. — Lay quietly in camp.

### OOLTEWAH, TENN.

I volunteered to go with a scouting party. We left camp at sundown, four of us, accompanied by Dr. Dorris, a loyal Tennessean. When Sunday closes we are still patroling the streets of Harrison. This we kept up until 2:30 A. M., searching every house and frightening women. By 3 o'clock A. M. we are asleep in the hotel, Dr. Dorris guarding our prisoner, Parker. We awake at daylight. We eat breakfast soon after sun-up, at the hotel, leaving town at 8 A. M., and reaching camp soon after 10 o'clock, weary and foot-sore, having searched every house in town, and captured one suspected spy.

My recollection is that Sergt. John Arehart was one of the four. The others I do not remember. My memory goes beyond my diary, recalling how we found some "Yankees" off their beat, and disturbed their peaceful slumbers by our midnight raid and rigid inquisition. As it now seems to me, our trip was attended with great danger, in that, at least, half rebel district. As I think of ourselves then, it was but "passtime."

It was Dr. Dorris' day to be avenged, and we were his "bloodhounds." We were harmless, however, and outside of what is narrated above, "did violence to no man."

S. C. Goss, Co. D.

We would like to ask Sergt. Goss if the "Yankees" referred to, wore No. 9 shoes. Perhaps Hi Brown and John Tritsch would like to know. — ED.

13th. — Four companies of the regiment were out on a scouting expedition.

14th. — Rainy. Preaching at the church to-day. Chilcote, says, "Our mess had a goose for dinner. Ovid Coleman got it while on the scout yesterday.

15th to 18th. — Lay quietly in camp.

16th. — Went out on another scout to-day.

17th and 18th. — Remained in camp.

19th. — Were paid two months' pay.

20th. Not quite so cold as it has been.

21st. — Preaching this morning, and prayer meeting at night.

22nd. — All quiet at Camp Ooltewah.

23rd. — Went out on a scout again.

24th. — Nice day. A detail was made to start in the morning, with two days' rations, to drive a lot of cattle to Red Clay, for the 2nd brigade.

25th. — The detail started for Red Clay this morning, and got there about noon, but our troops had left, so we followed them up, drove out to Tunnel Hill where our men were fighting, and had to turn back and drive the cattle 5 miles back to Dr. Lee's farm and go into camp. Marched over 30 miles.

26th. — Started back to Ooltewah, via Ringgold, and got to camp about sundown.

27th. — The regiment took another scout to-day.

28th to 31st. — Remained in camp. Got mail.

March 1, 1864, to 5th. — Nothing only the regular camp duties.

6th. — Dress parade. Preaching at Ooltewah, at 11 o'clock, by Hiram Douglas, an old citizen.

7th. — Skirmish drill this morning, and battalion drill in the evening.

8th to 11th. — Was spent in drilling, and other duties connected with the camp.

12th. — The regiment was detailed to guard a battery part of the way to Cleveland, Tenn.

13th. — Preaching this forenoon, and grand review in the evening.

14th. — Cold and windy. Drilled this evening.

15th. Drew clothing to-day. Had brigade drill in the evening.

16th to 22nd. — The time was spent in drilling, reviews, dress parade, etc.

22nd. — It was snowing this morning, and kept it up till noon. The snow was about 10 inches deep. We had a time snow-balling. Our regiment and one of the Kentucky regiments fell out and came near fighting, and with guns, too.

23rd. — Snow nearly all gone.

24th to 26th. — Windy, rainy, and bad weather, generally.

27th. — Preaching in the church. Review in the evening. Had a sermon preached to us at night in the regiment.

28th to 30th. — Drilled, when it was not raining, and did other camp duties. Nothing of importance to note.

31st. — The 31st Ind. regiment got back to-day, from home. There was an order that all regiments that had served two years or more, would get a 30-day furlough, if they would re-enlist for three years more. Many of the older regiments did so, and the 31st was one of them.

April 1, 1864. — The regiment drilled to-day.

2nd. — The companies policed (cleaned up) their quarters, and did some washing.

3rd. — Preaching this morning. Review in the afternoon, across in the bottom.

4th to 9th. — The same daily routine was gone through with, and nothing unusual happening.

10th. — This is Sunday. We were reviewed by Generals Thomas and Palmer.

11th. — Began target shooting. This was kept up for several days, the men making the best shots having their names reported to headquarters.

12th to 17th. — Drilling and shooting at targets, also doing picket duty.

18th. — The brigade was reviewed to-day by General O. O. Howard and staff.

19th. — Did not target practice to-day, but had brigade drill.

20th to 30th. — Was spent in drilling, getting ready for the summer campaign.

May 1, 1864. — Grand review and drill.

2nd. — Drilling as usual.

3rd. — Received orders this morning to be ready to march at 12 o'clock to-day, when we started toward Tunnel Hill, across on the W. & A. Railroad, south of us. Marched 5 miles and went into camp.

4th. — Resumed our march, and moved to Catoosa Springs, Ga., lay there until evening, then moved a short distance and drove in the rebel pickets, about 3 miles east of Ringgold, Ga., and camped on a ridge in the woods, in line of battle. — The boys had a "stag dance," then threw away their cards and were ready for the campaign. All through the night cow bells could be heard. The bells were not on cows, however, but were carried, as a ruse, by the enemy who lived in the vicinity, and were taking leave of home and families, preparatory to joining their comrades. Such is war. — ED.

5th. — Drew 3 days' rations. Some skirmishing to-day. — From this time until after the fall of Atlanta, Ga., I do not think there was a time when our regiment was out of hearing of guns. It was fight all the time, for 120 days. — Ed.

6th. — Still on the battle line near Ringgold.

7th. — Advanced on Tunnel Hill and drove in the pickets.

8th. — Still skirmishing near Tunnel Hill.

9th. — A detail went on picket. Still in the same camp.

10th. — Commenced firing on the rebel pickets at daylight, and kept it up all day. Our line did not advance any, but held the ground gained yesterday. Henry Emrine was wounded by a sharpshooter this evening as the pickets were coming out to relieve us.

11th. — At 4 o'clock P. M., our brigade made a charge up the side of Rock Face Ridge, to within a short distance of the enemy's works, then lay down and remained until dark, when they withdrew to their old position. — There was a narrow gap through which the railroad and creek ran. Across this creek the enemy had built a dam, and filled the creek full of brush. In the gap were the enemy's batteries. The writer was on the side of the mountain, on picket, when the charge was made. In the rear was a knoll on which we had a battery. Only a short distance in front and a little to our right was the rebel batteries in the gap. In front of us in the woods on the side of the mountain, were the enemy's infantry. When the charge was made, we were ordered to remain where we were. Our battery in our rear was throwing shot over us through the timber; our men were firing over us as they charged; the battery in the gap cut loose;

From a war-time photo.

MAJ. JAMES F. COOK.

the rebels in front with their rifles were shooting into us, and taking it all together, it made things quite interesting, as the brush cracked and the limbs fell. After our men withdrew, leaving their dead in the woods, it was still interesting. The Johnnies would start a rock rolling down, when we would fire in the direction from which it came, and, they seeing the flash of our guns, would let loose on us. Then all would be quiet for a short time, when the same thing would be repeated, and thus it was kept up all night. Some time ago, we saw where a comrade had made application for a pension for wounds received by being hit by a stone at Rocky Face Ridge, and we suppose he got it that night. — ED.

### ROCKY FACE, GA.

If no objection I will "carry a rail," in order to kindle the fire for a little warm coffee.

In regard to that charge at Rocky Face Ridge, at the railroad gap, let another eye witness relate an incident. Being on picket with a detail from our regiment and others, we charged the rebel pickets, drove them back and across the railroad track. I, being on the extreme left of the line, came right up by the gap. We all got on the track, shooting at the rebels while they were wading through the back water, or swamp. Lordy! we splashed water on them with our bullets, but the next moment they opened up to our left from the fort above that famous gap and let drive a solid 6-pounder at us who were on the track. It went past me at a great velocity, and not far from my head. I didn't know whether I was in Georgia or at home in Ohio, but one thing I do know, I nor no more of the boys stayed on the track very long. I stood on the left-hand rail, the shot struck the 7th tie back of me on the outside rail. Now, you can figure out the distance. A Co. F boy stood on the 7th tie, and it doubled him up and rolled him down the 15-foot embankment, his knapsack being on top half the time. Of course we gave the usual grunt, "Poor boy," as we thought him dead, but he was only stunned. After he got the knapsack off, he got up, and we all felt better, and I began to feel for my red handkerchief to wipe my feverish forehead, but I could not reach the top of my hat — my hair had pushed it out of my reach, or it seemed so, and my hair is gray yet.

Now, if that was not a Co. F boy, who was he?

Next morning the rebels had left and I counted that tie, and as the humorist, Mark Twain said, "There was just 7 of them." JOHN P. URBIN, Co. D.

12th. — Moved a short distance to the right and took position on the hill side.

13th. — The enemy evacuated the gap last night, being flanked by our troops. We started, went through the gap and through Dalton, Ga., just on the opposite side. Marched 8 miles and overtook them; had a little brush and routed them again, near the Coosa River.

14th. — Resumed our march at daylight, and at 10 o'clock we encountered the enemy near Rosaca, Ga. — Our brigade was on the extreme left of the line, in the woods, without any support. The 31st Ind. on the extreme left, our regiment next. Co.'s B and G lay to the left of a road on which the rebels had a battery, and were ordered to fall back with the 31st Ind., in case they had to fall back. Soon the rebels came up in front on a charge and were repulsed. Again they came, this time obliquely, and were repulsed again. A third time they came, and this time came in on the left flank, and Johnnies and Yankees were mixed together in a hand-to-hand encounter. The 31st Ind. and the two companies across the road were forced to fall back, and the regiment to swing to the rear. The object was to envelope our brigade and effect its capture. In the rear was a battery which the enemy very much coveted, and which was doing excellent work, and they determined to capture it. The battery double charged the guns with grape and canister. The rebels got close to the battery, and would have succeeded in capturing it, but just at that moment, and none too soon, General Hooker, who had double-quicked his men, arrived and saved us. The Johnnies were taken back faster than they came. It is said that 316 dead rebels were counted in front of that battery, but of course many were killed by musketry. We were relieved and placed on the reserve line, and did not take an active part in the battle of the next day. — ED.

15th. — This was the second day of the battle of Resaca, Ga., and heavy fighting has been going on all day.

16th. — The enemy evacuated Resaca last night, and this morning we moved out across the battle-field, through Resaca, crossed the Coosa River, marched 3 miles farther down the W. & A. R. R.

17th. — Had a hard fight to-day. They had to fight us in order to detain us while they got their wagon train and baggage out of the way.

18th. — The enemy having left during the night, we moved out through Adairsville and camped near the railroad.

19th. — Resumed our march, passed through Kingston, skirmishing with the rear guard.

20th. — Lay in camp at Cassville. Drew 3 days' rations.

21st and 22nd. — Lay in camp near Adairsville.

23rd. — Moved out about 4 miles and crossed the Ettowah River, marched about 6 miles and camped in a big wheat field.

24th. — Marched slowly all day. Were caught in a storm about dark, and then marched about 6 miles after dark.

25th. — Marched briskly all day, and at evening came up to where the 20th corps was fighting, formed in line and remained all night in the woods. — This was a dark, rainy night, and the groans of the wounded and dying could be heard all night. Men were searching the woods with torches for the wounded, and men were being carried out on stretchers. It was a sad, weird night. — ED.

26th. — Moved a short distance in line of battle, halted and drew rations.

27th. — Moved to the front line and relieved another brigade, but were soon taken back to the rear where we were massed, and remained until morning.

28th. — Moved about 2 miles to the left and erected breastworks, in the rear of Wood's division.

29th. — Finished the works and remained here during the day.

30th. — Went out on a hill to our left to support Stoneman's cavalry. We were relieved in the evening and returned to our works, but got orders to guard a supply train back to Kingston, and marched back to Pumpkinvine Creek.

31st. — Resumed our march toward Kingston.

June 1, 1864. — Moved on and arrived at Kingston, a distance of 30 miles from the front, about 10 o'clock in the morning.

2nd and 3rd. — Remained at Kingston while the wagons were being loaded.

4th. — Started for the front, going 8 miles, and camped for the night.

5th. — Marched to the Altoona Hills and camped.

6th. — Crossed the hills, passed Burnt Hickory, got on the wrong road, turned back and went about 6 miles and camped.

7th. — Moved on and reached the front, near Dallas, Ga, the rebels having retreated. During our absence the army had moved forward to near Ackworth, Ga.

8th. — We laid out a regular camp in the woods. Some of the boys got some cotton bales for bedding. Drew 5 days' rations.

9th. — We remained in camp.

10th. — Moved out in pursuit of the enemy, who showed himself in our front. We did not go far until we encountered the rebels, and fighting began. Having formed our line of battle, we advanced a short distance and erected works close to the enemy's position.

11th. — Moved about half a mile to the left and remained until evening, then advanced a short distance and built works after night.

12th. — Remained in our camp of last night; all day in a drenching rain.

13th. — The rain still continued, and we remained in the same place, with picket firing all day.

14th. — This afternoon we moved to the left a short distance and remained during the night.

15th. — The enemy left our front and we moved out in pursuit, marching over Bald Knob, where General Polk was killed; advanced out in the valley and found the enemy again entrenched. We took position and fortified. The charge on Bald Knob was made under the personal eye of Major General Thomas, and by his orders. The position had been taken once before by a brigade, but they failed to hold it, but the 90th succeeded in occupying, fortifying and holding it, until they were removed to the right to assist in holding another key position from which a regiment had been repulsed. This they did after night, fortified and held it. General Thomas issued a complimentary order in recognition of the gallant conduct of the 90th Ohio, in these engagements.

16th. — Remained in our position of last night until dark, then advanced.

### FROM MARIETTA, GA., TO KENESAW MOUNTAIN.

June 14, 1864, the Rebel General Polk was killed by a shot from the 5th Indiana battery, on Pine Mountain.

The 15th we occupied Pine Mountain.

On the 16th Valentine Cupp of Co. D, was wounded.

17th. — We were relieved by 3rd Division.

18th. — Jacob Westenberger, of Co. I, was wounded. This night the enemy abandoned their works, along a few miles north of Kenesaw Mountain.

19th. — Our batteries shelled them, with a vengeance.

20th. — Moved to the right and in front of Bald Knob. Here Wm. Springer, of Co. D, and James Church, of Co. I, were wounded.

Springer died July 12, and is buried at Marietta, Ga. Church died July 12, at Bremen, O., both wounded on the same day and both died on the same day, one in Georgia, the other in Ohio. — ED.

21st. — Charged and carried Bald Knob. This assault was severe. In an open field, with some dead trees, we fortified under fire of the enemy. I thought then this may be my last day, but really, I thought of everything, past and present. The heat was intense with frequent thunder showers from above, and Rebel bullets from the front. Joe Wilson, of Co. D, wounded severely; Wm. Eby, of Co. F, killed; Osborne Philips, Co. A, wounded.

24th. — Capt. Witherspoon, of Co. I, was wounded.

27th of June, 1864, we will always remember. The heat of the sun about 95 degrees in the shade, and with Rebel missiles flying, and within 150 yards of the Rebel works, was almost beyond human endurance. Sergt. W. H. Strode, of Co. D, was wounded; 1st Sergt. Amos S. Leist, killed; Paul Westenberger, of Co. I, wounded — a hole shot through his ear; Capt. W. A. Denny, wounded in the shoulder.

29th. — Armistice between the two armies was agreed to, when we buried the dead. In one trench we put 16 of our comrades, in a state of decomposition, with limbs burnt off by fire that was raging in the woods, a ghastly sight to behold.

July 3, 1864. — Took possession of Kenesaw Mountain; continued to march and skirmish, over hills, through ravines, underbrush, Rebel earth works, into gopher holes the Rebels had made. Four miles south of Marietta we found them in line, with a bold front.

July 4, 1864. — Independence Day we were shelled by the enemy, fiercely, at first, but we moved on to them, and drove them to a line where they had gopher holes by the wholesale. We were in one line of their abandoned works and they were in front of us, a few hundred yards, in a strongly entrenched position, defying the Yankees with a Fourth of July celebration, with leaden hail, cannon shot, shells exploding around, singing sweetly as they passed over us, while we were hugging the ground.

About 10 o'clock a. m. the scene was getting quite warm for a national holiday. George Spangler, of Co. D, who had been absent on sick leave, for a long time, happened to return in time to participate in the celebration. Wm. Beecher began to explode, himself. Just then Spangler was shaking like an aspen, in the gopher hole, the first time under fire.

Beecher was full of fun, and as he heard the shells sing in the forest around and about us, he exclaimed, "Oh how sweet, how lovely they sing the song, 'America,'

> " 'My country 'tis of thee,
> Sweet land of liberty.' "

Spangler raised his head and said to Beecher: "You ought to be ashamed to mock those shells, when we are in such a close place. We may all be killed before night.'

Beecher replied: "Don't get nervous, the Johnnies are only celebrating the Fourth of July, and I want to enjoy the glorious opportunity."

It created quite a sensation; some laughing; some angry; but the most were cold and defiant, and blazed away at the enemy.

Well, I never saw a man any cooler than Beecher was in that tussel with the Rebels. I enjoyed it. It gave me more courage and enthusiasm for the fray. Nothing like zeal, courage and determination in time of battle.
                                           S. D. SOLIDAY.

CoLUMBUS, O., Jan. 24, 1894.

A great many remember Bald Knob. I do, for I was one of the number that was on picket, and happened to be stationed direct in front of the Knob, in the edge of the woods, and was about 700 or 800 yards from the picket line, with quite a ravine between. The Rebs had rifle pits and were well protected, while we had trees for our protection. Every time either of us showed himself, "whiz" would come a bullet. I exchanged seven shots with a gray coat and he hit the tree several times that I was behind. We were ordered to charge their line, and you can imagine how the bullets did fly and whiz around us. They had to fall back, but we did not hold the line long, for they came up with their whole battle line. They got so

From a recent photo.

Color Guard S. S. Stover, Co. K.

near us before we saw them over the hill that they
halted us and called us names not appropriate for a
lady Sunday school teacher to use, and the way the
bullets were flying about us was a caution. Run for
your life, and you bet we did run. I had a hole shot
through my hat and one shoe heel shot off. They
worked both ends, but thank Providence, they didn't
hit the middle.

Charlie Church, by my side, was wounded in the
leg. He was a one year man, and had not been with
us long, but he was a brave soldier. He was sent
home, and I never saw him afterwards, but heard he
is dead.

We charged their line the next day (I don't recollect the date), with our battle line and took some
prisoners. While throwing up breast works and cutting out underbrush, we had six men killed, one after
the other, each had his head shot off. The Rebels
had range of us and it was a difficult job to cut out
space for our cannon, but when we got our gun in,
we soon settled them.

I was out three years, and I think that was about
as close a place as I was ever in.

Butler, how is the old Tom Cat and the banjo?

Yours truly,

NATHANIEL KNOTTS, Co. I.

17th. — The enemy again on the retreat. Marched
out, overtook them and skirmished until evening.

18th. — Advanced in a heavy rain, and mud knee
deep. In the evening moved to the right, under fire
of the enemy's artillery, and erected works at night.

19th. — Finding the enemy had met and left, we
moved out after them, had a skirmish and camped
in the woods.

20th. — Moved to the right half a mile and relieved a part of the 20th corps. In the afternoon

our skirmishers advanced and took a hill, but were driven back.

21st. — At 4:00 o'clock the 90th and 31st Indiana advanced, retook the hill, held and fortified it.

22nd. — Remained on the hill until night, when we were relieved by the 14th corps. We then moved to the right about a mile.

23rd. — Advanced a short distance, drove the Rebels back and fortified our position at night, but were relieved and went to the rear line.

24th. — Remained in our works.

25th. — Did not move until night, then moved out to the front line again

26th. — Skirmished all day and at night were relieved.

27th. — A grand assault was made on the Rebel works on Kenesaw Mountain, but without success, and our men were driven back with great loss. This is known as the battle of Kenesaw Mountain, Ga.

28th. — Skirmishing all day, but it ceased at night, when our men brought in and buried our comrades who had been killed the day before in the great battle.

29th. — Quiet during the day, but at night a brisk fire commenced, but did not last long.

30th. — All quiet, as getting ready for another fight. Each army watching the other.

July 1, 1864. — This proved to be another quiet day.

2nd. — Brisk cannonading commenced this morning and lasted about an hour, during which the skirmishers replied tellingly. Our Major, George Angle, of Logan, O., was killed during this fusilade.

3rd. — The Rebels evacuated during the night. We marched in pursuit. Close by Marietta, and about six miles beyond we again found the enemy entrenched.

4th. — We celebrated the Fourth of July by advancing our lines. We captured and drove in the skirmishers, and fortified close to the Rebel works.

5th. — The enemy is gone again, as usual. We marched to the Chattahoochie River and encamped.

6th. — Here we remained until the 10th and then moved up the river six miles.

11th and 12th. — Lay in this camp.

13th. — Crossed the river, moved down about 2 miles, where we went into camp and fortified.

14th to 17th. — We remained in this camp.

18th. — Moved out toward Atlanta, Ga., about 4 miles, where we again found the enemy.

19th. — Moved this afternoon about 2 miles, crossed Peach Tree Creek and fortified.

20th. — Marched toward Atlanta, drove in the skirmishers, and halted for the night.

21st. — Remained here all day, with but little skirmishing in our front. We are within three miles of Atlanta, the coveted prize.

It must be remembered by our readers, who were not soldiers, that the 90th was only one of hundreds of other organizations composing General Sherman's great army, and that this army, divided into corps, divisions, brigades and batteries, which the great general was maneuvering, flanking the Confederate commander out of the many strongholds. — ED.

22nd. — The enemy has fallen back to Atlanta, and we moved up close to their works and fortified. A big battle took place to-day, on our left, in which General J. B. McPherson was killed. This is known as the Battle of Atlanta, Ga.

23rd. — Erected quarters in camp, and remained until the

26th. — Moved at night about a mile to the rear and camped.

27th. — Remained in this camp all day and night.

28th. — Went back to Peach Tree Creek to guard a train, and returned to camp in the evening. Here we remained until

August 1, when we moved to the front near the railroad east of Atlanta, and camped. We remained here doing duty until the

16th. — This was the siege of Atlanta. Moved a short distance to the left where we remained until the

25th. — Then commenced our great flank movement, which caused the evacuation of Atlanta. We moved out quietly, after dark, marched around to the rear of the 15th corps, northwest of Atlanta, the Rebels following us.

26th. — Moved to the right, the rear guards skirmishing with the Rebels, who followed us closely until they came to the 15th corps, which had fortified to check them. We marched until evening and camped in the rear of the 14th corps, which was the extreme right of our army.

27th. Moved toward the Montgomery railroad, encountered the enemy in force, and fortified.

28th. — Moved at noon, marched until night and camped near the railroad, where we remained until the

30th. — When we resumed out march, crossed the railroad and camped close to where the Rebels were fortified.

31st. — Marched out, drove the Rebels from their works and camped near the Macon railroad.

September 1, 1864. — Moved to the railroad, early, and began tearing it up, which we continued to do until we overtook the Rebels near Jonesboro, Ga. We deployed, pressed forward, driving them before us. The battle raged furiously until dark closed the scene of carnage.

2nd. — The Rebels having evacuated Atlanta, joined the forces which fought near Jonesboro, south of the latter place. We moved on, overtaking them near Lovejoy Station. Here we remained until the

5th. — When we marched back to Jonesboro.

6th. — Remained at Jonesboro, Ga.

7th. — Moved early, and camped on a small stream.

8th. — Marched on this morning through Atlanta, and to the old battle ground, where General McPherson was killed, and went into camp. We remained there until October 3.

CROOKS, KY., Jan. 22, 1894

DEAR COMRADES: As our Editor has promised to put in print our letters, I have made up my mind to lend a helping hand. I have read the History with much interest and am truly sorry to find it brought to a close. Let us join in with our individual experience, thereby helping Comrade Harden out a little, and at the same time learn where many of the survivors of the bloody 90th reside. I have in mind the other name some of them gave our regiment, but will withhold it, for the present. But, as some of the boys have confessed to crimes, committed while in Dixie, and at the same time knowing that an open confession is good for the soul, I will relate a small part of my experience. It was after we fell back from Lovejoy, and went in camp at Atlanta, on the battlefield where General McPherson was killed on the 22nd of July, Sergt. Abe Trout, of Co. E, was on picket. While there fell in company with a captain belonging to the

Second Brigade of our division, and during their conversation, the captain said to him that he was very fond of milk, and that he had been fortunate enough to have plenty. During the campaign he had captured a fine muley cow, soon after our leaving Chattanooga, and he had a negro cook that never failed to keep that cow up and milked regularly. Therefore, he had all the milk he could drink. Comrade Trout came in and told me about it. I said, 'wouldn't she make good beef, as well as give good milk." He said: "I suppose she would, if we could get her." I told him we would try to capture muley. That night about 5 p. m. there came one of those quick thunder storms, and we started in pursuit of muley. We found her grazing in an old field. She had the head stall of a halter on, and was fat and sleek, and while the thunder rolled and the lightning flashed, and everybody got in their tents, I caught muley, and at the same time got full benefit of the rain, for I don't think it ever did rain harder. Away we went with our prize, unmolested. I led her about a mile, into a dense thicket, and tied her up, went back to camp and notified a half dozen of the boys to be ready at dusk, and we would have some beef. We started, and after hunting some time in the dark, and dark it was, could not have any light, we found her, and a nice job of butchering soon took place. My mess got one quarter and muley's liver, which was quite a change from "sow belly." Got to camp, dug a hole in the ground under the bunk, cut up our beef, put it in a box, secreted it under the bunk, without salt, for we had none. Next morning I was detailed to go on picket. We cooked the liver for breakfast, and soon after, I left for the picket line, with the understanding some one would get salt. The whole command was looked over for salt. Not one grain could be secured. I came in next morning with that blessed hope of feasting on beef. But oh, imagine my surprise when they told me it was all spoiled. Thus ended the life of muley, and it was not Chilcote's cow, either.

Now, comrades, I am going to close by saying, I was run over accidentally by a heavy loaded wagon, soon after the battle of Stone River; was wounded in the right leg on Saturday, at Chickamauga; shot in the arm at Rasaca, 14th of May; and shot at several times and missed, not saying anything about how many times I ran. The regiment never moved without me, when there was any fighting to be done.

Yours truly,<br>
H. S. Brown, Co. E.

October 3. — When we started back to Big Shanty, now called Kenesaw Station, after General Hood, who is in our rear. Camped 5 miles from Marietta, Ga., and 18 miles from Atlanta. From there the regiment marched over about the same ground it had marched in its advance on Atlanta. Every nerve was strained to intercept General Hood, who was makin his way toward Nashville. All the familiar, blood-bought scenes of the march were again viewed by the brave men, and while in camp, lying behind breast-works that had been constructed by Rebel hands, the story of their deeds were recounted and new resolves made.

Oct. 4th. — Marched through Marietta, and camped at the foot of Kenesaw Mountain.

5th. — Marched to Bald Knob, and lay there until the 8th, awaiting orders.

8th. — Moved to near Ackworth. The railroad is cut, and we get no mail.

9th. — Moved a short distance in the evening.

10th. — Marched through Ackworth, Altoona Pass, crossed the Ettowah River and camped late in the night.

11th. — Moved early, passed through Cartersville,

Cassville and Kingston. About noon marched toward Rome, Ga., a short distance, and camped.

12th. — Marched on toward Rome, until late at night, and went into camp.

13th. — Went on toward Resaca, Ga., until late at night, and went into camp 15 miles from Resaca.

14th. — Moved out, passed through Calhoun and Resaca, and camped on the old battlefield of Resaca, where we fought the preceding 14 and 15th of May.

15th. — Left camp, but did not follow the railroad, but marched across toward the old Chickamauga battlefield, where we fought a little over a year ago, up the valley about 4 miles, crossed Rocky Face Ridge into Snake River Gap, 7 miles from Resaca.

16th. — Marched again to-day and went into camp 12 miles from Dalton, in the Chickamauga valley.

17th. — Moved a short distance in the direction of Sommerville.

18th. — Moved southeast 20 miles.

19th. — Moved across the river and camped near Sommerville.

20th. — Started at daylight and went in the direction of Gailsville, Ga., and camped near that place until the

27th. — We then started toward Chattanooga and camped at Alpine.

28th. — Marched to Lafayette, Ga.

29th. — Left Lafayette, moved toward Chattanooga and camped at Rossville, 4 miles from Chattanooga.

30th. — Moved to Chattanooga, where our corps, the Fourth, all took the cars, except our brigade.

31st. — Our brigade moved across Lookout Moun-

CORP. W. G. MAUK, CO. E.

Several of his poems are in this book. He rose to the position of P. E. in the U. B. Church. His widow lives at Basil, O.

COL. N. F. HITCHCOCK.

He went out as Capt. of Co. H. His widow lives at Sterling, Neb.

LITTLE JOHNNY MOORE. Co. H.

He is the boy whom the Bushwhackers captured near Pulaski, Tenn. From a photo taken at Manchester, Tenn., 1863.

HENRY O. HARDEN. Co. G.— 1862.

He is the publisher of this book.

tain with the wagon train, and camped in Lookout Valley, at Wauhatchie.

November 1, 1864. — Moved down the Tennessee River, passed Whitesides, and camped at Brown's Ferry.

2nd. — Moved on down to Bridgeport, Ala., where we left the preceding January.

3rd. — Marched to Stevenson, Ala.

4th. — Marched only 6 miles. The roads were so bad the wagons could get no farther.

5th. — On the move again. Marched through Anderson, went 12 miles and camped at the base of the mountain at Tantalon.

6th. — Started up the mountains. Only got about 2 miles.

7th. — Marched to Cowen, Tenn, across the mountain.

8th. — Moved to Decherd. Held our election this evening.

9th. — Moved out through Winchester and Salem, Tenn., 15 miles and camped. It rained all day.

10th. — Marched all day through an unbroken forest, but came to a good country at night. Camped near Fayetteville, Tenn. Little Johnny Moore, of Co. H, was captured here, while returning from camp to the picket line, by bushwhackers, who had got inside our lines. We will let him tell the story of his capture and escape which is as follows:

### CAPTURED BY GUERILLAS.

Our brigade was left to guard the wagon train from where we left Sherman to Pulaski, Tenn. On our way we stopped at Fayetteville for the night. I was detailed on picket duty that night. Henry C. Laughman and myself were sent back by the corporal

for our rations of beef.  We got our beef and were
returning to our post.  Coming in contact with a big
patch of burrs, Laughman went on one side and I on
the other, when, lo, I heard the word "halt."  I took
a step or two more, when, O, horrors!  I was looking
right into the muzzle of a 44 pistol.  Wasn't I scared!
Well, I did some thinking.  I had run right into these
guerillas, one lying behind a log with his deadly
weapon pointing right at my heart, and one standing
with his gun right between my eyes.  I might die a
hundred times and not suffer the agony I did then.  I
knew I was captured by the worst class of men in the
South.  To be captured by guerillas we all knew meant
death.  Well, comrades, imagine if you can, how I felt.
My captors took me out, and we had not gone a rod
when here stood another one up against a tree.  I
thought my time was up.  We got out through the
picket line and went on, and as we walked I was
thinking.  I said to myself, "Good-bye, Colonel Yeoman; good-bye, comrades, you will never see little
Johnny Moore again.  Farewell, mother, sisters,
brothers, little Johnny is gone.  We went about a
mile from camp and stopped.  But, I am too fast.
They took me to the log where the one was lying and
questioned me concerning the number of troops we had
in our command.  I knew General Forest was hanging
around on our flanks, so I thought I would give them
a good one.  I told them we had a division, or about
6,000 men, besides teamsters.  One of them said,
"Have you that many men down thar?"  I said, "Get
up and look for yourself.  You can see the campfires from here."  He got up and looked a good while
and sat down and said, "Well sah, I believe you have
that many men down thar.  Who is commanding that
division?"  And right then I came near spoiling it all.
I told him it was General Kirby.  "Who is General
Kirby?"  Said he, "General Kirby, did you say, sah?"
"Yes, sir," I said.  "General Kirby is commanding
that division, as brave an officer as ever crossed Tennessee, sir.  He has lately been promoted for bravery."
"Well, sah, you are right, I guess."  Turning to the

others he said, "Forrest could not do anything with that many infantry." They said, "No, sah, it won't be worth while to send him word."

I shall always believe that is what saved our wagon train. If Forrest had known there was nothing there but a little brigade, he would have captured the whole thing.

Well, now for what became of little Johnny Moore. From where we stopped we soon got on horses and started on, got to a house and put up, it being about one o'clock in the night. One kept guard over me and the others lay down and slept. When morning came two of them started back toward camp for a canteen of whiskey. They went to a house where they kept that beverage, but, lo, Capt. Witherspoon with his twelve boys had voluntered to go out and hunt for little Johnny Moore, and they ran right into those fellows, capturing one, the other getting away. The captain gave him some short talk, but he showed up his protection papers as a citizen doctor, and Capt. had to let him go. He came back to where we were, the maddest man I ever saw, swore the hills were full of Yankees, but the captain had struck him right. He told him they were going to stay there two weeks, and were going to kill two men for one that was gone; were going to get the right ones if they could, and then were going to kill them. Thank you, Captain, that was what saved Johnny Moore.

After he got through with his conversation with the others, casting side glances at me, (I took in every move, for I expected my carcass would be thrown out and covered with leaves), two of them came to me and said they were going to take me up to an officer to be paroled. They got three horses, bidding me get behind one of them. They rode along, side by side, and right here they set a trap for me. I know I was awfully scared, but not enough to bite at their bait. The one I was on behind left his revolver stick out of his pocket so I would try to grab it and shoot him before he could interefere. I looked at the revolver, then at our partner. I found he was riding with his hand on his gun, ready, should I make a move. So I concluded I would let it go and wait further developments. They took me twelve miles from camp and did not parole me, as they could find no officer, they said. They considered the matter a few minutes and concluded to let me go, so they dumped me down on the ground and told me to go back to camp, and if ever they should fall into our hands to do all I could for them. I thanked them for their kindness while in their company, and started for camp. It was about two hours more of sun, and I twelve miles from camp; but I started in a walk until I got out of their sight, then I got into a dog trot, and I am not certain but that I ran as fast as I could part of the time, but I was so badly scared I don't know whether I did or not; but I do know that every leaf that was blown by the wind on the roadside, I was on the other side quicker than a sheep could shake its tail. I made twelve miles before sun down, but, oh, when I got to camp the brigade was gone. I took the trail and was almost tired out, when about two miles from their camp I saw a company of cavalry about half a mile ahead of me, I thought may be they are our men; but I had got to the place to be cautious. I let them pass over the hill, and went on. Seeing a little boy sitting on a gate post, I asked him if they were Yankees or Rebels that were on before. He said they had blue clothes on, and I felt relieved, but thought I would go on and look over the hill. So I did, but just as soon as my head appeared above the hill, one of them saw me and back he came. I thought I was gone again, but he rode up and proved to be one of our 1st Tennessee boys. "Are you the boy that was captured?" said he. I told him I was. "Well, just get on this horse and ride." I felt pretty good about that time. There was no fear of guerillas where the 1st Tennessee was. I stayed all night with them, and rode a big gray horse, bare back, the next day. He was sharp as a razor. I got to the regiment that night, being absent two days. I never shall forget that old gray horse. He made an "impression" on me that would be hard to forget.

I found the boys all right and looking better than I had even seen them. The Colonel certainly was the best man I ever saw.

Well, boys, I shall never be captured by guerillas again. I believe I am ten years older than I would have been had it not been for that capture.

Now, boys, farewell, for this time. We are all getting old and must soon answer the last "roll call."

LITTLE JOHNNY MOORE.

YELLOW SPRINGS, OHIO.

I enlisted in the Grand Old 90th, Aug. 13th, 1862. My mind has been very busy since the history of the Regiment has been in progress, reading over the accounts as quoted from the diaries of Chilcote and Mauk. By the way, boys, do you know that Chilcote and I were bunk mates for a long time? Of course I would not give anything away intentionally. When the Regiment broke camp near Nashville, in December, 1862, and marched out on the pike, the orders were for all sick to be sent back to Nashville. John and I were among the number sent back, the squad being in command of Captain McDowel. By some maneuvering of the Captain we did not stay long in Nashville, but were sent out nine miles to guard a stockade and from there to the regiment at Cripple Creek.

This was our only absence from the regiment while in the service. I still stuck to John for a bunk mate, for it was there (I think) that John went into the dairy business, and we drank milk from the same canteen, but to tell you the color of the cow, boys, I couldn't, if I was to be hung. John and I got some onions when on picket at Cripple Creek, from an old lady's garden, but it proved to be an uphill business at that time, for the old lady came to camp next morning and Colonel Rippey said, "boys there is a tariff on onions to the amount of $1.00 apiece. The old lady returned home happy, and I hope always remained so.

By reading the letters from the different members of the Regt., my memory has been refreshed, and a great many things I had forgotten have been brought back to me. The one from Jonas Chenoweth reminds me of marching through Kentucky, when Uncle Sam could not furnish you a pair of shoes. You marched on, barefooted, leaving your footprints stained with blood; too gritty, old boy, to go to the rear or ride in an ambulance. Another from little Johnny Moore. Yes, John, well do I remember the evening you were captured. The next morning a company of us went out to look for you and we got hold of an old citizen, tied his hands behind his back, and standing him up against a tree, threatening to shoot him. We got all he knew about the Bushwackers that captured you, and with a promise from him that he would deliver either message for us to them, that if they did not let you go, or if they killed you we would burn everything in twenty miles square. I think the old man lost no time in delivering the message, and I do know how glad we all were when you came to us. Thirty years have passed since then, yet my mind runs over the many incidents of our army life, they are as vivid as if they had happened but yesterday. I would like to read a letter from every comrade of the regiment. But, here, my letter is too long. I am like all of the boys. I am over the hill of life, going down on the other side; nearing the time when I will answer to the "last roll call."

With best wishes to you all, I am ever yours in F. C. & L.

B. Lott, Co. H.

Cheyboygan, Mich., December 18, 1893.

It is my sad duty to report the capture of William F. Lytle, of Co. I, by bushwackers. This occurred in the fall of 1864, while we were guarding the wagon train back to Pulaski, Tenn., from Chattanooga. One afternoon Lytle and I got permission of Capt. J. S. Witherspoon to go out foraging. The Captain cautioned us to be very careful and not get very far away. We were at a farmhouse, not over half a mile from the road and in plain view of the passing train. I was under a tree gathering apples, while Lytle and a man dressed in our uniform and riding a brown mule chased a pig near the top of a ridge. The man was on top of the ridge, and Lytle a few rods below. Lytle fired at the pig when the man on the mule rushed down on him with a carbine in his hand. Apparently he spoke a few words to him, when Lytle turned toward me, took off his hat and waved it twice at me to go, then he turned and ran up over the hill close behind the mule, and has never been heard of since, so far as I know. There were several men and officers there at the time, and I told them that the man was capturing one of our men, "Oh no," said they, "that is one of our men." I insisted I was right, but they would not believe it. Some thought I ought to have shot the fellow. How could I, when he was 600 or 800 yards away, and Lytle between us. I can not give the date, but think it was the evening of that day when two of Co. H's men were captured inside of our lines. One dodged and got away, and the other they liberated the next evening, when he came to us at Pulaski, Tenn., which has always been a mystery to me.

SYLVESTER RADER, Co. I.

October 11.—Marched hard all day and camped. W. G. Mauk says at Clifton, John Chilcote says at Boonville.

12th.—Marched 18 miles, and camped four miles from Pulaski, Tenn.

13th.—Marched to Pulaski, turned over the wagon train to the proper authorities, and reported to our division and went into camp on a high hill, where we almost froze. Remained here until

November 23rd.—Moved out in the direction of Nashville, and marched 16 miles.

24th.—Started early, passed through Linnville, and
arrived at Columbia, Tenn., in the evening.

25th.—Moved out, took position and fortified.

26th.—Worked on the fortifications all day.

27th.—Moved out across Duck river.

28th. Moved up the river a short distance and
fortified.

29th.—Moved to the left and rear a short distance,
formed in line of battle and fortified. Our army was
now racing with Gen. Hood, the Confederate commander, for Nashville. We remained till dark and
then withdrew, and marched on the Franklin pike,
passing close by the rebel camp at Spring Hill, and
arrived at Franklin at 10 o'clock next day.

30th.—Fortified our position, and at 4 o'clock P.
M., Hood's army came up and assaulted our lines re-
peatedly, but was repulsed each time. The battle
lasted until dark, when we abandoned our works,
crossed the river, and fell back to Nashville, arriving
there the next day. Franklin was probably the blood-
iest and most destructive battles of the war, for the
number of men engaged, and the time it lasted. The
Confederates lost many officers in the engagement.

December 1, 1864.—Arriving at Nashville, ahead of
Gen. Hood's army, Gen. Thomas at once began to con-
solidate the troops, and organize for the annihilation
of the rebel army under Hood. The troops were organized, the cavalry remounted, and Gen. Thomas
waited for suitable weather to begin active and offensive operations. The authorities at the city of Washington were very urgent that Gen. Thomas move out
and assault the rebel army, and they became so impatient that an order was prepared, relieving him, and
placing General Logan in command. Gen. Logan had

From a recent photo.

CORP. JOSEPH B. RIFE, CO. F.

His enthusiasm was one of the factors which brought out
this book, he offering to pledge his private means.

got as far as Louisville, but did not assume the
command, as Thomas was ready to begin opera--
tions.  Old Pap Thomas knew his business better than
the people at Washington, and when he got things in
proper shape, made a clean sweep.

### REMINISCENCES OF PULASKI, SPRING HILL, COLUMBIA, FRANKLIN AND NASHVILLE.

FORT WAYNE, IND.

The 20th of October, 1864, we reached our destination in pursuing Hood near Galesville, Ala.  While
remaining there, a detail was sent out for foraging, in
a northeasterly direction, about 20 miles from camp.
We were then living off the Southern Confederacy.
We filled the wagons with sweet potatoes, Irish potatoes, chickens, etc.  We also got a supply of beef,
pork, mutton, etc.

An incident I'll relate here.  While digging sweet
potatoes, the old lady came out to me, and was in the
act of striking me over the head with an old-fashioned
hoe.  I took the hoe and used it to dig potatoes, instead of the bayonet I was using.  She said: "You
dirty Yanks, you are taking everything we have. How
will we live the coming winter?"  Her daughter, a
pretty maid, came up in the meantime to reinforce her
mother.  "Why, mother, let them take everything, us
included.  We can live off the leaves of those trees.
I'll go and get them up a meal before they depart."
But we declined the invitation, hungry as we were.
We were a little suspicious of getting "Rough on
Rats," because they got too intimate with us so suddenly.  Or, else they were trying to detain us to have
us captured.  The enemy was only a few miles west
of us.

That night when we got to camp, about 10 o'clock,
orders were to move the next morning.

Nov. 10th. — Camped near Fayetteville, Tenn.
Some of the boys were out foraging about an hour be-

10  90 O V I

fore we camped, and Wm. Lytle of Company I was captured. Poor Bill, we never heard of him afterward, or what his fate was.

13th. — We reached Pulaski. The regiment was paid off, except Companies I and D. They received their pay at Bridgeport.

We will surely never forget the weary march from Pulaski to Columbia.

23rd. — In the afternoon we went through Lynville. That night the town was in ashes.

24th. — Reached Columbia.

26th. — Shifted to the west side of town.

27th. — Crossed Duck river, and Carter creek on the 29th, and 30th through Spring Hill early in the morning, and arrived at Franklin late in the morning, tramp, tramp, all night by Spring Hill, by rebel camps, by Hood's army, through Thompson Station a line of wagons, over dead mules, burned wagons—no rest, no sleep that night. About 4 o'clock the enemy came in full array for the fray. I had not time to finish cooking my sweet potatoes, so I poured off the water and shoved them into my haversack, half cooked, but were full cooked to fight.

After the battle we were glad to get to Nashville, 18 miles distant, and if it had been 118 miles we would have got there all the same. Daniel Welsh, of Company D, was wounded. (He died Dec. 30, at Louisville.—Ed.)

My diary says that Dec. 1st we lay quiet. We all felt like it. We were up and at them from Pulaski to Nashville. I suppose the Rebs felt the same way.

Dec. 2nd formed line, 3rd began to fortify for defence; 6th I was on picket, and 10th on the skirmish line. It is severe cold weather, snow on the ground and it formed a crust, making it very disagreeable for several days.

12th to 14th I assisted Capt. Biers to survey the fortifications. Received orders to move at 6 next morning.

### HIS LAST NIGHT ON EARTH.

My messmate, the brave boy, John Emick, on the night of the 14th, when we laid down to rest, said, and repeated it several times during the night: "Sol, I won't fare so well tomorrow as I did at Chickamauga. (He was wounded in the arm.) I'll be either killed or so badly wounded that I'll not live long." The presentment of that brave boy proved true. He was shot through the forehead in the charge in the evening, in the cornfield, on our way to the hill that our brigade carried. His brother-in-law, Martin K. Thomen, was wounded and died in two weeks at Nashville. No better soldier in Company D than John Emick. Always ready to perform his duty to his country and his God. He was but 18 years old when he enlisted.

H. C. Williamson was wounded in right arm which was afterward amputated. He was but 18 years old.

Jacob McDaniel, S. A. Parsons, Wesley Pugh, Ira Lines and A. K. Thomen, of Company D, were wounded the first day. Pugh was 20, Lines 21, Thomen 20, McDaniel 18, and Welsh, killed at Franklin, 18 years old—all boys.      S. D. Soliday, Co. D.

### A TRIBUTE TO A COMRADE.

#### PRIVATE JOSIAH LUKER,

Who was a bunk-mate of the author of the poem, and who was killed in the battle of Nashville.

The following poem was composed on the march through East Tennessee, by a soldier in the ranks of Company E, 90th O. V. I.

The author, Rev. W. G. Mauk, read the poem at the close of his memorial sermon at Frazeysburg, O., May 26, 1889.

In eighteen sixty-four, in the month of December,
The time and the place I clearly remember.
A battle was fought, our Union to save,
Which stained many fields with the blood of the brave.

It was to Nashville, in the state of Tennessee,
That we overpowered, had hastened to be,
Where we could recruit our ranks now depleted
By many hard fought battles before we retreated.

With audacious boldness they followed us close,
Determined to crush our receding host.
But there, close before them, our fortress in sight,
We camped until ready to give them a fight.

All things being ready, we marched to the fray,
To take Johnny in or drive him away,
The battle now opened, all things going fine,
Orders were given to assault their whole line.

Then whiz after whiz, came ball after ball,
And one after another did our brave heroes fall,
The cannons wild belching, boom after boom,
And the rebels soon saw they were meeting their doom.

Then seized with a panic, they flew to the rear,
As we in our battle array pressed near.
A few minutes more, the fray was all o'er,
The field was now dangerous to Yankees no more.

The rebels were captured by tens and by scores,
As we scaled their works by divisions and corps.
How grateful were we who did survive
The bloody engagement and came out alive.

Now anxiously looking, my comrades to see,
I missed one who had often fought beside me.
I searched all around through the smoke of the storm,
Now passing over to see that one form.

But there in the ranks he could not be found.
Alas! he was prostrate upon the cold ground.
Then hastening rearward, I soon found the place
Where he had fallen upon his young face.

On nearing the spot where my comrade was laid—
That life had departed, I felt much afraid;
For there he lay, bleeding, pale, speechless and faint,
His eyes turned to heaven, without a complaint.

Then close by his body in silence I knelt,
His face and his hands and his pulses I felt,
In that solemn moment quite anxiously near,
I, from those pale lips, a faint whisper did hear.

"O give me some water," he chokingly said,
"I am mortally wounded and soon will be dead."
A few moments silent, he looked up and smiled,
And said, "tell dear mother the fate of her child."

"Do tell her," he said, and then he did falter,
"I die upon my own dear country's altar."
"Tell mother and father, sisters and brothers,
THAT ONE, I love, beside many others."

"The foe, he is vanquished, and it is all right
That I am now dying in this gallant fight,
Though far from my kindred, I've nothing to fear,
My Jesus is coming—I feel He is near."

Thus saying, he whispered, his face growing bright
With a smile, as if lit with angelic light,
"My joy is ecstatic, my vision sublime,
And I am now sailing to a celestial clime,

"Where war clouds n'er gather to darken those skies,
Where carnage unknown, nor tears, dim my eyes."
As night was approaching with damp, chilly breath,
That body lay captive to cruel monster death.

The spirit set free, had taken its flight
To sweep through the gates where cometh no night.
There was victory on earth, there is victory above,
Where he basks in the sunlight of Infinite love.

### THE BATTLE OF NASHVILLE.

FORT WAYNE, IND.

I will relate an incident of the first day's battle,
at Nashville. When we lay in a ravine, in that corn
field, Col. Yeoman got in front of the regiment and
gave the command, "Forward! double quick, 90th
Ohio!" We were glad to go forward. Where we
lay, it seemed as if every bullet stopped in that de-
pression. Nobly did we execute that command. Over
the sharpened brush that the enemy had placed in
front of their fortifications, when I saw our always
brave Captain J. M. Sutphen, had worked his way over
the brush, I followed suit, and a few others of the
company got over about the same time. We all made
a leap and got on top of the entrenchments. Four
Johnnies jumped and began to run away. Captain Sutphen demanded them to drop their arms. First they
refused. He commanded me and a few others to
shoot. As we raised our Enfields they reluctantly surrendered. A rebel flag lay within ten feet of us, but
we were more interested in those four stubborn rebels
than the treasonable flag. I wished after, I had taken
it in, so I could have had the honor of going to Washington City. All soldiers who captured rebel flags were
sent there, and received a medal of honor. But too
late now, but it has been a great regret to me, for
many years, that I let such an opportunity slip.
Captain Sutphen was, just at the time taking in
Johnnies, and I wanted to remain by him. A braver

man I never saw. Always, during our service, he was always ready to do his duty to his comrades and for his country. Long may he live and enjoy the laurels he won.
S. D. SOLIDAY.

The regiment lay in camp near Nashville until December the

15th. — When the army moved out to the attack of Gen. Hood. We moved out in line of battle, attacked and drove the enemy from his position in our front. We made a charge, took their works and captured a lot of prisoners.

16th. — Attacked again, drove the enemy from his second position, routing them with great loss to their army. This was the last stand Hood's army ever made.

17th. — Followed up the retreating army, and marched to Franklin, Tenn., where we were so roughly handled on November 30th, a little over two weeks before. Things were now going our way.

18th. — Moved on to Spring Hill in pursuit of Hood's retreating forces.

19th. — We moved back a short distance.

20th. — Marched to Duck River, but the high water prevented our crossing, as the bridges were destroyed.

21st. — Remained in camp at Duck River.

22nd. — Moved out at dark, crossed Duck River, marched through Columbia, Tenn., and camped on the south side of town.

23rd. — Marched 6 miles, attacked the enemy's rear guard, killing a captain, and dispersed them.

24th. — Marched 12 miles, passing through Linnville, Tenn.

25th. — Moved on through Pulaski, Tenn., overtook their rear guard, put them to flight, capturing prisoners, wagons, ammunition, etc. This is Christmas, and Sunday, also. — Last Christmas we were at Bridgeport, Ala. We noted a year ago: "Where will we be next Christmas, and what will be the changes." Since then we have been through Georgia to Atlanta and Lovejoy; have fought at Tunnel Hill, Rocky Face Ridge, Dalton, Resaca, Bald Knob, Marietta, Kenesaw Mountain, Atlanta, Jonesboro, Lovejoy; and then returning over the same ground to Chattanooga. Then through to Pulaski, Tenn., fighting all the way to Franklin, Tenn., and then taking part in the bloody battle of Franklin; thence to Nashville, Tenn., and on December 15th and 16th, fighting the battle of Nashville. How many of our comrades have been killed, and are sleeping in Southern soil! How many have been wounded, and are in hospital, some slightly, some mortally, and some with arms and legs shot off! Now, we wonder what another Christmas will bring forth. Will the war be ended and we be at home with our loved ones? We hope so. — Ed.

26th. — Remained in camp to draw rations.

27th. — Marched to Sugar Creek, a distance of 12 miles.

28th. — Marched 15 miles and camped at Lexington, Ala.

29th. — Remained at Lexington two days.

31st. — Marched 15 miles and camped at Gordonsville, Ala.

January 1, 1865. — This is New Year's Day. Marched 3 miles to Elk River.

2nd. — Lay in camp all day.

3d. — Marched to Athens, Alabama.

The First Gun at Chickamauga, Ga., Reed's Bridge. One Federal
soldier was killed, and ane wounded.

4th. — Marched on again. Went 18 miles.

5th — Marched 5 miles, through Huntsville, Ala., and went into winter quarters, 20 miles east of town, at the foot of Mount Sinai, where we lay until March 13th, 1865. We built very nice, comfortable quarters, and had a very pleasant time. While we lay here, Mrs. Yeoman visited her husband, Colonel S. N. Yeoman. The Colonel had a very comfortable cabin, and Mrs. Yeoman received many courtesies. A church was built here, and the chaplains from other regiments also preached in it. A kind of revival service was held, and the church would be crowded. The boys were not so bad, and when not fighting Johnnies were about the same as other people. — ED.

March 13, 1865. — Broke camp, marched to town and boarded freight cars, something we were not used to, and went east to Stevenson, Ala.; thence through Chattanooga, Tenn., and on to Knoxville; passed through Knoxville and arrived at Strawberry Plains in the night of the 14th of March. Here we lay until the

24th. — When we pulled up and started on east, marched 15 miles, through Quakertown and New-market, Tenn. Were called out at midnight and marched a short distance to guard a train of cars. Half of the regiment got on the cars, but the left wing remained until morning and marched with the brigade.

25th. — Marched 15 miles, passed through Morristown and Rosewell, Tenn.

26th. — Marched 8 miles, and arrived at Bull's Gap, East Tennessee.

27th. — Marched 6 miles to Lick Creek, and camped. We lay here until the 3rd of April, guarding the railroad and bridge. Details were made to cut railroad ties.

April 3, 1865. — Started on a raid to Asheville, North Carolina, at 3 o'clock, P. M., marched through Evansville and went into camp at 9 o'clock at night. We made 12 miles.

4th. — Marched 22 miles, crossed Nollichuck River, over the Smoky Mountains, passed through Paint Rock Pass, came to the French Broad River, and marched 6 miles up the stream.

5th. — Marched up the French Broad River 17 miles, cleared out much timber and rocks by which the road had been blockaded by the enemy, and camped at Marshall, N. C.

6th. — Marched 20 miles, attacked the rebels 2 miles from Asheville, N. C., where a small skirmish took place, but we had orders to not bring on a general engagement, the object being to hold the force here, so they could not re-enforce Gen. Joe Johnston. Some of the boys were in the town, though. We learned afterward, that the force here was not so large as was represented. In this little fight Parces Sweet and Joseph Tatman were wounded. We withdrew and marched 16 miles over the route we had come, through an extremely dark night. Halted and got our breakfasts, remained here until the

8th. — At noon, when we started and marched 8 miles.

9th. — Marched down stream, through Paint Rock Pass, re-crossed the Smoky Mountains and camped at their base.

10th. — Marched 15 miles, and camped near Greenville, Tenn., the home of Andrew Johnson. Here we heard of the surrender of Lee's army in Virginia.

11th. — Marched 16 miles, passed through Blue Springs and arrived at Camp Lick Creek, from where we started.

MOUNT STERLING, O., January 21, 1894.

I enlisted in Co. A, 90th O. V. I., July 19, 1862. I never shall forget our march from Lexington to Louisville. The intense heat and thirst was enough to kill a mule; yet the brave boys pushed on. Do you remember the maneuvering about Louisville, and that pretty girl that followed our regiment in the city? Ask Sergt. Griffith. My memory goes on to Wild Cat Mountains, then back through Kentucky, and after a while we come to the state line between Tennessee and Kentucky. How the boys did hollow. Still farther on, and at last we come to the Cumberland River. See the boys plunge into the water. Next I see the old 90th going into the battle of Stone River. Many brave boys answered the "last roll call" there. Do you remember when we had to fall back and form our lines anew? Right there, boys, some Johnny gave me a New Year's gift that I shall carry to my grave. Next I see of the 90th is at Cripple Creek. That is where McDowell got his dun horse and where Chilcote milked the cow, where Sam Law did free banking.

On to Chattanooga and Chickamauga, comrades, that memorable Sunday, September 20, 1863! I was the third man to Adjutant Kingery when he was killed, helped to lay him down by that old stump. Do you remember that poor cannoneer who was mangled by that shell, arm shattered and one side of his face torn to pieces? This took place behind Co. A., September 20, 1863.

The siege of Chattanooga; on to Bridgeport, down Hog Jaw Valley. Ask Abe Lane and Tom Lee who got Lieut. Riggins' sow.

On to Atlanta. Those days are as vivid in my mind as if though it were but yesterday.

At Huntsville. What peaceful hours we enjoyed there! How sweet their memory still!

Strawberry Plains; Bull's Gap; on to Asheville, N. C.; at Nashville.

Comrades, those days are gone, our deeds are done, and by and by we will have to answer the "last roll call."

Comrades, I could write a whole day and then not tell it all.                Yours truly,

FRED OWENS.

## THE OLD BLUE HEN.

SEGO, PERRY CO., O.

Coward as I was, I was promoted to Corporal after the battle of Stone River. Held that position for a short time, resigned to go into the elite company that was being raised by detail, but the order was countermanded and that left me a high private. Co. E boys called me Co. H's Little Corporal. I went by the name of "Little Johnny Moore," in our company.

When on the march from Knoxville, close to the Virginia line, we lay in camp for a few days. John Chilcote and my mess thought some chicken would not go bad, so we concluded that four of us would slip through the picket line and go in search of the southern rooster that Chilcote heard crowing the morning before. All being ready we went out to a farm house, probably a half a mile beyond our picket line. There we found six old hens and that rooster. One guarded the house and Chilcote went for the chickens, handing them out to the other two to wring off the heads, until every chicken was out — seven all told. We then started to camp, had to hug a creek bank very close to get around the pickets. One of the boys made a misstep and in the creek he went. (I wonder who it was.) We got to camp all right and divided our chickens, three of them falling to my mess. Well, there was one old blue hen, very large. We dressed her and got eleven hard shelled eggs and two more full sized, and a number of little yellow ones, out of that old blue hen. Now, comrades, don't fly up and call me a liar. Who ever knew a soldier to tell a lie? JOHNNY MOORE.

12th to the 19th. — We lay in camp. While here we received the sad news of President Lincoln's assassination. It was the saddest and gloomiest day we had known since our enlistment.

19th. — Broke camp and marched to Bull's Gap.

20th. — Remained at the Gap until 8 o'clock in the evening, when we boarded box cars and went to Morristown, toward Knoxville, where we remained until morning.

21st. — Moved down 4 miles, cleared from the track the ruins of a burnt train of cars, then proceeded to Knoxville, where we arrived in the evening.

22nd. — We went to Cleveland, Tenn., then on to Chattanooga and lay there until 10 o'clock in the forenoon, then went on, arriving at Stevenson, Ala., at 12 o'clock. From here we started for Nashville, arriving there on the 23rd.

23rd. — Moved out about 5 miles west of Nashville, near the Cumberland River, and went into camp. — This camp was called Camp Harker, in honor of Gen. Harker who was killed at the battle of Kenesaw Mountain, Ga. We lay here in camp until June 14, 1865. We were mustered out June 13, 1865, and started for Camp Dennison on the 14th, to receive our pay and discharges, the war now being over. We had a good time while in Camp Harker, plenty to eat, and not much to do, and lots of fun. The boys knew the war was over, and camp guard was a mere form. Here we saw one of the grandest processions we ever witnessed. Lights were ordered out, one night, and the boys thought it none of the officers' business, and lighted candles and stuck them on their tents. They then climbed trees and stuck candles on the limbs. They then started out in procession with candles stuck in the muzzles of their guns. They visited Colonel Yeoman at regimental headquarters; then went to Gen. Kirby's headquarters, and intended to go to division and corps headquarters, but Generals Kimball and Stanley were not there, so they returned. The next day transparencies, mottoes, pictures, and every conceivable device was fixed up. The Adjutant of the 21st Illinois painted a life sized portrait of General Stanley on a piece of shelter tent, with a shoe blacking and a brush made from a stick. Underneath the portrait was inscribed, "The hero of Franklin." A transparency carried in the First brigade was a very correct representation of the taking of Bald Knob, near Kenesaw Mountain, by General Kirby's command, June 21, 1864, and was inscribed with General Stanley's order to the brigade commander, General Kirby,—"Take that hill, Kirby." One was carried representing a covered wagon, on which was inscribed, — "The war is over, now for home." All these were improvised and made in one day. The night was still and dark, and about 6000 men formed in line, officers and all, and started for corps headquarters. Generals Stanley, Kimball, Kirby and others made speeches, and it was certainly a great event. The boys were soldiers, through the war, they were citizens now, they thought. It was a grave question with some as to what would be the result of turning so many soldiers loose. The result was that each went to his home and pursued his avocation, just as he did before — quiet, peacable citizens. No other people on earth could have done this. Think of two great armies, so lately opposed to each other in deadly warfare, now turned loose! Many from the North returned and settled in the South, marrying and intermingling. Northern boys married Southern girls,

Southern boys married Northern girls. What other country would, or could pardon and franchise those who fought against the government? And when, in 1898, "Old Glory" was insulted by the Spaniards, the sons of the Southland and the sons of the Northland marched shoulder to shoulder — sons of the men who fought against each other in 1861-1865.

We have now, in the past few months retraced our steps, as it were, and passed over the marches, fought the battles of nearly 40 years ago, with our comrades, and while writing and compiling this little book, it sometimes seemed to us we were actually experiencing the scenes described. — ED.

### THE 31st INDIANA VETERAN VOLUNTEER INFANTRY BID THE 90TH O. V. I. "GOOD-BYE."

On the evening of June 12, 1865, as the 90th Ohio Volunteer Infantry was about returning home, the 31st Indiana Veteran Volunteer Infantry paid a visit to the 90th, to express their appreciation of their services as patriotic soldiers, and their love for them as comrades. The following preamble and resolutions were unanimously adopted, not as a favor, but as an expression of their hearts' sentiment:

WHEREAS, The 90th Ohio Volunteer Infantry are about returning to their homes, to again assume their citizenship, after three years' faithful service in their country's defense; and,

WHEREAS, We of the 31st Indiana Veteran Volunteer Infantry have been intimately associated with them while in the army; shared in their dangers, their hardships, their privations, and in their victories— forming affections and ties as lasting as life itself; therefore,

*Resolved,* That we hail with joy the order that allows our comrades of the 90th O. V. I. to again assume the duties of civil life, amid the tragic influences of home associations, and home endearments.

*Resolved,* That mutual dangers and common interests during the long struggle for national life, has begotten a feeling of love and friendship between us that can never be forgotten, and can only be appreciated by soldiers, and that along with comrades brave, who have fallen by our sides in battle, will be cherished our associations with the 90th O. V. I.

*Resolved,* That in the future all the happiness and honor, the peace and prosperity ever vouchsafed to man we most cordially wish to attend the members of the 90th O. V. I.; and that ever hereafter the talismanic watchword that shall leap over all the conventionalities of society, and appeal directly to our hearts' best sympathies and love, shall be, "I belonged to the 90th Ohio Volunteer Infantry."

*Resolved,* That a copy of these resolutions be *not* furnished to the Cincinnati *Commercial,* or to any other paper for publication, but be treasured in our memories as the utterance of our hearts' deepest sentiments.                              GEORGE M. NOBLE,

Captain 31st Indiana Veteran Volunteers.

### GEN. NATHAN KIMBALL'S TRIBUTE.

HEADQUARTERS 1ST DIVISION, 4TH ARMY CORPS,
        CAMP HARKER, TENN., June 11, 1865.

*Col. S. N. Yeoman:*

You, with the officers and men of the 90th Ohio, after three years of gallant devotion to the cause of our common country, in this war against rebellion, are now about to return to your homes, with honor unstained, and with reputations bright with glory. Your deeds will live forever. In nearly every battle, from the southwest, you have been engaged; Louisville, through Perryville, Stone River, Chickamauga, Resaca, Rocky Face, Dallas, Franklin and Nashville, you have borne the flag of the Union, and banner of your noble state to victory over the foe, who would have destroyed the government and Union made by our fathers.

From a recent photo.

CAPT. T. E. BAKER, CO. G.

God has given us the victory. Remember Him; and, now that the war is over, the rebellion at an end, remember those whom you have conquered. Use victory as becoming true men and brave soldiers; return to your homes with enmity toward none and charity for all.

I know you will be the best citizens, because I know you have been the best soldiers. While we live, enjoying the honor and privileges which our victory has won and saved, let us cherish ever, as the idol of our hearts, the memory of our comrades who have given up their lives for the salvation of their country; who fell by our sides battling for right. Remember the widows and orphans of our dead comrades; be true to them as our comrades were true to their country.

My comrades, accept my gratitude for your devotion to me personally. You have been true and noble soldiers, and brave men. May God ever bless you, and crown your lives with happiness, and each of you with peace and plenty. Be as you ever have been— true to God, to your country's friends, and to yourselves.

Good-bye, comrades; again, God bless you.

NATHAN KIMBALL,
Brevet Major-General Commanding.

### LETTER FROM THE 31st INDIANA VETERAN VOLUNTEER INFANTRY.

ROCKVILLE, IND., AUGUST 16, 1886.

*Col. S. N. Yeoman, Washington C. H., Ohio.*

Dear Colonel — On the 7th and 8th proximo, some three hundred and twenty-seven of the three hundred and eighty-four survivors of the once long list corresponding exactly to the year of our Lord, above written, of the old 31st Indiana Veteran Volunteer Infantry, will once more meet around the camp-fire, built from the undying sparks of that continuing loyal flame that has always burned in the patriotic hearts of all our boys. And, in fancy, as the bugle

sounds the assembly, for an imaginary forward, on
a long, weary and dangerous march, I notice a momentary halt, and watch another proud body of men
file into line.  The smile on the faces of our men
tell as plain as words, that it is the gallant old 90th
taking her place.  And, as it was then, so it is now;
our marches and fights and camps are incomplete without the 90th in her place.  And I am enjoying the
thought of the sight of those three hundred and
twenty-seven caps high in the air, and the shout of the
boys around the fires, as the 90th came into line.  God
bless them all.

Come as many as will, and we will take good care
of you.

With high regards, I remain, very respectfully,

JOHN F. MEACHAM.

HEADQUARTERS DEPARTMENT OF TEXAS.

SAN ANTONIO, TEX., AUGUST 19, 1886.

DEAR COLONEL — Your invitation to join the survivors of your gallant regiment in their reunion on
the 31st inst. came duly, and I am sorry to answer
that the great distance, and my official cares will prevent my being present.

There is no regiment from Ohio or other state
more indelibly impressed upon my brain, than the
brave and efficient 90th Ohio.  For good order, good
discipline, sound health, and readiness for work, for
cheerful courage, always ready for any daring, I com-
mend and shall ever remember yours as a model regiment.

I know I would greatly enjoy your meeting, and
am really sorry I can not come.

Very Truly, Your Obedient Servant,

D. S. STANLEY,
Major General Commanding.

Col. S. N. YEOMAN, Col. 90th Ohio Vol. Inf.,
Washington C. H., Ohio.

SERVICE CERTIFICATE.

WASHINGTON, C. H., OHIO, August 31, 1886.

This is to certify that David C. Goodwin was enlisted in the 90th Regiment, Ohio Volunteer Infantry, as a Private, on the 22nd of July, 1862; was detailed by Col. C. H. Rippy from Co. E, after the battle of Stone River, to carry the colors of the Regiment. Whilst carrying the Colors at the battle of Chickamauga he was severely wounded and placed on the Roll of Honor by General Order of Maj. Gen. Rosecrans, for his gallant conduct. He is now in receipt of a pension on account of said wounds. He was a faithful, meritorious soldier during his three years service in the 90th O. V. I. He served as Color Sergeant without promotion, upon detail and without appointment as Color Sergeant. He is, and has been a good citizen ever since his honorable discharge at the close of the war. He has always had the confidence of the commanding officers and fellow comrades. He took part with the regiment in thirty-two skirmishes and battles.

S. N. YEOMAN,
Lieut. Col. Commd'g 90th O. V. I.
JAMES F. COOK,
Maj. 90th O. V. I.
A. W. MOSURE,
Lieut. Ord. Sergt. of Co. E, and 1st Lieut. Co. G.
J. M. SUTPHEN,
Capt. Co. D,
J. M. SUTPHEN, Capt. Co. D.
P. H. EBRIGHT, Co. D.
A GETHMAN, Co. H.
C. E. BARNES, Co. K.
A. R. KELLER, Capt. Co. C.
JOSEPH COLLINS, Co. E.

THE COLORS OF THE 90th O. V. I. THE FIRST ON THE
   BREASTWORKS AT THE BATTLE OF NASHVILLE,
   TENN. A BRAVE ACT.

The following appeared in a Washington C. H.
O., paper, about twenty-five years ago:

Mr. Jacob S. Cockerel, a farmer living a few miles
from this place, was a member of Company C, 90th
O. V. I., and served well and faithfully during the three
years the regiment was in the field. He was Color
Sergeant for a long time, and at the battle of Nashville, in December, '64, he did an act of bravery which
should not have been allowed to sink into oblivion like
a common, everyday occurence. During that memorable battle the 90th Ohio occupied a position some
twenty steps in advance of the line occupied by the remainder of the brigade ( 1st Brig., 1st Div, 4th A.
C. ), and when General Wood gave his order, "charge,
Kirby, charge!" the gallant 90th was the first regiment
of the brigade to reach the rebel works, and the colorbearer, Jacob S. Cockerel, was the first man to mount
the works, where he planted the flag, amid the din and
smoke of the firearms and the whistling of death-
dealing bullets and shells. As the flagstaff entered the
earth a rebel soldier — frightened, perhaps, and excited — put forth his hand as though to grasp the
colors, when one of the colorguard brought his gun
to bear, and the man exclaimed, "For God's sake, Sergeant, don't let him shoot me! I didn't intend to touch
the colors!'" The gun was thrust aside, and the
man's life was spared. 'Twas a brave act by a brave
man, and was made the subject for special mention
by the Colonel ( Yeoman ) in his report to his super-
iors.

The Sergeant was given the choice of either having
a medal or being recommended for a commission.
Being rather of a modest nature, he chose the medal.
The necessary papers were made out, Col. Yeoman
saw personally that they were properly endorsed as

high up as Corps headquarters, and there the matter ended. The medal has never been heard from, and the honest, brave soldier who did his whole duty, is thus robbed of the memento which would have served as a monument in his family to perpetuate a brave act.

This is what Comrade Cockerell says, in a recent letter:

"I couldn't say, sure, myself, for I was not in a position to see all along the line, nor was I looking up and down the line, just at the time. At the encampment at Columbus, a few years ago, I asked Gen. Kirby what he thought about our colors going on the works first. He said he had no doubt of it. I know this much, there was none on the works where I went, until I went on. Several of our boys went on just as I did. I can think of two; J. W. Harper and E. L. Janes. We were pretty badly mixed up all along the line by the time we got to the works. I was tired when I got to the works, and stuck the flag staff in the ground, when one of the rebs took hold of it. Wils Allen was going to shoot him, when he threw up his hands and said, "Sergeant, don't let him shoot me, I wasn't going to take your flag."

Now, as regards the medal. The Colonel asked me which I would prefer, a commission or a medal. He said I could not be mustered, as there was no vacancy. I said I would as soon have the medal. I saw, when it was too late, that I had made a mistake. I was not caring anything about commissions at that time. I was thinking more about coming home.

A TRIP BY H. O. HARDEN AND HIS DAUGHTER, FLORENCE, TO THE BATTLEFIELDS AROUND CHATTANOOGA, TENN., OCTOBER, 1900.

Monday morning we started out to see the city. We went back on the high grounds where the position of the old forts, batteries, and general headquarters are marked by an iron tablet. The Holsten Conference of the M. E. church was in session, and one of the ministers took us through the church. It is a very fine building, both inside and out, especially inside.

About nine o'clock we took a street car for Mission Ridge, and left the car at Gen. Bragg's headquarters, the fare being 10 cents. Here is a fine steel tower, 75 to a 100 feet high. The monuments are very numerous at this point, and are mostly Illinois'. The state of Illinois has erected a fine monument near Bragg's headquarters, about 60 feet high, at a cost of about $25,000.00 The old Confederate battery is planted here, as it was at the time of the battle. The government has constructed a fine boulevard or driveway, along the ridge, from one end to the other. We walked south on the ridge, noting the monuments to the different regiments, marking the place where they came up the ridge, at the time of the battle. Thence we turned north to the point (Long's) where there is another tower, a number of monuments and a battery, where Turchin's men came up. We especially noted the point, about a mile north of Bragg's headquarters, and directly opposite Orchard Knob, where stands the First Ohio, where our comrade, M. J. Dilger, received his dose, and although we saw no blood, we imagined we saw a very rich spot of ground, but we didn't see a chicken near. Before leaving Bragg's headquarters, our daughter concluded to climb to the top of the tower, which she did. Having a camera with us, we got some fine pictures on the ridge.

From Long's point, we retraced our steps to the first road, and walked down the ridge and across to Orchard Knob, where General Grant and his officers watched the battle, the Confederate General Bragg also watching it from his headquarters. Orchard Knob belongs to the government, and is walled in with a nice stone wall, with a wide boulevard around it. On the knob are some grand monuments and several guns. The old works are still there. We got some good pictures here. At the time the 90th was in Chattanooga, this was in possession of the Confederates. It is about half way from our old camp, northeast to the ridge. The street car line passes over the ground where we stood picket, and where we met the Johnnies and traded tobacco, coffee and papers.

From Orchard Knob we walked to the street car line and rode as near to the National Cemetery as the line runs. We then walked to and around the cemetery, which contains 75 acres. It is kept very nice. In it are buried over 13,200 soldiers, including those of the Spanish war, and of this number over 4,000 are unknown. The most of the unknown are those who were killed at Chickamauga, and were buried by the Confederates, and afterwards re-interred. Their first places of burial can be seen yet, at different points on the battlefield. The Confederate dead, a soldier told us, were taken to Marietta, Ga., for interment. The Union dead all have a marble marker, and if name is known, it is cut on. The Spanish-American war soldiers have no marble markers as yet, but a head-board, giving their name and regiment. They will be marked by marble head-stones, in due time. Here are buried the Andrews Raiders, who have a fine monument erected by the state of Ohio, in 1890, on which is a small bronze engine, the "General," which they captured. We got a very fine picture of this monument. We were present ten years ago, when it was dedicated, and met the relatives of the men who were hung, including the widow of Slavens, one of the men.

It was now about night, and as we had walked 8 or 10 miles, we felt tired enough to quit for that day and walking to the street car line, rode into the city, well pleased with our day's sightseeing. Before leaving this point, we wish to say for the benefit of Comrade Dilger, that we got a picture of the tablet, placed at the foot of Orchard Knob, from where his regiment started on the charge across the plain and ridge.

While we are in the city, we will describe a little tramp we took on Thursday morning. We were desirous of finding the camp of the 90th, while in Chattanooga, when we got half a cracker and three grains of coffee for a day's rations; when the boys gathered up the corn the horses dropped, washed and ate it. So we started out, making inquiries, and learned that the "Old Brick House," the only brick in that part of the city, was still standing. We finally found the old house and it looks very natural, only that it has been painted. It was then a farm house, now it is on a fine street, the street being cut down and a stone wall in front of the house. The ground where our camp was, is all built over, yet the location looks quite natural, as we view Mission Ridge and Lookout Mountain. The "White" house (Craven's) on the side of the mountain was burned, but has been rebuilt, and looks about like the old one.

We were shown a little, six-cornered frame building, about ten feet across, on one of the streets, used as the office of the U. S. Paymaster during the war. It is now used by some colored people as a peanut stand, or something of that sort. The ground which the "Old Blacksmith" vacated in order to give the army room, after the battle of Chickamauga, is still there, but we were unable to locate it. Think it was Market street, down to the "Old Government Bridge," over to Waldron's Ridge.

Tuesday morning we go to the Central Depot, and at eight o'clock take the train for Battlefield station, nine miles out from Chattanooga. This railroad runs to Rome and Atlanta, on the west side of the battlefield, and parallel with the Dry Valley road, past Crawfish Spring, and has been built since the war.

Alighting at the station, we found hackmen ready and willing to take us over the field, but we had decided to walk, and in company with a former Ohio man, a contractor in Chattanooga, we walked to the top of the low ridge about a quarter of a mile north of where General Lytle was killed, where he left us, as he came out to attend a government sale of lumber and other property used during the Spanish war. We sauntered on east, past the Dwyer house, where is the headquarters of the Park Commission, and where are piled several hundred cannon not yet mounted. From here we go on east to the Brotherton field, and stop on the west side to read the tablets, which give a history of the battle at that point. We then cross the small field to the old Brotherton house. On the north side

The Battle of Kenesaw Mountain, June 27, 1864.  The mountain
᾿ is seen in the distance.

of the house are planted two Confederate cannon, and on the south side, two more. Here was a deadly conflict, and it was here that Longstreet's men under Hood, pierced the Union lines, doubled them back, drove them across the Dwyer field, where General Hood lost a leg, and to the top of Snodgrass hill. There is a family by the name of McDaniel, living in the Brotherton house, and we got a very fine pictu> of the house, the mother and children. Five years ago, last September, we attended a Confederate reunion at this house, and heard one of the Brotherton daughters, who lived there at the battle, say, that she and her sister returned the next day after the battle, and that she could have walked all over their yard on dead men, they lay so thickly.

From here we went north on the LaFayette road to where we camped five years ago. The place looks quite natural, and we almost imagined we could hear Abe Smith snore, and see Adam Getman, Dave Goodwin, E. E. Rickett and others sitting on the pile of rails the government had hauled up for our use. But, poor Getman has answered the last roll call, and the others are scattred over a large territory.

We crossed to the east side of the road, opposite the site of the Poe house which was burned during the battle, to the Poe field, where the state of Georgia has erected a monument, costing $25,000.00. It is built of Georgia granite, surmounted with bronze figures representing the different arms of the service, and 60 to 70 feet high, with a circular esplanade around it. Here we met Mr. M. Reed, of the First Georgia regiment, who fought in the battle, and whose home was, and is yet, at Reed's bridge where the first shot of the battle was fired. He introduced us to Col. Gordon, a relative of Gen. John B. Gordon. He also lived near the battlefield. While we were talking, who should come up but Capt. Brandt of Carroll, Ohio. We soon had quite a crowd of men and women, mostly of the South. We got an excellent picture of the monument, and it so happened that there were three old Confederate soldiers sitting on the base, two of whom were Reed and Gordon, the other we do not remember, and a man from Florida. Mr. Reed had his wife, son and daughter with him.

Crossing to the other side of the road, we took in the situation around the Poe house, visited the monument of the 17th Ohio, and that of the 31st Ohio. While at the 31st monument, an old Confederate Virginia Bugler came up. We asked him to sit for a picture, which he readily did. Sitting on the base of the monument, he unfastened his old army bugle and placed it upon his knee. It is one of the best pictures we took. He then started off toward the Georgia monument, giving a few blasts on the old bugle. It is doubtful if he could be induced to part with it.

Again we move north on the Lafayette road to near where General Thomas spent the night of September 19, 1863, and crossing the field to the east, we enter the woods where the Confederates turned Thomas' right. We follow the line of the "Horse-shoe," around and to the top of the low and woody ridge, where, at the toe of the "Horse-shoe," stands the battery just as it was in action that day; the 90th Ohio, 31st Ind., 1st and 2nd Kentucky monuments. These formed the brigade. Here we lingered long thinking of those whose lives went out that day, or were wounded or captured or both. We ate lunch while sitting on the base of the 90th monument. We went out in front, across the ravine, and to the left where General Helm, C. S. A., was mortally wounded. Got some fine picture-scenes in the vicinity of the 90th monument, one the tall pine tree near it, showing the scars made by shot and shell 37 years ago.

Here we will explain the Battlefield Park. Some have an idea that it is a small piece of ground, planted with flowers, something like a city park. That is not the case. The Park is about 4 miles wide, east and west; and 6 miles long, north and south. It was nearly all woods at the time of the battle, and is yet, only an occasional field being cleared. At the time of the battle the undergrowth of pine and scruboak was so thick in places that a man could hardly get through, and most of the fighting was done in this brush, neither side seeing what was in front. The ground is comparatively level, somewhat rolling except Snodgrass Hill, and since the Government has bought it the thick underbrush has been cleared up, the old fences all taken away and a person can see quite a distance in the woods. Many trees are still standing, marked with shot and shell, but the balls were all cut out as relics before the government bought it. Now nothing is allowed to be molested. If a tree dies it is cut up for wood. The roads are kept in the same places, and there are many of them, but the principal ones are graded, there being 50 miles of the finest drives in the world. But where a road has been graded or cut down, there is a tablet stating the fact. Where a house was burned the same is told. We suppose there has been a million dollars spent for monuments alone. Ohio has spent nearly one-tenth of that sum. The monuments are placed where the batteries and regiments did their hardest fighting. The batteries both Union and Confederate, are placed in the same position they occupied during the battle. Sometimes we see one lone gun in the woods, then two, and at others whole batteries. In many places the guns of both sides are dangerously near to each other.

The state of Georgia has marked the position of all her troops in the battle, and in passing around the "Horse-shoe" to the north from the 90th monument, there is nothing but Georgia markers, and as the regiments had become decimated, they stand thickly, only 50 to 75 yards from each other, and only a short distance on the inner line stand the monuments of the Union troops, the two lines close enough together that a rifle shot would kill a squirrel from one to the other, and the old trenches near, where the dead was first buried show how deadly the conflict was. At one place between the lines there is a cleared piece of an acre, perhaps, and while standing here, Mr. Reed and family, of whom we spoke, drove up. They stopped, and as we had met several times that day were quite well acquainted. It so happened that where we stopped was near the marker of his regiment, the 1st Georgia, and we got him to stand beside the marker for a picture. They were on their way home, and insisted that we go and stay over night with them, but as we had more to see, could not go, but if we ever go there again Mr. Reed will have a Yankee soldier to keep over night. With "Good byes" we parted. Will we ever meet again?

Keeping on around the "Horse-shoe," we came to the Lafayette road south of Cloud Spring, at the north end of the Kelley field, where stands the Kentucky monument. Passing south a mile or so, we turn west on a road leading to Snodgrass Hill, on which Gen. Thomas had his headquarters on Sunday, Sept. 20, 1863, and which the Confederates tried so hard to capture, after having driven Gen. Rosencrans from the south end of the battlefield into Chattanooga. If they had succeeded in capturing this hill, instead of there being a "horse-shoe," it would have been a circle, and the army of old Pap Thomas, the "Rock of Chickamauga," inside of the circle. But Old Pap and his men held the hill until night, and then silently withdrew, saving the army.

While on the hill, where monuments stand thickly, we met a German soldier from Indiana. He said, "Right here I was shot through the neck and shoulder, depriving me of the use of my arm. I was carried into the Snodgrass house and my wounds dressed, I did not think then, that I would be here in 37 years."

We had been tramping all day, and, the female portion was about tired out. A man drove up with a two-seated rig, and we asked him what he would charge, to drive us to Lee & Gordon's Mill, down past the Viniard house. He said it was a little late, but he guessed he could make the trip, and that it would be about a dollar. We climbed in and he jogged along, down the Lafayette road to the Viniard house. Here is where Sheridan did such hard fighting, and where he was repulsed and driven back to the Glenn Hill, where Gen. Rosecrans had his headquarters. We drove on up to the Lee & Gordon Mill, where we got out and walked around. We then went into the mill, and the head miller, a man from Steubenville, Ohio, showed us through. They do a big business, and have a fine roller system. The mill is run by water, as of old, and the outside looks as it did in war times. The old saw mill had been torn away, and a wareroom erected in its stead.

The sun was about two hours high, and we asked the driver if he could not make Crawfish Spring, yet. He allowed he could, as it was moonlight. So we drove to the Spring, about two miles farther, and getting out, went down and took a drink—of water. The dam has washed out, and the spring looks as it did in war times. The big hotel is not open. It was used for a hospital during the Spanish War. The Rome & Atlanta railroad crosses just below the spring. This is the finest spring of water we ever saw, and is so clear. It is strong enough to run a mill. After taking a view of the Lee house, where Gen. Rosecrans first had his headquarters, we got into the rig and started back, going by Cave Spring, and then over the Glenn Hill, where stands the Wilder monument, and where Gen. Wilder with his mounted brigade with Spencer rifles did such deadly work, but were driven off by Longstreet's men. Here is where the monument of the First Ohio Cavalry is located and where Col. Val. Cupp, of Baltimore, Ohio, was mortally wounded. We drive on over the raise of the ground where Gen. Lytle, the poet General was killed, and where a monument, in pyramidial form, is erected of cannon balls, as is the case all over the battlefield, where a general officer was killed, either Union or Confederate.

We got to the station about dark, and asked the driver how much we owed him. He said he would not charge us anything extra. He was a Wisconsin man, but lived near Lookout Mountain, in the country. The train was late, and we did not get into Chattanooga till 8 o'clock. We attended a Masonic Street Fair, after supper, and got to our lodging place some time in the night.

We will mention an incident that took place on the battlefield that day, and close for this week.

Two old Confederate soldiers, one from Texas and the other from Mississippi, started from the Lafayette road, north of Lee & Gordon's Mill, to trace their first line through the woods. Coming to a monument of cannon balls, the Texan asked what it was. A man standing near, said, "It is a monument." "Whose monument?" asked the Texan. "General Deshler's," said the man. "General Deshler?" said the Texan. "Yes." "Who put it there?" said the Texan. "The Government,' said the man. "Which Government?" said the Texan. "We only have one Government." said the man. "Do you mean to say that the Government erected that monument to one of its enemies?" "Yes." "Well," said the Texan, "I thank God for two things, I thank Him that General Deshler was a noble man and citizen, and a brave soldier, and I thank Him that we have a Government so magnanimous as to erect a monument to one of its enemies." He pulled out from his pocket an old handkerchief and wiped the tears that were streaming down his face. The Mississippian looked around in the woods, and said, "I guess this is the place."

In this battle the Union, loss was:
Killed ................................... 1,656
Wounded ............................... 9,749
Captured ............................... 4,774
                                        ―――――
    Total ........................... 16,179

Confederate loss:
Killed ................................... 2,389
Wounded ............................... 13,412
Captured ............................... 2,003
                                        ―――――
    Total ........................... 17,804

Total killed, both armies ................... 4,045
Total wounded, both armies .............. 23,161

It is thus seen that 27,206 men were shot during the two days' battle. Hundreds of the wounded died after.

Wednesday had been set apart by us for the trip to Lookout Mountain. Henry M. Stanley, the explorer, said while standing on the point of the mountain, "This is the finest view in the world."

After breakfast, while standing on the street corner waiting for a car to Incline Plane, we looked into the street and saw Henry Conrad coming toward us, and looking across to the Rossmore hotel, whom should we see but Sam Law, as large and natural as life! We did not know that either was in the city, and that we had been missing each other for two days. After a chat, we took a street car for Incline, and at its first stop the German soldier from Indiana, whom we spoke of last week, and his party boarded the car, bound for the same place. Alighting from the car at the base of the mountain, we enter a station of the Incline. This railway runs up the side of the mountain, and is 4,800 feet long, or nearly a mile, and one can see from one end to the other. It is the steepest incline in the world for its length. It averages 37 feet to the hundred, and where it passes through the palisades, for about a quarter of a mile, is 67 feet in a 100, that is for every 100 feet you travel you are raised 67 feet higher, and when you reach the top are suspended 1,800 feet high, and can see clear to the bottom. Some are very nervous, while making the first trip, and some are jolly, while others stand out on the platform. It is like going up in a balloon. We noticed that the ladies, as a rule, were nervier than the men. It takes about 10 minutes to make the trip, up or down, as while one car goes up the other comes down. People who travel it often, don't mind it. We noticed a small school boy coming down, and they stopped the car about half way down, and let a lady get off. The mountain side is all dotted over with houses. The old standard guage railroad has been torn up, except on the top of the mountain, where it is used for the electric cars, there being a system of electric railroads on it. There is an incorporated town on the mountain, postoffice, school house, church, town hall, etc., and is, of course, called "Lookout Mountain." There are no graded streets, and no cleared land except where the houses stand, and you would think you were in a forest instead of a town, yet there is a government road or boulevard around the west side back to Lulu Falls and Lulu Lake, 8 miles. The mountain is 86 miles long, with only three gaps to cross. Down on the west side of this mountain was the route taken by Gen. Rosecrans and most of his army, and crossing through the gaps and getting between General Bragg and Chattanooga. When Gen. Rosecrans went down on the west side, Gen. Bragg left Chattanooga and marched in the same direction on the east side to keep Rosecrans from getting in his rear and cutting off his supplies. Rosecrans crossed through the gaps, Bragg marched back towards Chattanooga on the east side of Chickamauga river, and Rosecrans on the west side. Thus the two lines, about six miles long, lay facing each other the night of Sept. 18, 1863, the night before the battle of Chickamauga.

There is a large hotel on the highest point of the mountain and is called "Lookout Inn." It is 365 feet long, four stories high and has 350 rooms. It is only open three months in the year.

On leaving the incline we noticed the one-legged Confederate soldier whom we had got acquainted with five years ago. He asked if we wanted dinner, and said his folks would furnish us dinner for 35 cents each. So when dinner time came he sent us around to his house in a cab. We had a very good dinner and the ladies were very sociable.

In the forenoon we had gone to the "Point," from which a look into seven states can be had, those of South Carolina, North Carolina, Virginia, Tennessee, Kentucky, Alabama and Georgia. It is a grand view, indeed, and one never tires of looking. Here we got some fine pictures of "Umbrella Rock," "Lovers' Lane," etc.

From a photo by H. O. Harden, 1900.

An old Confederate Bugler, from Virginia, with his old army
bugle on his knee, Chickamauga, Ga.

Standing at "Umbrella Rock," one can look down on the "Point Hotel," a large hotel built at the foot of the palisades. Here one gets a good view of Chattanooga, Moccasin Bend in the Tennessee river, 1,750 feet below; of Missionary Ridge, etc.

There are two guns planted on the "Battery Rock," and the old Confederate magazine, dug in the ground and covered with timber and earth, is still seen.

South of Lookout Inn, on a high knoll, is the old Confederate fort, and bank on one side is yet ten feet high, and several good sized trees have grown on the bank since the fort was built. In the center is the standpipe of the waterworks of Lookout Mountain.

In the afternoon we made the acquaintance of Capt. Arrowsmith and wife, and several ladies from Pulaski, Tenn. Capt. Arrowsmith belonged to the 32nd Tennessee regiment, C. S. A., and was stationed on the mountain at the time of Hooker's battle. He showed us where he stood on the rocks and looked down, but could see nothing on account of the fog. It was called "The Battle Above the Clouds." We found the captain and his party very sociable, and have received several papers printed in his home town, since returning home. We picked mountain huckelberries, which were then just getting ripe. He told how he had made meals of them while in the army. He said he spent several months at Indianapolis in 1862, being a prisoner of war, having been in the surrender of Fort Donelson.

From the Point one can look down on the Craven house, about half way down the mountain. The old house was burned during the battle, but has since been rebuilt and looks like the old one. We called it the "White House," and it was from here that Gen. Walthal's battery threw shells into our camp when we were cooped up in Chattanooga, in 1863. The family of Craven took refuge in a stone milk cellar during the battle. There are some fine monuments erected at this place.

An excavation has been made near the Point on Lookout Mountain, by the state of New York, for a $100,000 monument, to be erected by them. The ground cost $10,000.

We started for the natural bridge, but missed the way in the woods and wandered around on the west side of the mountain, two or three miles, but finally got around to the bridge. Here is some grand scenery, and one could spend a whole day here and not tire of of it.

While on the mountain we saw some colored boys "barbecue" a hog. They dug a square pit, filled it with wood, and when they got a bed of coals, put green sticks across, on these placed half a hog, and then basted it. It smelled as good as Jim Collins' roasted 'possums. The colored boys were a lively, happy barefooted lot.

Buying a few trinkets from our Confederate friend, we take the car for the city, and arrive safely. After supper we went around to the Rossmore hotel, and Sam Law and the writer accompanied Henry Conrad to the depot, as he was determined to go home. We then returned, and had a long chat with Sam and his sister, Mrs. Melvin, of Washington C. H., Ohio.

The following is from an article written by the Editor, after a visit to Chickamauga, in May, 1891:

The Snodgrass house still remains, and looks just as it did at the time of the battle 29 years ago. We were in the house which is occupied by a branch of the Snodgrass family. Snodgrass' wife, now an old lady being one of the inmates.

Mary J. Mercier *nee* Snodgrass, lives near the railroad, and owns a part of Snodgrass hill. She was a young lady of about 19 years, and lived at home, when the battle was fought. We will give her story as near as possible, which is as follows: "Living off here in the country, we little dreamed of the horrors of war. I was the oldest of six children. My father was greatly troubled when the battle opened the first day, as he could not imagine what the "Yanks" (here the lady

excused herself, knowing we were from the north, but
we told her to just go ahead and call them "Yanks,"
and "Johnnies,") would do with him, as there had
been none in that part of the country before, and he
had no correct idea as to what they were. I told him
to stay at home. Some of the family wanted to go and
hide. Finally, he said he would stay right here, let
the consequence be what it might. About this time a
Confederate Cavalry officer rode up with a sack of
meal and asked me to bake him some bread. I told
him it was a poor time to think about baking. He said
to me to bake it, and if he was not back in an hour,
eat it ourselves, or give it to some d———d Yankee.
I baked the bread, but the officer did not call for it,
but a Yank did. Dinner time came, and all was confusion. I said I was going to eat some dinner. So,
I and my stepmother and the children sat down at the
table on the porch, and finally we persuaded father
to do so. We ate our dinners, and in the afternoon
fighting began. We were ordered to leave for a place
of safety. We went to Mrs. Mulled's house, whose
husband was in the Confederate army. This was about
a quarter (quarter of a mile) from our house. Here
we stayed the first night. Things became too hot,
and on Saturday we all went to Mrs. Cooper's, whose
husband was also in the Confederate army. Here we
spent the second night. Sunday we were obliged to
move again, and we went about a mile back into the
woods. Here we spent Sunday night. At this time
our party consisted of 63 women and children, with no
male protectors, around log fires, with nothing in the
world except what we had on our backs.

I afterward went back to the house, but found bed-
clothes and everything torn up for bandages for the
wounded. When the battle commenced, and before
we left our house for the last time, men were brought
in, bleeding as if they had been cut with a butcher
knife. Our house was taken for a hospital, and was
also Gen. Thomas' headquarters. I did not mind seeing this at the time, but I could not bear it now. I
could have walked all over the field, near our house on

dead men. When the Yankees were beaten back they went in great confusion, throwing their knapsacks, cartridge boxes and some would bend their guns, by striking them against a tree.

The Yanks were buried in a square hole dug in the ground. A row was put in, and then they were laid across the other way. (The holes are yet visible.—ED.) When they were dug up and taken to Chattanooga they were placed in rough boxes and hauled away. (This accounts for so many unknown in the Chattanooga cemetery. It was impossible to tell who were there, being buried in this way.—ED.

The first Yankee money that was in our neighborhood, I got by getting a soldier a bucket of water. (It was a 25 cent shin plaster.—ED.)

We did not go back to our house to live for two years after the battle. The first pair of shoes I had after the battle, I got by the sale of bullets and other things which I gathered up on the battlefield, and sold in Chattanooga. I have talked about this a great deal, and years ago could tell you a great deal more than I can now."

Heavens, thought we, isn't this enough?

## REMINISCENCES, LETTERS, POEMS, ETC.

I was the first man who enlisted in Deer Creek township, under the first call for troops, in April, 1861. I was in the first battle of Bull Run.

Although our time was out, we volunteered to go into battle. During the battle a call was made for volunteers to go back to a spring with canteens for water, and I was one. We slung half a dozen canteens over our shoulders, went and filled them, but when we returned the regiment was gone. I started out, and looking across in a corn field, the corn about hip high, I saw a man with a plug hat and long linen duster, running for dear life through the corn, and a Johnny Reb after him. He was a congressman who had come out from Washington to see the battle, but Johnny got him. I saw no more of the regiment till I got to Washington.

August 7, 1862, I enlisted in Co. A, 90th O. V. I. On our march through Kentucky and Tennessee, I and my partner would play cards, every chance we got, at 25 cents. Lieut. Willoughby threatened, often, to tie me up to a tree. I told him not to go off and leave me tied up, the Rebs might get me, but if he did leave my hands loose so I could handle my gun. He never tied me up. We were not paid off for several months, and down in Tennessee the boys got pretty short of money. Lieut. Willoughby was one of them, and he wanted some rations. He asked me if I had any money. I said I had. He asked me to loan him five dollars. I told him I made it play-

181

ing cards, and of course he would not want it. He begged for the money. Just then another officer asked me the same question, and I promptly loaned him five dollars. Then Willoughby begged again, and said he would never say anything more about cards, and I loaned him the money.

While on the Atlanta campaign, a squad of us were going out on the skirmish line. It was somewhere near where General Polk was killed. It was a damp, foggy morning, and we could not see far. There was a bunch of haw bushes in front of me, and when I was within about twenty feet, a Johnny fired at me, being so close that the smoke came in my face. The only way I can account for his shot not killing me, is, that the ball had been loose in his gun, and had rolled out, as was sometimes the case. The Johnny jumped and ran into the brush before we got a shot at him.

On the same campaign a number of us were sent out on the skirmish line in command of Captain Denny. After all had been placed but myself and another man, Denny said we'd go on further and see what was there. I cautioned him. We came to a road where there was a small cleared patch. Denny wanted to go across, he said he heard men talking, and that they were our men. I said, "Yes, they are our men, but we'll have to catch them first. He insisted and we bounded across the road to the fence, where they let loose on us, and made the splinters fly. Then Denny wanted to get back, and finally we made a run and got back, none of us getting hurt.

At Kenesaw Mountain we went on picket, in the timber, one night. We could not see, it was so dark, could not tell what was in front of us, or how close we were to their lines. We stopped behind a big log, which was long enough to shelter our whole company. Denny wanted me to get over the log and chop a tree down. I told him I'd be d——d if I did, that the Rebs were not fifty yards away. He insisted and so did I. He finally got another man to get over the log, when he was shot in the leg. I told Denny there would be plenty of good shooting around there in the morning, and so there was. Denny was wounded in the shoulder, early in the fight. This was June 28, 1864. JONAS ROSS, Co. A.

OCEAN GROVE, N. J., Aug. 26, 1901.

*H. O. Harden, President, Stoutsville, O:*

DEAR SIR AND COMRADE: — Your kind invitation to attend the Annual Reunion of the 90th O. V. I., received. I am glad that the Boys keep up the Reunion, and would be glad to know how many unite in it. I suppose, of course, that many have gone to the "Bivouac of the Dead." It will not be possible for me to come this time, as I am at the seashore recuperating my health. Last February I had a break-down at my 5008th successive meeting, but am on the mend. I often mention the 90th O. V. I. in my addresses over the country, and have written of it occasionally. I am writing a book now of 300 pages in which I tell the story of my life in Kentucky with the dear old Regiment.

I enclose a circular, by means of which we may keep in touch, if you wish, also, send you report of the Old Jerry McAuley Water Street Mission, in which my brother, the superintendent, kindly mentions my name and prints my picture.

Will you kindly drop me a line and tell me what sort of a time the Boys have at the Reunion, and what Company you were in?

I am a member of Alexander Hamilton Post, G. A. R., New York City.            H. H. HADLEY,
*Private Co. H., 90th, and Capt. and Brev. Lieut. Col., 119th U. S. C. T.*

The story of Comrade Hadley is pathetic. He says in his "The Miracle of My Conversion": "When I was 20 years old the war broke out, and shortly afterward, enlisted as a private in the 90th O. V. I., Co. H, which went from New Lexington. My mother bore it resignedly, but could not consent to my going. Father restrained his feelings, but when I ran back to kiss mother once more, I found her on the floor in a heap, crying as if her poor heart was breaking — and it was. Four years after I was mustered out, having attained the rank of Captain and Brevet Lieutenant Colonel. But the temptations of the army had captured me and I was a slave to drink. Father and mother had died, the farm was sold and I went into business with success, and but for drink would have become rich."

He then tells of his terrible struggles till 1886, when he was converted at the Jerry McAuley Mission, New York City. He and his brother are devoting their lives to saving fallen men and women. — ED.

———————

On Sunday, Sept. 20, 1863, at the battle of Chickamauga, a sharp shooter in front of the 90th, kept picking off the officers. Adjutant Kingery was killed and Captain Angle was wounded. Colonel Yeoman

From a recent photo.

SERGT. JAMES DOBBINS, CO. G.

asked for volunteers to go out and capture him. Eight
men of Co. I volunteered, among whom were John
Seaman, Nathan Knotts, James H. Foster, R. R.
Pierce, P. B. Wilcox. The names of the others we
do not know. Colonel Yeoman bade the boys good-
bye, as he said he did not expect to see them again.
The boys found the Johnny in a large pine tree, and
he, like Davy Crocket's coon, came down without much
ceremony. He had nailed cleats on the tree to climb
up and down.

----

### CHILCOTE'S COW.

An aged lady lived in Dixie,
   Who, we hope, is an angel now.
But away back in the sixties,
   She owned a Brindle Cow.

John Chilcote, then a lad of the 90th,
   Who is along in years now,
Regularly, morning and evening,
   Milked the Old Lady's Cow.

That cow was gentle, kind and true,
   So is Johnny now,
For at every opportunity
   He milked the old Brindle Cow.

It seems that John hadn't been weaned,
   But we hope he is now;
For regularly as the day dawned,
   He looked for the old Brindle Cow.

Our 90th Butchers got on a bum;
   We recall the incident now,

And on that bright and moonlight night
They butchered Chilcote's Cow.

By this unfortunate butchers' bum
   John received a very hard rub,
But he endured it like a soldier brave,
   And settled down to army grub.

---

Comrade Parsons tells a good story on S. D. Soliday, of Co. D. Parsons says that on leaving the battlefield of Chickamauga, Soliday stuck the bayonet of his gun in the ground, leaving the gun, which had been injured by a shot. Parsons said, "Sol, what did you do that for?" Sol said: "By ——— the war will last six years, and I want a new gun." Parsons said: "Yes, but I'll report you, and you'll have the gun to pay for." Sol said: "Yes, but Sergeant, you will not report me."

At Chattanooga arms were issued, and Soliday was allowed first choice.

---

Talking with Samuel Timberlake, of Co. G, he said: "I got a furlough at Bridgeport, Ala., and came home. If I were to be in the army fifteen years, I'd never go home till I went to stay. I was married and had four children. My wife and the children, by this time knew what war was, and I tell you it was the hardest trial of my life, when I started to return. My wife had me around the neck, and a child hold of each leg, crying. I never want to experience such a thing again."

Just before the storming of Rocky Face Mountain, or Buzzard Roost, we were drawn up and ordered to pile our knapsacks. We well knew what that meant, and there was no levity, as we all stood with blanched faces. A young man approached us, gave the address of a young lady in Delaware, O., to whom he was engaged, and asked that we write to her, informing her of his fate. This incident we will never forget. We did not write to his girl, as he came home safe and married her. — ED.

---

PEEKSKILL, N. Y., April 24, 1894.

COMRADE HARDEN: I have observed, with a great deal of interest, that in your history of the Regiment, hardly any part of its service surpassed in importance and excitement, the period between the date of muster and the battle of Stone River. With interest, because I was unfortunate enough to break down with the trials of that period, and was discharged on Christmas day. Up to the day of my discharge I had been with the regiment, although excused from duty while in camp at Nashville, and I had always felt a keen disappointment in not having been able to continue in the service, and until reading the history had felt as if I had not been through a real soldier's experience. Now, I know better, for it seems that the regiment encountered little more that was trying, than during those few months.

I left the regiment this morning; it broke camp for a movement which none of us thought meant importance. On reaching Nashville, a defect in my papers occasioned my remaining there nearly three weeks and perhaps a sketch of some things transpiring in the city during that time may be pleasing to some.

I was quartered in the Zollicoffer House, called the "barracks." There were probably two thousand there at intervals, nearly all "convalescents." There was plenty to eat, of army rations, of course, and the commandant exercised good discipline, so quietly to be a marvel to me. It was a habit of mine to know what was transpiring around me, and I used to take walks, about camp, of evenings, to note how soldiers lived. So in the barracks — it was an immense building — but I made the acquaintance of every room in it. On the second or third morning of my tours I was astounded to find one room occupied by a squad of thirteen from my own company, who had been sent there as unfit to march with the regiment.

They were not there long, and one morning, after vainly searching the house for them, I made inquiries and learned they had been removed to a convalescent camp outside the city, all but one of them, and I could tell you a most pitiful tale of a poor comrade I found in deplorable condition, in an unlathed room, where the same cold rain swept through that was making battling experiences dreadful for our regiment at the front. He was helpless. I took him to the surgeon of the establishment, who gave me a ticket for the sick man's admission to a hospital. I took him to the hospital, and was the last of his company to see him alive. He was then awaiting discharge papers, but when the papers came he was at rest.

I was not slow to find the convalescent camp, and visited my comrades every day, and exchanged items of news concerning the fighting towards Murfreesboro. Harrowing tales we heard. A commissioned officer had been given his discharge papers on the field, and he started at once for home, but left with my friends a report of the losses our regiment was sustaining. One member of my company whom I particularly liked, a big, black whiskered, hearty souled, good fellow, this officer said had been killed, and he had seen the body — riddled with bullets. So I mourned for my friend, Sam Shaeffer.

What excitement prevailed in Nashville that week of the fighting! Spare troops were gathered together and pushed forward; additional hospitals were improvised to accommodate the wounded that came in by the hundreds. A church opposite our barracks was thrown open, was filled, and many scenes were transpiring there to fill both soul and heart to overflowing. I recall one little sight that seemed so full of a touching story. Many bodies were encased and shipped to friends at home, and one, enclosed in a tin covered box had a small bible secured to the top by strips screwed across it.

One afternoon there were rumors of reverses at the front. Terror and consternation were in the rumor. The weather was dull, cold, windy and rainy, as disagreeable as could be imagined. About 10 o'clock that night the long roll was sounded. Perhaps the most solemn sound heard upon earth is that of "taps" by the bugle, over the soldier just lowered in the grave, as I heard it at a military funeral at West Point a few weeks ago. Can anything be more thrilling than the sound of the "long roll" in time of impending danger! How the convalescents, who were able to do anything, tumbled out and took their guns and places in the ranks. Fortunately for Nashville and the nation "Old Rosy" with the 90th as part of his persistent force, sent all the consternation to the south side of Stone River.

There is always a humorous side to the trials of life. During my enforced stay in Nashville, I never obtained a pass to go about the city, but I wandered all over it. Perhaps every day I went to the State House where Provost headquarters were stationed. Of course I wasn't disturbed there, for no guard imagined any fellow without a pass would venture near them. From the appearance of the interior of the State House I judged some regiment had been newly clothed there, and it had left its old shoes and garments in the representative chamber. I used to sit in the seats and picture to myself the bold Tennesseans making the beautiful stone arches ring with their demands for secession and the destruction of the union, and laugh all by myself, thinking they had to skedaddle after doing it.

One day, though, I had distinct visions of the guard house. I had asked for a pass out of the city to the convalescent camp. My request has been misunderstood, and in place of a pass I was given a transfer. I never used it, and always went to and from camp without a pass. One day, however, I went to the suburbs to get a little look at Fort Negley. Suddenly a mounted patrol came bearing down upon me at a furious gallop. With a spring from his horse he landed by my side and demanded my pass. I was scared and won't deny it. I either did not show my fright or he did not know a scare when he made it. I at once thought of my "transfer," so, without any idea it would help me out of a scrape, I produced the piece of paper. He opened it and read the big printed heading, "Headquarters 14th Army Corps, Army of the Cumberland" — and without going further he neatly folded up the paper, and politely handed it back to me, saying "that's all right." I enjoyed looking at that man's back and thanked his ignorance.

The battle of Stone River ended. My papers failed to materialize, and after another week I was advised to go to the front after them, they having been sent there for correction. So I started with a wagon train, and rejoined my company, 30 miles beyond Murfreesboro. As I got off the wagon on which I had jolted 60 miles, the first man I met was my bullet riddled friend, Sam Shaeffer. The squeeze of his hand wasn't what one would naturally expect from a riddled man but there was no disappointment in my finding Sam as sound and good as he always had been. Let me tell you the rest of it. A week later when I was in Lancaster, I of course corrected the report that had reached there of Sam being riddled. Three days later when I was preparing to leave for Peekskill, New York, where my father had moved while I was with the 90th, I was told an old gentleman wished to see me. It was Sam's father who wished to be sure that I knew what I was talking about before he believed my story. Said he, "Me and Sam's mother have been mourning for him as dead. Now I don't want to go home and tell her he is alive, and find after all that he is gone. Is there anything about the man you know, that you can tell me, so I can be sure that the Sam you know is my Sam?" I had to think a moment, then I remembered something. I replied, "Yes, there is. This man had lost the first joint of the fore finger of his left hand." Before I had quite concluded my remark, the old gentleman grasped my hand, and as great tears met a glad smile on his lips, he exclaimed, "That's my boy! Now I must hasten home and tell his old mother he is alive." Why, comrade, I felt as though I had received my injury, which troubles me to this day, on purpose to be discharged to carry this good word to the soldier's father.

On my return to Nashville, I spent a night in Murfreesboro, and slept on a counter in a store where were some of our wounded. Medical attendance was so poor that I was told that where I slept, the night before a soldier had died with vermin in his wounds. The next morning I walked across the battlefield, and looked at a brick house I think some of you know about. If you know of my comrade who forgot to "return rammer," he may be glad to know I brought home a piece of a ram rod I found at an angle in the ground, as if it had been shot from a gun. Amongst my curiosities I have two bullets that met in mid air and united in one. I found it on the rebel works at Petersburg, the Sunday following its capture.

I stopped also at the hospital of the 90th which I believe was the only tent hospital that had been established. It was full and I have learned since, from an article I saw in relation to it, that it was of great service. Not only the hospital, but our surgeon was highly commended for what was done during those awful days, to the wounded.

How long ago was it, comrade, all these things happened? When I begin to write about them it seems as if I could account for every hour of time, recall every incident, find room for mirth, and so much for pathos — why when one comes to really analyze it a soldier's life is all pathos — but if I don't stop —

Sincerely yours,

HOMER ANDERSON.

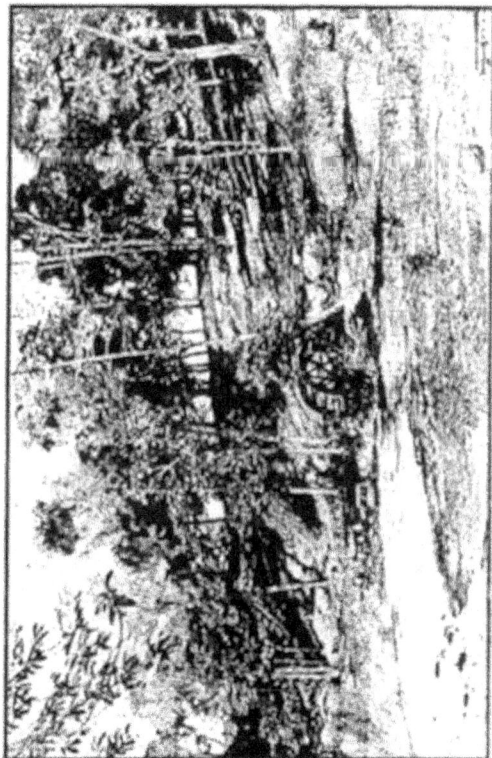

From a war-time picture.

Crawfish Spring, near Chickamauga.

WELCOME, 90TH O. V. I.

BY C. B. TAYLOR, 86TH O. V. I., 1ST O. H. A.

AIR : Happy Land of Canaan.

'Twas in 1862
These brave men put on the blue
And went forth the old flag to defend,
And from private up to colonel
Midst shot and shell infernal
They stood by the colors to the end.

CHORUS:

Oh! Ho!
Our town is all aglow,
Listen and I'll tell you the reason why,
For we welcome here to-day
The soldiers old and gray,
The veterans of the 90th O. V. I.

On Stone River's bloody field
These men refused to yield,
But boldly they held their colors high,
And in Chickamauga's fight
They battled for the right,
These veterans of the 90th O. V. I.

God bless the stripes and stars
That they followed to the wars,
And bless the men who dared to fight and die,
Yes, bless the whole caboodle,
Hail Columbia! Yankee Doodle!
These veterans of the 90th O. V. I.

Welcome every old galoot
That e'er hollered, "Grab a root"

13  90 O V I

Welcome to our hearts and homes and chicken pie;
The cake and coffee's on the shelf,
Every fellow help yourself
You dear, old blessed 90th O. V. I.

And when your time is done
And your earthly race is run,
May the angels far above the starry sky,
The celestial choirs above
Welcome with a song of love,
The veterans of the 90th O. V. I.

The singer was recalled by cheers, when he added
the following verse:

O, we like to have you cheer
You old pension grabbers dear,
It sounds like your old battle cry,
When amidst the shot and shell,
You answered back the rebel yell,
You veterans of the 90th O. V. I.

----

ADDRESS DELIVERED BY H. O. HARDEN AT THE
REGIMENTAL REUNION, AT McARTHUR, O , SEP-
TEMBER, 1895.

"The committee assigned to me an address, without
stating the subject. I suppose that they intended that
I should choose my own. I have thought over the
matter, and have concluded that I would like to interest the younger people — those who have come among
us since the war. I will take as my subject, "Going
to War." Now, what is war? General Sherman said
on one occasion, "War is hell." On another, he said,
"War is civilized barbarism." And he knew.

In 1861, as you have all read, our nation was in
peril. Armed rebellion was seeking to destroy the
government. Troops were called for to suppress it.
We had no regular army, or but a very small one. The
soldiers to be, were from all the walks of life. Farm-
ers, mechanics, merchants, teachers, doctors, ministers — all were represented.

"Going to war" meant a great deal. They did not
go for the paltry sum of $13 a month. They went
because they felt it a duty they owed their country;
because their property, their homes, would be useless
without a government to protect it. Somebody must
go, why not they?

What did it mean when you went to war? It meant
that when you signed your name to the muster roll
and took an oath of fealty to the government, that
you placed your life on the altar of your country. You
said, by that act, that you would bare your breast to
the bullets of the enemy. You said you would make
long marches through the dust day by day, and sleep
at night, with the ground for your couch and the
sky for your roof. You said you would march through
mud by day, and make it your bed by night. You said,
by that act, that you would march over frozen ground,
thinly clad, barefooted, leaving your footsteps stained
with blood. That you would risk capture and con-
finement in prison. That you would walk your lonely
beat, on picket, while those at home were sleeping
soundly in their soft beds.

It meant, that if you were a husband and a father,
that this act would make your wife a widow, and your
children orphans. With the young man, it often meant
the breaking of a heart dearer to him than his own life.
In the case of the boys, it meant the tearing of the

heart strings of an aged and loving mother. It meant sorrow, and weeping for those dear friends at home.

Now, I will draw you a picture of war times. In the little village, or at a country school house, may be, a war meeting is held. Drums are beating, fifes are playing and speakers are urging enlistments. The recruiting officer, perhaps the man who is to be an officer of the company, is present. You feel it your duty to go. You finally step up and sign your name. When you tell your family, what sorrow. It seems as if some of the family were dead.

The day comes when you are to go to the front. The husband, with his wife's arms about his neck, weeping, his children clinging to him, bids them a last good bye, and is gone.

Who can measure the depth of sorrow in that household?

The husband is at the front. He writes and tells his wife of his army life, of his marches, his hardships, and anxiously awaits a reply. This goes on for months. A great battle is fought. It may be Bull Run or Shiloh; Gettysburg or Stone River; Vicksburgh or Antietam; Frederickburgh or Chickamauga; Nashville or Chancellorsville — no matter. A daily paper is received at the village post-office. In it are the names of the killed and wounded. One of the neighbors glances over the list, and there finds the name of this husband among the killed. Who will break the awful news to his wife? They talk it over, and a neighbor and his wife go to the little home of the woman. She sees by their blanched faces that they have bad news. "Tell me quick," she said, "Is John killed?" They break it gently as possible, then she sits and stares, like a figure of stone, not a tear dims her eyes. Then the fountains of her sorrow break up, and she now realizes the awful situation, and in anguish she exclaims, "My God, I am a widow and my children are fatherless."

This is only one case among many thousands.

I will draw you another picture. If any of you young ladies are ·in love, you can appreciate it. This thing "love," is too lightly spoken of. "God is love." Young men and young women have fallen in love in all ages past, and will continue to do so, so long as there is a pair left.

A young lady and gentleman have, through a long courtship, agreed to walk together through life, as man and wife. This cruel war comes on and the young man feels it his duty to go to war. His sweetheart begs of him not to go. He still insists that it is his duty to go, that a home without a government to protect it would be mockery. She consents and her lover enrolls his name. The time comes for him to leave for the scenes of strife and bloodshed. And that last parting. It is enough to make angels weep. They each pledge fidelity to the other, no matter what comes. How eagerly she watches for his letters, and how she steals softly to her room and reads them. Then she reads again and again. How she wrestles with hope and fear for his safe return. He, as eagerly waits for her letters, and when out on a lonely picket post, he is thinking of her. He sits in his tent, or walks out to some secluded· spot and reads. Then he draws from his breast pocket a tin type of a pure and noble girl, and he looks, and he looks at it, and perhaps speaks to it, perchance he kisses it.

One day this girl receives a letter from the army. It does not look like the handwriting of her lover. Her hand trembles and she shakes like an aspen. She opens it, and finds that the letter was written by one of her lover's comrades. He tells her that James, her noble lover, is dead. That he waited on him, and promised that if he died he would write and tell her. He tells her how they dug a grave beside an oak, wrapped him in his blanket and gently laid him away, and marked his grave with a piece of board with his name cut thereon. Oh, what depth of sorrow in that pure, young girl's heart. None but a Christ could fathom it.

This, too, is only one picture of many thousands all over this land. What is true of the North, as to suffering loss of friends, is also true of the South, though they were fighting on the wrong side.

Though I fear I will tire you, I can not refrain from drawing one more picture—one of these gray-haired veterans will know.

I see before me, a large army of soldiers, confronting as brave and determined an army as their own. They march and countermarch in the enemy's own country. Footsore and hungry they march, and march all day and far into the night. Hungry and thirsty, they lie down to sleep and dream of home and its comforts. They dream of frugal meals at the old homestead. They dream they have been to the little country church and have associated with their neighbors. They see the wife of their bosom and their dear little prattling children. They see their dear old father and mother. They see that dear, young lady who has promised to be their wife. It may be the angels were hovering over them, and caused them to dream, which was an oasis in the deserts of their hardships. They wake —it was only a dream. On they go next day, and next day—for weeks perhaps. They meet the enemy. A hotly contested field is fought over, and then fought over again.

Their comrades fall all around them. They know not how soon they will be numbered among the dead or wounded. Night comes on. It is dark and rainy. They grope their way over the field among the slain, amid groans, uttered with anguish tongue can not describe, looking and hunting for their fallen comrades.

They are gathered and buried in one long trench, their tomb unmarked, their names unknown.

The living go on, from one hard fought field to another, for four long years, sleeping on the cold ground, exposed to rain and snow, many times hungry and but little to eat. Some are captured and spend long, long months in prison. Many die there—but few return. These men, or boys, by their hardships, contracted disease from which they will never recover. Though they may look reasonably healthy, there is disease sapping away their lives. These men come home and resume their respective avocations in life. Just as they were good soldiers, so are they good citizens. They often think of their comrades who were left behind. They remember where they buried them. They never forget those who shared the hardships with them. Their comradeship is cemented with ties that can never be broken, for they are ties bound and cemented by the blood of their fallen comrades.

Is it any wonder then, that we make so much of each other at these reunions? I believe that the grand old 90th will keep up these fraternal meetings so long as two of them are left, and should I be fortunate enough to be one of the last two, I will endeavor to meet the other one somewhere, and when we are all gone, let us hope that we'll have a full regimental re-union on the other side of the river that marks the boundary of our earthly pilgrimage.

---

THE 90TH O. V. I. IN NORTH CAROLINA.

LOGAN, OHIO, *March* 26, 1898.

It was in April, 1865, and we were encamped on Big Lick creek, in East Tennessee, near Bull's Gap. On or about the 4th of April the first brigade of the first division of the Fourth Corps, was ordered to make a raid into North Carolina, to a place called Asheville, the county seat of Buncombe county, and about 100 miles distant. Asheville was the headquarters of a large force of guerillas, and it was reported that they had quite a large amount of supplies stored there, and we were ordered to go there and destroy them. General Kirby was in command of the brigade, and he was told to take the brigade and two sections of artillery and two ambulances, make the trip, do the work and return as quickly as possible. His orders were to take the place with a skirmish line if possible, but not to risk a battle so far away from support, as we could not care for the dead and wounded. So everything was put in order and we started, with five days' rations for each man, for we were expected to make the trip in five days. We went from our camp to a little place called Midway, on the railroad track and then struck across the country to the mountains, near the state line between Tennessee and North Carolina. Here the brigade was halted, and General Kirby rode along the line and told us that when we got into North Carolina we could have all the fresh pork we wanted. So we

D. C. GOODWIN, CO. E.          ADAM GETMAN, CO. H.

He served in the German army
before coming to this country.

thought, of course, we would live fat while in that state.

We crossed the mountains at a place called Paint Rock and struck the French Broad river. I suppose it takes its name from being so very broad and swift, also, very shallow and rocky. The river runs between two mountain ranges all the way from Paint Rock to Asheville, about 75 miles, and at no point were we more than 100 yards from the river, as there is no valley, and at some places, when the road was built, they had to build stone walls along the edge of the water so as to make room for the road. One day we halted at noon to rest, and we saw a man, and a woman with a babe in her arms, come down to th: edge of the water on the opposite of the river to get a good look at the Yanks, as they had never seen any. Now was our time for some fun. Col. Yeoman had a field glass, and he put it to his eyes, and we thought he'd never get through looking at them, for we wanted a chance ourselves with the glass, and we got it. All that we saw would not look well in print, in regard to their condition, but the tobacco juice was running out of the corners of her mouth, dripping off her chin on the breast and running down on the babe. The Colonel told the old man that Richmond had fallen, and asked him to give us three cheers, but the old man said, "I only have *two stools* in the house." We spent about an hour talking to the old man and getting our dinner, and after using the Colonel's field glass to our satisfaction we resumed our march. That night we went into camp near a little town called Marshall. It looked very much like rain, so Joe Collins, Sam Poland and myself went up on the side of the mountain and crawled in under a shelving rock to keep out

of the rain. We had hardly got comfortably fixed
when Sam Poland said something about rattlesnakes,
and then our hair began to raise, but I was in the
middle, so I told the boys to lie still and the snakes
would not bother them, so we slept there until morning.

The next morning we resumed our way and nothing transpired until about ten o'clock. Our regiment
(90th) was in the advance that morning, and I was
straggling ahead by the side of Co. A and just behind
the Colonel. We came to a place where the road
wound around a hill, and just as we got there Colonel
Yeoman saw a man on the other side of the river on
a gray mule, going down the river. He commanded
him to halt, but the fellow paid no attention to the
order, but put the spur to his mule and away he went.
The Colonel turned to the captain of Co. A and told
him to let one of his men fire at the man. The captain told one of his men to fire, but when he fired
every man in the regiment who had a load in his gun,
blazed away, and the fellow went as if he were shot
out of a gun, and I don't think there was a bullet hit
him or the mule. I would like to hear that Johnny
tell his experience on the French Broad. I think he
had more lead fired at him than any other man in the
Confederate army.

About one mile further up the river, we struck
what they called a country hotel. Here was a bridge
across the river, the only bridge we had seen on the
river. Here, also, was the gun and cartridge box that
belonged to the Johnny on the mule. We halted here
to rest, and as all soldiers like to eat, we went into the
house to see what kind of grub they had. As we entered the dining room the landlady was trying to clear

the table, but we were too quick for her and began to help ourselves. She "kicked," but kicking did not go with us when we had a snap. While we were eating, the General commanding the brigade, came in and the old lady began to tell him how the boys were treating her. The General turned his back and listened to the old lady tell her story, and once in a while he would look back over his shoulder and give us the wink, so we got all there was on that table. While scouting around the negro cabins I found a small roll of butter, which served me and the mess for our suppers. Butter and hard tack are not so bad to take. Our stay was short, as we were bound for Asheville.

When we were about eight miles from Asheville, we stopped at a house where we found two sick Johnnies, and an ambulance in the barn yard. We took the ambulance and threw it in the river, but the Johnnies we had no use for and left them.

When we were one and a half miles from Asheville, we passed a negro cabin and we asked them if there had been any rebels out that road that morning and they said six guards passed, going around the hill into town. All soldiers know that a general's orderlies are brave, so they rushed around the hill and captured the whole squad without firing a shot. The prisoners stated that their troops were holding a court-martial in the court house, and the troops were all in town without their arms, and that there were no pickets on that road, so there was another soft snap for staff officers and orderlies. They put spurs to their horses and rushed into town, up Patton Avenue to the court house, then turned and rode out again, while the infantry was yet a mile away, so that by the time we got there they would be out to their camp, had their arms and were ready to give us a warm reception. When we drew up in front of town they had their line deployed along a rail fence running up a small hill, and two pieces of artillery planted on a small elevation behind the infantry. As soon as we appeared in sight they opened fire on us with infantry and artillery, but we had the advantage in the lay of the ground and they did not do much harm.

While we were there a negro came to us from town, and we arrested him as a spy, and told him that we wanted him to tell us all he knew about the rebels. He got down on his knees and said he could not tell us anything, as he did not know anything about them. But we told him we did, and if he did not tell us we would hang him on a tree, but the poor old darkey protested and prayed to the Lord that he was telling the truth, but the boys said we would have to hang him. One of them got a rope from a wagon and we put one end around his neck and led him to a tree and threw the rope over a limb and told him this was his last chance, and that his time had come. The old darky thought he was a "goner," for certain. We gave him a chance to pray, and he got down on his knees and held up his hands and told the Good Lord that he was no spy, and that he was telling the truth, and if we would let him live he would never tell a lie. As we had had enough fun, we let him go.

We skirmished around the town all the afternoon. They had about three companies of infantry and two pieces of artillery, and they would fire a volley and then give a yell to make us believe that they had a large force."

Since the above was written we met Charles Vandemark, of Co.I, and he explained the shooting at the man on the gray mule, although he says it was a gray horse.

In 1874 a Doctor J. J. Johnson, of East Tennessee, located in Amanda, for a while, and he called on him one day for some medicine, as the other doctors were not at home. The doctor spoke of being from East Tennessee. Vandemark then related the incident to him. The doctor said he was a surgeon in the Confederate army, that he owned the brick house near where the man was when the boys shot at him, that he was well fixed but the war had ruined him. He was then about 70 years old. He said the man, whose name Vandemark has forgotten, was shot through the elbow, and that he dressed his wound.

Vandemark has a silver spoon he picked up in the doctor's yard, and on it is engraved "J. J. J."

Vandemark says he is satisfied the old doctor was telling the truth—ED.

"The boys wanted to charge them and take the town, but General Kirby would not allow us to do it. We told him that we were willing to take our chances, but he said no, and we had to obey orders.

During the afternoon we lost two men and one gum blanket. Perces Sweet, of Co. E, was shot through the leg, and Joe Tatman, of Co. G, was shot in the hip, and Fred Saumering, of Co. E, had five or six holes shot through his gum blanket. That made him mad, for he said it was a good blanket. At last night came on and it began to rain and got very dark. We had captured eleven prisoners and had our fun with the old darkey, and then came orders to withdraw and return to camp. We started on our return with eleven prisoners, just after dark, the boys all feeling blue because we did not get into the town. We marched all night

through the rain and it was so dark we could not see
our file leader, and every once in a while we would hear
some one fall into the river, then we would hear a yell.
Quite a number of the boys got a ducking that night
but they did not mind it. When morning came we
only had four prisoners, the others had got away during the night, for it was so dark all they had to do was
to step out of the ranks and we could not see them.

The next day the sun came out and it was nice and
warm and some of the boys said they were going to
float down the river in a dugout, as there were plenty
along the river. So they took several of them and put
four or five men in each one and started down the
river. The water was very swift and they could go as
fast as we could march on the road. But the fun was
to come. They had not gone far until they struck a
whirlpool and the dugout upset and threw them into
the water, but they held on to the boat, as the water
was only about three or four feet deep. They emptied
the water out and got in again, but the same thing
occurred three or for times, but they did not mind it
as they were having plenty of fun. What a sergeant
can not do is not worth doing, so Barrah Moore said he
could steer one of them all right. He took his seat
in the stern, with an old fence rail to guide it, they
started. Everything went smooth for about half a
mile when they came to another whirlpool. The sergeant told the boys to keep cool and he would take
them through all right. He had hardly spoken when
she struck a rock and over they went into the water.
The sergeant's feathers dropped. The boys told him
the stripes on his sleeves looked very nice, but that
he didn't know a thing about steering a boat.

Before the war this road was a stage line, as we saw quite a number of the old rockaway coaches at several barns along the road. When night came we were near Paint Rock again, on our return, so we went into camp until morning. The next morning we resumed our march, crossing over the Blue Ridge mountains at Paint Rock. Nothing of importance transpired during the day, until evening when we were going into camp near Greenville. Just as we were leaving the road going into the field to camp, word came that Lee had surrendered, and then the boys went wild, for they thought the war was over. We all said, "now we will get to go home, as the war is over." But there were still a few rebels that had not surrendered.

The next morning we passed through Greenville, the place where Gen. John H. Morgan was killed about seven months before. Some of us boys stopped at the house where he was killed, to see the place. A woman lived there by the name of Williams, and it was in her back yard that he was killed. Hiram Brown said that Morgan was trying to crawl in a cabbage hole, but after examining the place we found it was a mistake as the hole was too small. The house was a story and a half brick, and stood near the edge of the town. It had two rooms up stairs and two down, with a hall between with the front and back door. Our cavalry rode up to the front gate, dismounted and rushed to the front door, for they knew Morgan was in the house. It was between midnight and morning, and as they broke open the front door Morgan and three or four of his staff rushed out the back door into the yard to make their escape. The cavalry ran to the back door and saw four men, three of whom were climbing the high board

fence, and one was in the middle of the lot. They fired
at them and the one in the lot fell, but the others got
away, but one of them was supposed to have been
wounded as they found blood at the fence.   Mrs. Williams was a Union woman and she sent word to our
cavalry by her daughter that Morgan and his staff
were at her house.   She showed us all through the
house and the backyard and told us all about it.   John
Cage says if he had been there he would not have
killed Morgan, but would have taken him prisoner so
that he could have made a mule driver out of him, for
he was a good horseman.   That night we arrived back
to our old camp, and the boys were very tired and mad
to think that Gen. Kirby would not let them capture
Asheville, as the boys wanted the fun of sacking the
town from one end to the other.   We arrived in our old
camp on the evening of the eleventh, feeling good over
the surrender of Gen. Lee, but on the evening of the
fourteenth we received word that Lincoln had been
assassinated and our hopes seemed to go down, but the
Government moved on and things came our way.   After remaining at our old camp a few weeks, we were
finally ordered to Nashville to be mustered out of the
service.   We moved about two miles to a little railroad
station near Bull's Gap, to wait for a train to take us
to Nashville.   While we were waiting for a train a
company of rebel cavalry passed through our camp on
their way to Knoxville.   They belonged to General
Vaugan's command, and had surrendered and were
on their way home.   Some of the command belonged
in that little station, for they stopped at a house to talk
to some of the ladies and I heard the ladies inquire
after several that had gone from that place.   There
was one Johnny Reb with an old black mare that was

HIRAM S. BROWN, CO. E.

The 90th Poet and Singer. Also one of the Little Browns.

just about played out, who brought up the rear. He was an Irishman and had on a small citizen's cap. He looked quite comical. He was walking and leading the old mare. He said the Confederacy was played out and he was bringing up the rear with the old black mare, as she was a fair representative of the Confederacy.

That night we took the train and ran down to Morristown, where we arrived at about two o'clock, but when we got there we found that the rebels had burned up a train about a mile below, so we had to stay there until morning. When daylight came we got on our train and ran down about a mile where we found a long box-car train burned up. Colonel Yeoman ordered us to stack arms and get some fence rails and throw the trucks off the track, as they were too hot to take hold of with our bare hands. While we were working we heard some one behind us hollowing, and when we looked around we saw a man coming down across the field with his hat in his hand waving it with all his might, and when he got close to us he said he was never so glad to see the Yanks in his life. He proved to be the engineer of the train that was burned, and he said when the rebels fired into the train he jumped off on the other side and broke for the woods and climbed a tree. He said he heard the rebels in the woods all night hunting for him, and he was afraid to come down until he saw us. There was no one hurt on the train, and in a couple of hours we had the track clear and boarded our train for Nashville. When we got to Chattanooga, we stopped a couple of hours, and Joseph Collins went over into town to see a sutler and came back with a box of fine cigars, and we had something to smoke. After leaving Chattanooga we made

14 90 O V I

no more stops of any length of time until we reached Nashville, where, after remaining in camp a couple of weeks, we were mustered out of the service, June 13, 1865, then taken to Camp Dennison, near Cicinnati, Ohio, paid off and discharged.

Two years ago when I was at the Dedication of the Chickamauga Park, I met quite a number of the boys in Gray, and they told me that if we ever had war with a foreign nation, that we would all be one and fight side by side, and I believe them. I there met Gilbert Montjoy, of Sweet's Battery, and he told me that it was his Battery that fought that artillery duel at Kenesaw Mountain. He said his Battery was placed down among the rocks and they gave us the best they had, but the old 5th Indiana was too much for them.

JOHN W. TRITSCH, Co. *E.*

## "SHELL ANNIE."

The following story is founded on facts, and as we remember them, they are as follows. On the march to Atlanta, Ga., on one of the many battlefields, a child was born in a cabin during the engagement. A shell passed through the cabin where the mother attended by a negress, were. The men and officers were drawn there, through curiosity, and one of the officers proposed naming the child, and it was agreed to call her "Shell Annie." The soldiers then emptied from their haversacks, crackers, coffee, sugar and bacon a large quantity, as the mother and negress were destitute of eatables, and left them well provided for in that line. — EDITOR.

"Nobody expected General Sherman to come into Atlanta from the south.

"Oh, no, in the natural course of events he must have certainly shouldered his way right straight on from the north, and accordingly the grim and grimy, frayed out fragments of Hood's confederate army wallowed in the stifling trenches all along the vast semi-circular line of outworks that faced the valley of the Chatahoochee and commanded the approaches from the Altoona hills beyond.

But he of the eagle eye was a strategist. He wanted to cut off and coop up the gray jackets in the city, and for that reason he quietly marched the larger part of his army up the western bank of the river eight or ten miles, flung them across the river, and with a mighty swing of that ponderous trip-hammer of war he struck them from the south, thus cutting off their lines of supplies by the Georgia railroad. Then followed those terrible days which wound up with the fierce onslaught of July 22, when the hopeless, half-starved southern men, the gallant men of the west, met in a mighty gladitorial contest which resulted in the fall of Atlanta.

These are matters for the historian, but what I am going to recount is one of those wild, weird romances with which this terrible conflict was so fraught, and here is the strange story:

"On to the sea," was the watchword of Sherman's armies, and the sullen and dogged retreat of the confederates to Jonesboro was the first movement of the defeated and despairing confederates.

Jonesboro was a little inland town, nestled amid field and forest, interspersed with beautiful undulating hills and grassy valleys green with the hope of the harvest, but little suited as a defensive point for the bruised and battered legions who were recoiling slowly toward the southern sea.

Breastworks had been hastily thrown up flanking the line of the Central railroad, and in the ditches behind them the straggling remnants of obstinate Confederates were entrenched.

It was a gloriously beautiful summer day when the skirmish line of the northern hosts debouched from the works and took up position in front of these breastworks.

Taken by surprise after relying in vain on the ability of the southern troops to check the onflow of the legions of the conquering hosts, the women and children, led by the lame and the halt and the aged men of the country, were fleeing for life, panic-stricken and utterly demoralized.

As the sun rose over the swelling ridges the eyes of the soldiers of either army caught the gleam of a little white tent, half hidden in a wood just a little to the left of the line of attack, and above it fluttered a tiny white flag, no bigger than a man's hand.

It was a woman's handkerchief, and all the chivalrous feelings of the American soldier were aroused as the grim veterans caught sight of that little appealing bit of cambric floating there through the uprising mists of war. The order was passed to respect that flag, and when the great guns began their work and shot and shell were hurled blazing and crashing across field and wood from either direction, never a gunner trained his piece toward a point near that little white house.

The battle was fiercely fought, but the combat was of short duration, and as the shadows length-

ened eastward the southern troops were seen in full retreat, leaving the field to the triumphant victors.

As they swept forward a drummer boy, Otto Barden, of a Pennsylvania regiment, passed by the little
white tent in the wood.

Guards in blue uniform surrounded it, and while the
smoke of battle swirled above and around there was
a plaintive cry from the tent and emerged followed
by an old negress, bearing in her arms a tiny, white
bundle.

"Please God, marsa, if you gwinter take us off
ter de nort?" wailed she, with the big tears cours-
ing down her withered face. "It'll sho' kill Miss Annie
ef yo' does."

"Not a bit of it, old lady, not a bit of it," replied
the good-natured surgeon with a smile.

"Hello, Otto, you're the very boy I want. This
is your prize, as you are nearest her age, and we are
going to detail you to take charge of this wee prisoner
and see that the little reb don't escape."

The rough soldiers came crowding around for a
peep at the prisoner, and many eyes filled with tears
of tenderness as they gazed on the baby that had first
seen the light in such grewsome surroundings.

"Ain't it a wonder that she and the mother were
not blown to pieces?" said the sergeant.

"It is, indeed," replied the corporal, "for look there
where a stray shell cut its way through the bushes,
clean as a knife."

"Well, boys, she is our prize. Let us christen her,
for time is up, and the Johnnies are waiting for us behind some brush down the road."

"Come, Otto, speak up. You shall have the honor
of naming the little miss," said the surgeon.

"Call her Shell Annie," said the boy, as his mind reverted to his own orphaned days, "because she was saved from a shell."

"Good," cried the surgeon.

"Shell Annie," chorused the corporal and the sergeant in a breath.

"Here, give me your canteen, Otto," said the surgeon. "Hold her head up, auntie," said the surgeon, and sprinkling a few drops of water on the tiny head, said, "Shell Annie, I baptize thee in the name of the Father, Son and Holy Ghost."

Twenty years after the furling of the flags the battlefield of Jonesboro was a corn field. Peace and plenty reigned, and the one-armed veteran of the north was hobnobbing with the peg-legged veteran of the south as they laughingly recounted the experiences of the war.

Asheville, N. C., had become a great resort for summer visitors.

As the train slowed up at the little station a man, apparently blessed with all the activity of youth, but bearing about him that unmistakable air of maturity that indicates intimate knowledge of and rough experience with life, stepped on the platform and strolled up the hill toward the hotel.

The dusky twilight of the dying summer day softened the rugged outlines of the gloomy mountains, and the tinkle of a crystal stream made music in the thickets below.

Suddenly the stranger was startled by a wild cry, and around a turn of the road came a horse at full speed, and in the buggy, swaying to and fro at his heels, there was a flutter of white.

Springing forward and dropping his belongings, the stranger clutched the reins of the frightened animal and arrested his mad career, but the shock was so sudden that the occupant of the buggy was tossed into the bushes by the roadside.

Releasing the horse, which stood trembling with fear and excitement, the stranger lifted the prostrate form, and as the crowd from the hotel came rushing to the spot she opened her eyes in a dazed and startled way.

"Are you hurt much?" asked the stranger.

"No, thank you; I was only frightened. I had just gotten into the buggy and was going for a ride when he became frightened and ran away. Oh, how can I ever thank you?"

"Best by not mentioning it again," said the stranger, brusquely, handing her his card as he resigned her to her friends and walked away.

On the following morning the stranger arose late after his fatiguing journey, and when he went down to breakfast beside his plate was a little perfumed note, and he opened it and read it, half amused and half in wonder.

"OTTO BARDEN : — Permit me to thank you and to convey to you the grateful feelings of my friends for your brave action in rescuing me from my perilous position yesterday. As a partial recognition of your kindness I wish to extend to you an invitation to enjoy a picnic excursion with us to-day. It is my birthday. Please do not fail to come.

Gratefully,

"ANNIE FONTAINE."

On a blank leaf from his note book Barden wrote a line accepting the invitation, and then leisurely finished his breakfast.

The day was perfect, and, as the special guest of the heroine of the day, he thought he had never felt quite so near at peace with himself and all mankind as he did while lounging on the grass beneath the shadow of the tall hemlocks at the foot of the mountain, with pretty Annie Fontaine.

Chatting ·a desultory way, Barden suddenly recalled the day and the drama of twenty years ago.

"Do you know," said he, "that I was one of those Yanks that marched with Sherman to the sea?"

"Indeed? Why, you must have been a very youthful soldier."

"I was a drummer boy, and this day twenty years ago I was in the battle of Jonesboro."

"And so was I," said she with a saucy smile, "for that was my birthday and the place of my nativity."

"What!" he cried, springing to his feet excitedly. "Then you are, you must be —"

"Shell Annie," she replied.

The Pennsylvania drummer boy now owns one of the finest fruit farms around Jonesboro, and the mistress of his home is "Shell Annie."

———————

### GOD BLESS YOU.

WRITTEN BY CAPT. A. W. BLACK, CO. F, 90TH O. V. I.

God bless you, dear old comrades,
So honest and so true.
You are the boys who feared no noise —
'Twas then you wore the blue.

CHAPLAIN W. C. HOLLIDAY.
Rev. Holliday is now (1902) living
in Columbus, O.

SERGT. T. S. MELDRIM.
Co. E.

PRIVATE JOHN CHILCOTE.
Co. H.

His diary is much quoted in
this history. From a photo
taken at Camp Circleville, O.,
in 1862.

You left your homes, and sweet-hearts, too,
Like soldiers brave and true;
Marched forth on many battle-fields —
'Twas then you wore the blue.

Dear wife, I am grieved to leave you
And our little children, too;
But Sumter it has fallen,
And I must don the blue.

Three years is my enlistment,
I'll now bid you all adieu,
My country calls and I must go,
For I have donned the blue.

On our long and weary marches,
With Sherman, it is true,
They never flinched from duty —
The boys that wore the blue.

Now the battle rages,
We have met the foe, 'tis true,
With shot and shell we made them go —
The boys that wore the blue.

When God had crowned our efforts,
We had a sad task to do;
Our dead were strewn on battle-fields —
The boys that wore the blue.

## THREE YEARS IN DIXIE.

### BY HIRAM S. BROWN, CO. E.

CROOKS, KY.

I composed the following about the close of the war. I used to sing it, and then after a few years I held the "Little Browns" on my knee and sang it to them.

I do not claim to be a Longfellow nor a Tennyson, but I guess it 'll do.

It was in the month of August,
In eighteen sixty-two,
When I, with many others,
Bade our friends adieu.
We left the city of Circleville
Enroute for Dixie's land
To reinforce our comrades
And check the rebel band.

It was at the town of Perryville,
Where first we met the foe —
Where many a brave companion
Did fall to rise no more.
We never shall forget them,
Our comrades true and brave,
They have fallen for their country,
And filled a soldier's grave.

Next came the battle of Stone River,
On the Cedar Plain;
And after nine days' fighting,
We hurled them back again.
The contest was most fearful
Amid the storm and rain.

And on that bloody battlefield
Many there were slain.

On Chickamauga's bloody field,
As I remember well,
Our forces were outnumbered —
To retreat we were compelled.
For many a long hour
The cannon loud did roar,
While many a heroe's heart did cease
To beat forever more.

On Chattanooga's rugged heights —
They soon were stationed there,
And Rosecrans' army
They thought to soon ensnare.
But from the old Potomac
Soon came the twentieth corps,
Which reinforced our number
Full twenty thousand more.

Way down in Lookout Valley
Were formed our boys in blue,
The mountain was in front of them,
And all the Rebel crew.
The signal sounded "forward!"
And they quickly did obey,
When General Bragg and officers
Were forced to ride away.

The rebel ranks were breaking
And fleeing to the rear,
Close followed by the Western boys —
The noble volunteer.
Then we had gained the victory,

There floats the stripes and stars
Where but one hour ere that time
They waived the stars and bars.

Both conquered and demoralized,
They were forced to Tunnel Hill,
While many of the southern defenders
Were captives on the field.
They reorganized their army
And fortified once more,
Determined when the Yankees came
That they would lay them low.

Then came our noble Sherman,
With a heart both loyal and true,
To command the Cumberland army,
And the Rebel hosts subdue.
But we remained all silent
Until the first of May,
When the bugle sounded assembly
And we soon were on the way.

We fought them down at Tunnel Hill,
Also at Resaca, too,
And hurled them down through Kingston,
So close we did pursue.
They halted at Altoona Pass
And fortified once more,
To check the advancing column
Of General Hooker's corps.

For two long weeks we fought them —
We fought both day and night,
When we surprised and flanked them,
And again they were put to flight.

At Kenesaw they formed their lines
For many miles in length;
But we soon were hovering 'round them,
Once more to try their strength.

Atlanta was our destination;
Possession we did obtain
By hurling back the rebel force
Step by step we gained,
Then they became so weary;
They thought that we were done
And they would call us back to Nashville,
To where we first begun.

Then General Hood with his followers,
Soon commenced the raid,
When Billy Sherman showed to them
That they could only trade —
Hood, he went to Tennessee,
And Sherman to the sea —
General Thomas down to Pulaski
To meet the rebel host.

General Thomas was our commander,
And Hood we did pursue,
When at the town of Franklin
An engagement then ensued.
But we, being overpowered
When the day had passed away,
We retired from the battlefield,
To meet some other day.

When we arrived at Nashville,
After many weary steps
We gained our reinforcements,

And on the field we met.
Full forty-eight hours we fought them —
We fought them hand to hand,
When General Hood exclaimed to them
"We can no longer stand."

Then they were almost conquered,
Both in the east and west;
To fight the Yankees longer
They did not think it best.
And then they all surrendered
And soon gave up the ghost,
Jeff bade adieu to Richmond
Clad in petticoats.

Oh, ye Southern sympathizer,
It is time to close your mouth.
Just think whose bones are bleaching
All o'er the sunny South!
Think of the many patriots
That fought this cruel war,
While you remained at home
Without a single scar!

God bless the orphan children,
And the widows all!
Also the many heroes
That in the field did fall.
But, now the war is over,
And the fortunate ones returned,
Once more to enjoy the freedom
Our many hardships earned.

EXPERIENCE OF 90TH BOYS IN SOUTHERN PRISONS.

We were captured at the battle of Chickamauga, Ga., September 20th, 1863, and were sent to Richmond, Va. When we got to Atlanta, Ga., we were marched from the railroad through the streets of the city to the stockade and kept there over night. As we were being marched through the streets, we were treated with contempt and insult by some of the citizens. In retaliation, we commenced singing: "Old John Brown," with the chorus: "and we will hang Jeff. Davis on a sour apple tree, as we go marching along." This enraged the Rebs so, that they threatened to shoot us, if we did not stop our singing. So we were compelled to be silent.

As we passed into the stockade we were relieved of our blankets, canteens and such other articles as the Confederate officers saw fit to take. We were taken out of the stockade the next day and sent on to Richmond, Va. We arrived at Richmond about the 1st of October, and were put in Libby prison, where we remained until the latter part of November, when we were sent to Danville, Va., where we were kept in tobacco warehouses.

While we were in Richmond, we learned that there was a quantity of flour, sugar and salt stored in the basement story of the building we occupied, and as our rations were short, we concluded to get some of these articles. We cut a hole through the floor, and helped ourselves to the sugar and salt. The flour we could not use. There was a notice of this in the Richmond papers, and they stated that we had taken between 7,000 and 8,000 pounds of sugar before the "Yankees" were detected. For our surprise we were not punished for this "sweetnees."

We remained at Danville, Ga., until about the middle of May, 1864, and were then sent to Andersonville, Ga. During the winter at Danville, we had no fire in the building to keep us comfortable, and we suffered very much from the effects of the cold. Our blankets had been taken from us, and the bare floor was our bed.

During the month of December, our government sent us blankets and clothing, which we received the latter part of the month, and this added greatly to our comfort.

During the month of February, 1864, the small-pox broke out amongst us, and quite a number of our boys were carried off by this loathsome disease.

During this month, some of us decided to try to make our escape by tunneling out. We got into a small cellar on the east side of the building in which we were confined, and sunk a hole down about three feet, and then started our tunnel, using a butcher-knife and a bayonet with which to dig, and a half of a canteen for a shovel. We had a small box to use in taking the dirt out of the tunnel and depositing it in the cellar. We had been working about six weeks on our tunnel, and had it almost completed, when, by some means we were detected in our work, and our plans were thwarted, and then we were more closely guarded than we had been heretofore.

We arrived at Andersonville, Ga., about the 20th of May, and found, to our sorrow, that we had come from "bad to worse." The prison was an open stockade, without any shelter, or provision made for our comfort. Language fails us, to properly describe the wretchedness and suffering of that horrible prison pen. Starvation, suffering and death were the ruling features

From a war-time photo.
The old John Ross House at Rossville, Ga., 4 miles out from
Chattanooga, Tenn.

of Andersonville prison.   We had some hard characters·
among us who went to robbing their fellow prisoners·
of whatever valuables they might possess.   A vigilance
committee was organized, and a number of arrests were
made, and those arrested were tried by a jury of 12 of
our own men.   Six of the men who had been arrested
were found guilty of grave offenses, and were sentenced
to ball and chain.   The rebel authorities refused to
keep them separate from the rest of the prisoners, and
gave the committee their choice, to either execute them,
or to have them turned loose amongst us.   The committee decided to execute them, and on the 11th day of
July, 1864, they were hanged inside of the stockade.
When the drop fell, one of the ropes broke, and the man
fell to the ground, but he was immediately taken back
upon the scaffold, the rope readjusted and he was
swung off.   This man had assumed the name of "Mos-
by," and was a hard character.   After this execution,
robbing was seldom heard of among the prisoners.   It
was about this time in July that the famous "Providence
Spring" broke out in the prison pen, and it was certainly a God send to us, and added greatly to our comfort.   On the 3rd of July, three of us organized a
prayer meeting in the stockade.   Sergt. James M.
McCollem, of Newcomerstown, Tuscarawas Co. O.;
Corp. W. C. Rose, of Granville, O., and the writer of
this, were the three who organized this meeting, and it
was kept up daily as long as we remained there.   And
many hearts were comforted by these devotional services.   There were about 35,000 of us confined in Andersonville prison at one time.

During the month of August the death rate was
fearful, and among the number that died were two
of the boys of Co. B, of the 90th O. V. I., namely: Mark

Tinley and Joseph Wyatt. Both died from the effects of scurvy.

About the 1st of September they commenced sending the prisoners away from Andersonville, and on the 9th of September, 1864, we were taken out of Andersonville and sent to Charleston, S. C., and at this place we received better treatment than any place we had been. We remained here but a few days, and were then taken to Florence, S. C., and imprisoned in a stockade there. This was a small prison, only about 10,000 of us there, but our treatment was the worst that we had met with any place we had been. It was an open stockade, and our rations were issued to us in a raw state, and they failed to furnish us with any cooking utensils with which to cook what little they gave us to eat. They gave us only one cord of wood to every 1,000 men per day, with which to do our cooking, and it is needless to say that it was necessary for us to use the wood very economically. We had to get our wood, and carry it to the prison gate. When the men were taken out to get wood, they were required to make oath that they would not attempt to escape while they were out. As it was a relief to get outside the stockade, we went out to get wood, and were put in charge of 100 wood carriers. There were five wood squads, but some of them contained considerably less than 100 men. One day two of our men decided to leave, and as we did not report that they had left, the Rebel authorities took those in charge of the different wood squads, and put them in the dungeon, where we were kept two days and two nights. The dungeon was wet and cold, and we suffered very much while we were in there. When we were taken out of the dungeon, we were turned back into the stockade.

After this exposure, the writer's health began to decline, and finally we became helpless, and for some six or seven days were unconscious most of the time. Finally we rallied, and before we were able to walk alone we were brought to our lines at Wilmington, N. C., at which place we arrived on the 2nd day of March, 1865, and on the 10th of March we arrived at Annapolis, Md., and were taken into the hospital on the Naval Academy grounds, a mere skeleton, with but three articles of clothing — a blouse, pants and shoes. We gradually recovered, and are still among the living at this date, February 5, 1902.

After we returned home, we learned that the captain of our company had ordered our name to be entered on the company roll with the remark — "reduced to ranks," and gave as a reason for doing so, that he did not consider it fair for another man to perform the duty of a 1st Sergeant, and the man in prison receive the pay. We reported the matter to the authorities at Washington, D. C. An investigation was made, and the result was, that we received pay as 1st Sergeant for the entire time, and now hold a certificate, with the statement, that "this man's rank is 1st Sergeant."

J. G. MILLER,
Co. B, 90th O. V. I.

## UNCLE SAM'S COMMISSARY.

TARLTON, OHIO.

Uncle Samuel's Commissary was, at times, rather slim. One evening no supper; morning came and no breakfast. I went out in the woods to see what I could find. I found a bush full of grapes, gathered a quart, put them in a pan and stewed them without sugar. It made a good strengthening meal. Some of the boys who had some pumpkins; held them in the fire till they were hot, then ate them.

Near Rock Castle River I came into camp about two hours behind the regiment. They had gone on picket. I got a pan and started out prospecting, not for gold, but something to eat. Found a wagon, the driver asleep. I found a barrel of rice, made a requisition for one gallon of rice and signed Quarter Master's receipt. I got a three gallon kettle, filled it with water, and commenced to cook my supper, and in a short time there was astonishing results, rice around the fire shoe top deep.

They issued three days' rations of wormy crackers to do five days, and in three days the worms had gotten away with them, and for the next two days parched corn, or anything we could get, and washed it down with muddy water.

Marching from Wild Cat Mountain to Nashville, the writer was barefooted, marched through snow, mud and over the frozen ground in company with some others. Thomas Mains had no pants to wear. He took a blanket to make him a pair. He being a poor tailor, only had one leg to them, and put them on over his head. Bill Bumcrots had no coat and was barefooted.

Sometimes we got behind, but John Morgan would hardly have taken us in if he had seen us.

At Chattanooga, for thirty days or more, we got an ounce of meat, half a cracker for a day's rations. Coffee and sugar to make a cup of coffee every other day. From there to Shellmound. There they threw out a load of corn. My mess got twelve ears, parched and ate all of it, and I was never so sick in my life.

JONAS S. CHENOWETH, Co. H.

---

### COMPANY I'S POET.

He says he was born a poet, with "tomfoolery" predominating; that he has irrigated his ink stand and ground his pen, and says in regard to the by-word, "Grab a Root":

While soldiering in the Army of the Cumberland,
Some Johnnies to shoot,
We stubbed our toe, fell down in the mud,
And the boys, hollowed, "Grab a Root!"

The origin of the word we never heard,
Yet, it always seemed to suit,
For, no matter what to you occurred,
They would tell you to "Grab a Root."

The Colonel of the 31st rode a mare —
A scary sort of a brute —
At the Catoosa Springs she threw him,
When one of the boys hollowed, "Grab a Root."

A new recruit was stealing meat,
Because he thought it cute,
But when the guard marched him off to Gen. Cruft,
The boys hollowed, "Grab a Root."

At Ooltewah we were crossing on a log
With a canteen full of old jute,
When we lost our balance and in we went,
And Smith hollowed, "Grab a Root."

A drunken bummer rode a mouse-colored mule —
A bucking son-of-a-galoot —
And when he threw him and nearly broke his neck,
The boys hollowed, "Grab a Root."

A goose hissed at us when we foraged,
As a disloyal old brute,
But when the Major ordered us front in disgrace,
George Harney whispered, "Grab a Root."

Down in Hog-Jaw Valley we heard a gun,
For some one in the distance did shoot.
But at the command, "Attention! I heard a gun,"
Some one remarked, "Grab a Root."

We shot the load from our gun in camp,
When there was positive orders not to shoot;
But as the General was placing us on the General's
    staff,
The boys hollowed, "Grab a Root."

A dude of a Sergeant got full of beer;
He sang a song he thought was cute,
But at the end of every verse he sang,
The boys hollowed, "Grab a Root."

The Sergeant got mad and wanted to fight,
And finally began talking shoot.
Then he stormed and raved till he foamed at the mouth,
And the boys hollowed, "Grab a Root."

An officer swore it was cowardly to dodge
When the Johnnies too near would shoot,
But when he dropped at a shell passing high in the air,
The boys hollowed, "Grab a Root."

                         SYLVESTER RADER, CO. I.

A NEW OLD FRIEND.

INDIANOLA, IOWA, November, 1901.

*Comrade Harden:*

Through the medium of your paper I have found our old comrade, Capt. Jas. K. Jones. Inasmuch as you reported me dead, I thought I would go down to Missouri and show "Kim" that I am alive.

Well, it was but a small thing to traverse the little strip of prairie intervening between us — a country rich enough for the Garden of Eden, and beautiful and delightful to behold.

So, it was only a few hours until I stepped off the train at Sheridan, Mo. Walking up from the station with a hotel man, I asked him if he knew Capt. Jones.

"Who? Kim Jones? Yes, I should think so. He is in town now, I think."

"How long since you met him?" said he.

"Over 30 years," said I.

"Do you think you would know him?"

"Don't know — I think so."

"Do you think that he would know you?"

"I'll risk it."

Up the street a few steps and we enter a hardware store, where my companion slyly points to a man in gray whiskers, and in earnest conversation with another man. We stopped to listen to the conversation. What it was about, I can never tell you, for my thoughts were elsewhere. I stood and looked for some of the ancient landmarks. There was, it is true, something of the snap left in the dark eye. There was something familiar in that resonant voice, and the emphatic gesture. But, Kim Jones! What a change! And must I part with the very image of my old friend? How often in my daily labors and in hours of loneliness has that image been before my eyes. But now it must be displaced, abrogated, banished. Henceforth he is not the "Boy in Blue," but the man in Gray! Oh, we can sit at eventide and see the sun gradually descend into shadowy dimness beneath the rim of the horizon and feel a spirit of resignation, but why should it grow dim at mid-day? The picture I have carried on my heart for almost two score years is that of my friend of 22, and now, in a twinkling he is changed to a man of 60. But now I must make the sacrifice. I cannot retreat. So I stand and wait. Surely he will know me. I have not changed. Very few are the gray hairs I carry. And still I wait. Finally I enter into conversation with him, expecting to be recognized, but again disappointment awaits me. Can it be that I, too, am changed? Can it be that my old friend will not recognize me as the companion with whom he ate with, slept with, marched with, away back in the 19th century? Have I, too, grown old? How hard it is to shake off the illusions.

We move past the cars standing on the switch and imagine that they and not we, are moving. We float in the boat away from the forest shore and imagine that the trees are fleeing from us while we stand still in the water.

After a brief conversation, during which he confessed that he did not know me, said, "It might be J. L. Hatfield," but when I had told him, he scarcely seemed to believe it, and had to wait until he saw some of the old landmarks, when he came at me for the second shake.

"Get in the buggy, there. I live over here."

CAPT. ALONZO W. BLACK, CO. F.

Such was the language of the man I must hereafter accept as a substitute for Kim Jones.

We go through the beautiful Platte Valley, which in spite of the absence of rain the past summer, is interspersed with large fields of corn, that by no means indicate a famine.

"There," said my new-old acquaintance, as we drew up to a large white house on the hill, "there's where I stay." And though there did seem to be something familiar about, it did not much resemble the ancient headquarters of Co. G. There were nice groves of oak and elm, but not a twig of cedar. There were barns and cribs, but not a single "pup tent."

There were the usual sounds from barn-yard and feed-lot, but not a single martial note. Evidently Lon Hanks' fife was not in the country. Lon Hanks' fife! Was there ever another piece of wood, or metal, from which floated such grand, clear, soul-stirring strains as came from that instrument in the hands of our Old First Kentucky Fifer?

However, I must acknowledge that Capt. Kim Jones was there, and with the same energy and faithfulness which characterized him while in the service, back in the 60's, he now holds sway over a fine farm of 1100 or 1200 acres, with its cattle, hogs, horses, and tenants, and is meeting with the success he deserves.

May great happiness surround him in these declining years.      Your Comrade,

J. L. HATFIELD.

# PERSONAL HISTORY.

Colonel Isaac N. Ross resigned April 14, 1863, on account of ill health.

Lieutenant Colonel Charles H. Rippey promoted Colonel April 14, 1863; resigned October 24, 1863. .

Major Samuel N. Yeoman promoted to Lieutenant Colonel April 14, 1863; to Colonel October 20, 1863, but not mustered; Brevet Colonel March 13, 1865; mustered out with the regiment.

Major Alvah Perry promoted to Major from Captain Co. D April 14, 1863; resigned October 23, 1863.

Major George Angle promoted from Captain Co. E November 23, 1863; killed July 2, 1864, near Marietta, Ga., while in action.

Major Nicholas F. Hitchcock promoted from Captain Co. H September 8, 1864; Brevet Lieutenant Colonel May 30, 1865; mustered out with the Regiment.

Richard H. Tipton, surgeon, served as brigade surgeon; mustered out with the Regiment.

Henry W. Carpenter, assistant surgeon, resigned May 26, 1863.

Jefferson L. Wylie, assistant surgeon, resigned November 5, 1862.

Charles P. O'Hanlon, assistant surgeon, mustered out with the regiment.

John G. Coates, asssistant surgeon, resigned December 18, 1863.

COL. CHAS. H. RIPPEY.

He is now (1902) living in Los Angeles, Cal.

Daniel N. Kingery, adjutant, killed September 20, 1863, in the battle of Chickamauga, Ga.

William Felton, Adjutant, promoted to Commissary Sergeant from private Co. D, August 29, 1862; to Second Lieutenant Co. A, January 27, 1863; First Lieutenant Co. A, December 21, 1863; Adjutant January 30, 1864; promoted to Captain Co. A, February 15, 1865; mustered out with the Regiment.

Henry F. Leib, promoted to Commissary Sergeant from private Co. D, June 17, 1863; to First Lieutenant Co. C, August 11, 1864; Adjutant February 22, 1865; mustered out with the Regiment.

Jacob Orman, Regimental Quartermaster; promoted to Captain Co. I, March 18, 1865.

William J. Webb, Regimental Quartermaster, appointed from First Lieutenant Co. H, April 18, 1865; transferred to Co. H, June 7, 1865; mustered out with the Regiment.

John N. Arehart, Regimental Quartermaster, promoted from First Sergeant Co. D, to date April 18, 1865; mustered out with the Regiment.

George L. Kalb, Chaplain, resigned May 12, 1863. William C. Holliday, Chaplain, mustered out with the Regiment.

Frederick W. Flickardt, Sergeant Major, discharged on Surgeon's certificate of disability, May 7, 1863.

Samuel W. Stuckey, Sergeant Major, promoted from Sergeant Co. C, June 17, 1863; to First Lieutenant Co. E, January 1, 1864; to Captain Co. C, December 30, 1864; mustered out with the Regiment.

John C. Bateman, Sergeant Major, promoted from Corporal Co. H, February 3, 1864; to First Lieutenant

Co. C, May 18, 1865; mustered out with the Regiment.

John W. Harper, Sergeant Major, promoted from First Sergeant Co. C, May 25, 1865; to Second Lieutenant, May 30, 1865; but not mustered; mustered out with the Regiment.

Edward P. Garaghty, Quartermaster Sergeant, discharged February 15, 1863, on surgeon's certificate of disability.

John S. Beck, Quartermaster Sergeant, promoted from private Co. D, July 18, 1863; to Second Lieutenant, May 30, 1865, but not mustered; mustered out with the Regiment.

Daniel S. Snyder, Commissary Sergeant, promoted from private Co. H, August 23, 1864; to Second Lieutenant May 30, 1865; but not mustered; mustered out with the Regiment.

Albert L. Kinnear, Hospital Steward, discharged March 19, 1864, on surgeon's certificate of disability.

Samuel S. Platner, Hospital Steward, promoted from private Co. I, April 22, 1864; mustered out with the Regiment.

Francis G. Philbrick, Principal Musician, mustered out May 18, 1865, at Camp Dennison, Ohio.

Abram Vlerebome, Principal Musician, promoted from private Co. F, January 4, 1864.

Robert F. Price, Principal Musician, mustered out with the Regiment.

John A. Clark, Principal Musician, mustered out with the Regiment.

## COMPANY A.

Captain Francis M. Black, resigned December 2, 1862.

Captain William A. Denny, promoted from First Lieutenant December 21, 1862; wounded in action June 28, 1864; discharged November 30, 1864.

Captain William Felton, promoted from Adjutant February 15, 1865; mustered out with the Company.

First Lieutenant Andrew J. Willoughby, promoted from Second Lieutenant April 14, 1863; resigned August 5, 1864.

First Lieutenant Edward A. Elliott, promoted from First Sergeant Co. K, August 11, 1864; to Captain Co. B, May 30, 1865.

First Lieutenant Jonathan Ellis, promoted from First Sergeant Co. K, May 30, 1865; mustered out with the Company.

First Sergeant William D. Hudson, promoted to Second Lieutenant, but no record of muster, November 27, 1863; to First Lieutenant Co. I, July 13, 1864.

First Sergeant Benjamin F. T. Yoakum, promoted from Sergeant July 20, 1864; promoted to First Lieutenant May 30, 1865, but not mustered; mustered out with the Company.

Sergeant Henry R. Markley, died January 18, 1863; in field hospital, near Murfresboro, Tenn., of wounds received December 31, 1862, in the battle of Stone River.

Sergeant Charles W. Thrall, appointed from Corporal January 14, 1863; mustered out with the Company.

Sergeant David Pritchard, promoted from Corporal October 1, 1863; died at Ooltewah, Tenn., March 8, 1864.

Sergeant John E. Ashbrook, appointed Corporal September 28, 1862; Sergeant, January 10 1863; died January 28, 1863, at Murfreesboro, Tenn.

Sergeant William S. William, appointed Corporal July 10, 1864; Sergeant, August 13, 1864; died December 19, 1864, near Bowling Green, Ky., of wounds received December 15, 1864, in the battle of Nashville.

Sergeant Henry Shannon, appointed Corporal September 28, 1862; Sergeant, April 27, 1863; wounded September 19, 1863, in the battle of Chickamauga, Ga.; mustered out with the Company.

Sergeant John H. Huffman, appointed Corporal August 7, 1863; wounded September 19, 1863, in the battle of Chickamauga, Ga.; promoted to Sergeant July 20, 1864; mustered out with the Company.

Sergeant John W. McGuire, appointed Corporal January 9, 1863; Sergeant, January 1, 1865; mustered out with the Company.

Corporal James W. Anderson, appointed August 26, 1862; discharged November 27, 1862, at Bowling Green, Ky.

Corporal Isaac H. Gray, died May 12, 1863, at Camp Chase, Ohio.

Corporal James Hardesty, died February 1, 1863, at Nashville, Tenn.

Corporal George Ater, appointed January 10, 1863; mustered out May 18, 1865, at Camp Dennison.

Corporal Erastus Furnis, appointed January 10, 1863; mustered out with the Company.

Corportl William McKinley, appointed October 1, 1863; died May 21, 1865, in Pickaway County, Ohio.

Corporal James Ramsey, appointed October 1, 1863; disharged March 23, 1865.

Corporal Samuel Brantner, appointed June 1, 1865; mustered out October 3, 1865, at Victoria, Texas.

Corporal Joseph Tatman, appointed July 10, 1864; wounded April 6, 1865; in action near Asheville, N. C.

Corporal George. W. Dennis, appointed January 1, 1865; muserted out with the Company.

Corporal Simeon Garrett, appointed January 1, 1865; mustered out with the Company.

Corporal Martin E. Neff, appointed January 1, 1865; mustered out with the Company.

Corporal William Watson, appointed June 5, 1865; mustered out with the Company.

William S. Snook, Musician, discharged April 28, 1863, at Columbus, Ohio, on Surgeon's certificate of disability.

John I. Radcliff, Musician, mustered out with the company.

William Bateman, Wagoner, mustered out with the Company.

Sampson Adkins discharged May 20, 1863, at Columbus, Ohio.

William Adkins, transferred to Co. C, 5th Regiment, Veteran Reserve Corps, January 10, 1865; mustered out at Indianapolis, Ind., July 21, 1865.

Jacob Ater, mustered out with the Company.

James Ater, mustered out with the Company.

Thornton Ater, died November 27, 1862, at Bowling Green, Ky.

Seymour Bolin, wounded in the battle of Stone River, December 31, 1862; mustered out with the Company.

Lewis C. Bower, died January 15, 1863, in hospital at Nashville, Tenn.

Joseph Briggs, died July 23, 1863, at Manchester, Tenn.

Joseph Brobeck, killed December 15, 1864, in battle of Nashville Tenn.

William Brown, died December 5, 1862, at Nashville, Tenn.

Nelson D. Cady, drowned December 3, 1863, in the Tennessee river, at Bridgeport, Ala.

James Crabill, mustered out with the Company.

Martin Crabill, died December 12, 1862, in hospital at Nashville, Tenn.

Albert Dolby, mustered out with the Company.

Harrison Eagleston, wounded in action; mustered out October 3, 1865, at Victoria, Texas.

William England, transferred to First Regiment, U. S. Veteran Volunteer Engineer Corps, August 7, 1864; mustered out June 30, 1865.

Thomas B. Frazee, mustered out with the Company.

William J. Furnis, discharged March 31, 1863, at Columbus, Ohio.

Daniel Gouchenour, died February 15, 1863, at Bowling Green, Ky.

Samuel Graham, mustered out with the Company.

Stanley Gray, wounded at Kenesaw Mountain, Ga., and Franklin, Tenn; mustered out with the Company.

Johnson Guseman, mustered out with the Company.

Robert Houskinson, died September 2, 1863, in hospital at Tullahoma, Tenn.

Jacob Hiles, mustered out with the Company.

Charge of the First Brigade, of which the 90th O. V. I. was a part, made on
the hill between the Granny White Pike and the Harden Pike,
in the battle of Nashville, Tenn., Dec. 15–16, 1864.

Elias F. Hines, wounded May 14, 1864, in battle of Resaca, Ga.; mustered out May 25, 1865, at Louisville, Ky.

John Hines, discharged October 31, 1862, at Louisville, Ky.

John W. Hook, mustered out with the Company.

William J. Hodges, discharged December 31, 1863, at Bridgeport, Ala.

Doctor F. Hott, mustered out October 3, 1865, at Victoria, Texas.

John M. Justus, died December 24, 1862, at Nashville, Tenn.

Elias Justus, died August 13, 1864, at Chattanooga, Tenn., of wounds received June 27, 1864, at the battle of Kenesaw Mountain Ga.

William H. Karnes, mustered out October 3, 1865, at Victoria, Texas.

Isaac Lance, died December 17, 1862, in hospital at Nashville, Tenn.

James Lowe, discharged September 23, 1863, at Louisville, Ky.

John McDonald, mustered out with the company.

William J. McGath, transferred to Co. F, First Regiment, U. S. Veteran Volunteer Engineer Corps, July 27, 1864; mustered out at Chattanooga, Tenn, June 27, 1865.

George W. Markley, mustered out with the Company.

Daniel M. Martin, discharged December 24, 1862, at Nashville, Tenn.

William Marsh, discharged March 16, 1863, at Cincinnati, Ohio.

John Michael, wounded May 14, 1864, in the battle of Resaca, Ga.; discharged October 7, 1864.

James W. Miller, transferred to Veteran Reserve Corps, from which mustered out.

John W. Miller, mustered out with the Company.

Jonathan Minton, discharged, to date August 5, 1863, at Columbus, O.

Jacob Morris, died January 15, 1863, at Nashville, Tenn., of wounds received December 31, 1862, at battle of Stone River.

George S. W. Neff, mustered out with the company.

Joseph A. Neff, mustered out with the Company.

Nathaniel Neff, mustered out with the Company.

Benjamin S. Nutter, discharged March 14, 1863, at Louisville, Ky.

Frederick Owen, wounded December 31, 1862, in battle of Stone River; mustered out with the Company.

James R. Patterson, mustered out with the Company.

Osborn Phillips, wounded May 21, 1864, in action, near Cassville, Ga.; mustered out with the Company.

Jesse H. Pritchard, died December 15, 1862, at Nashville, Tenn.

Jacob Purcell, mustered out with the Company.

Jerry T. Pursell, mustered out with the Company.

Robert B. Rice, mustered out with the Company.

Lancelot S. Robinson, transferred to 124th Co., Second Battalion Veteran Reserve Corps, December 31, 1863, from which mustered out.

Jonas Ross, mustered out with the Company.

Stephen Ross, mustered out with the Company.

Thomas Ryan, discharged January 4, 1863, at Nashville, Tenn.

Jared Septer, transferred to Veteran Reserve Corps, December 15, 1863, from which mustered out.

Levi Septer, mustered out with the Company.

John W. Sheets, wounded and captured September 19, 1863, in battle of Chickamauga, Ga., paroled on the field; mustered out with the company.

Floyd Shisler, discharged August 25, 1863, at Dunlap, Tenn.

Jacob Smith, discharged July 29, 1863, at Nashville, Tenn.

John Smith, killed September 19, 1863, at the battle of Chickamauga, Ga.

Aaron Stephens, mustered out with the company.

William H. Tilton, died May 28, 1863, at Nashville.

John Timmons, mustered out October 3, 1865, at Victoria, Tex.

Luther Tumbleson, mustered out with the company.

Henry Vanvickle, wounded December 15, 1864, in battle of Nashville; mustered out July 12, 1865, at Camp Dennison, O.

Thomas B. Whitehead, mustered out October 3, 1865, at Victoria, Tex.

John Weigand, died December 3, 1862, at Bowling Green, Ky.

John F. Williams, mustered out with the company.

William S. Williams, discharged January 6, 1863.

John H. Wilson, wounded May 21, 1864 in action near Cassville, Ga., mustered out with the company.

Pleasant F. Wilson, discharged January 15, 1863, at Bowling Green, Ky.

George W. Wood, killed December 31, 1862, in battle of Stone River.

Joshua O. Yates, mustered out with the company.

## COMPANY B.

Captain John S. McDowell, promoted to Major August 11, 1864, but not mustered; resigned May 1, 1865.

Captain Edward A. Elliott, promoted from First Lieutenant, Co. B, May 30, 1865; mustered out with the company.

First Lieutenant John S. Witherspoon, promoted to Captain Co. I, April 14, 1863.

First Lieutenant Augustus R. Keller, transferred from Co. I July 18, 1863; promoted to Captain Co. C January 1, 1864.

First Lieutenant John L. Halfield, appointed First Sergeant from private, September 7, 1862; promoted to Second Lieutenant January 1, 1863; to First Lieutenant January 1, 1864; resigned August 5, 1864.

First Lieutenant Archibald M. Rodgers, promoted from Second Lieutenant Co. C August 11, 1864; in command of company from May 1, 1865; mustered out with the company.

Second Lieutenant Joshua G. Gibson, resigned December 14, 1862.

First Sergeant Christian Rudolph, appointed from private January 1, 1864; promoted to Second Lieutenant May 30, 1865, but not mustered; mustered out with the Company.

First Sergeant Jacob G. Miller, appointed from Sergeant to date from July 1, 1863, by order of War Department; captured September 20, 1863, at the battle of Chickamauga, Ga.; exchanged; mustered out July 25, 1865, at York, Pa.

Sergeant John Schreckengaust, died December 18, 1862, at McArthur, O.

Sergeant Nathan H. Curry, died August 22, 1863, at Louisville, Ky.

Sergeant Henry Zeigler, appointed from Corporal May 1, 1863; mustered out with the company.

Sergeant George R. Dickerson, appointed from private April 1, 1864; mustered out June 3, 1865, at Camp Dennison, Ohio.

Sergeant Robert Hewitt, appointed Corporal May 1, 1863; Sergeant January 1, 1864; mustered out with the company.

Sergeant James Jones, appointed Corporal May 1, 1863; Sergeant January 1, 1864; mustered out with the company.

Sergeant George L. Derry, appointed from Corporal December 3, 1862; discharged June 19, 1863.

Sergeant James K. Jones, appointed from private April 21, 1863; promoted to Second Lieutenant, Co. G, to date April 10, 1863; promoted to Captain, Co. H, September 24, 1864; mustered out with the Company.

Sergeant Joshua R. Martin, appointed Sergeant from private September 1, 1862; discharged December 1, 1862, to enlist in the 4th U. S. Cavalry.

Corporal Cyrus Devault, mustered out with the company.

Corporal Samuel Defigh, discharged March 15, 1863.

Corporal Richard W. Kennard, died May 9, 1863, at Covington, Ky.

Corporal Willis Parcels, mustered out with the company.

Corporal Thomas W. Jefferson, killed September 20, 1863, in battle of Chickamauga.

Corporal Andrew W. Karnes, appointed June 30, 1863; mustered out with the company.

Corporal Henry Dozer, captured at the battle of Chickamauga, September 19, 1863; mustered out with the company.

Corporal Emery F. Redfern, appointed April 1, 1864; mustered out with the Company.

Corporal John H. Broyles, appointed April 1, 1864; mustered out with the company.

Corporal Benjamin P. Ansel, appointed April 1, 1863; mustered out with the company.

Corporal Sylvester Wyckoff, appointed May 1, 1865; wounded and captured at Stone River; exchanged; mustered out with the company..

Harrison E. Redfern, Musician, transferred to Veteran Reserve Corps, October 22, 1863, from which mustered out.

Joseph Wyatt, Musician, captured September 20, 1863, at battle of Chickamauga, Ga.; died August 31, 1864, in Andersonville prison.

Robert Fagan, Wagoner, mustered out with company.

George Andrews, discharged September 8, 1864.

Moses B. Andrews, mustered out June 19, 1865, at Camp Chase, Ohio.

Christian Betts, mustered out with the company.

John Burns, missing December 31, 1862, in battle of Stone River, Tenn.; never heard from.

David Burr, discharged January 22, 1864.

James R. Boyles, mustered out with the company.

John Campbell, mustered out with the company.

Orison Champlin, mustered out with the company.

George W. Clark, discharged December 1, 1862, to enlist in the 4th U. S. Cavalry.

John B. Claypool, mustered out with the company.

Wilson H. Claypool, mustered out October 3, 1865, at Victoria, Texas.

Samuel Dearth, transferred to 1st Regiment U. S. Vol. Engineers, August 7, 1864, from which mustered out June 30, 1865.

John H. Derry, discharged April 15, 1864.

Joseph L. Devault, transferred to 1st Regiment U. S. Vol. Engineers, August 10, 1864; mustered out June 30, 1865.

Francis Doyle, discharged May 11, 1863.

David D. Drake, mustered out with the company.

William Eagan, transferred to Vol. Reserve Corps March 15, 1865, from which mustered out.

James A. Eichor, discharged April 6, 1863.

William Eidson, died January 18, 1863, at Nashville.

Joseph W. Ewan, transferred to Veteran Reserve Corps March 16, 1864, from which mustered out.

John R. Gardner, mustered out with the company.

Lewis Gardner, mustered out with the company.

Lafayette Gaston, transferred to Veteran Reserve Corps October 28, 1864, from which mustered out June 30, 1865.

James C. Groves, discharged January 29, 1863, at Camp Dennison, Ohio.

Aaron Harkless, mustered out with the company.

Harry Hawk, died January 14, 1863, at Nashville, Tenn.

William Hesseldon, discharged March 9, 1863, at Camp Dennison, Ohio.

James A. Howell, mustered out with the company.

Alexander Hoyland, mustered out with the company.

Andrew H. Hubbard, transferred to Veteran Reserve Corps February 2, 1864, from which mustered out.

John Irvin, mustered out with the company.

George W. Johnson, discharged May 16, 1865.

Henry Johnson, died January 25, 1863, at Nashville.

John Johnson, discharged December 4, 1862.

David A. Kreible, severely wounded May 14, 1864, in battle of Resaca, Ga.; mustered out with company.

John Lavelle, mustered out with company.

William A. Ledlie, died April 20, 1863, at Cripple Creek, Tenn.

Abner C. Linn, mustered out with the company.

Thomas J. Livingston, mustered out with the company.

David McQuaid, discharged March 17, 1865, for wounds received in battle of Resaca, Ga., May 14, 1864.

Thomas S. Miller, killed December 31, 1862, in the battle of Stone River.

Lafayette Mollihan, died May 31, 1864, at Chattanooga, Tenn.

John North, mustered out with the company.

Lee Ogan, captured September 20, 1863, at battle of Chickamauga, Ga.; exchanged; mustered out June 23, 1865, at Camp Chase, Ohio.

Thomas Parrish, mustered out with the company.

Jasper Pennell, mustered out with the company.

1863.         1902.

HOMER ANDERSON, CO. I.

Levi Peskey, wounded May 14, 1864, in the battle of Resaca, Ga.; mustered out with the company.

James H. Phillips, discharged March 7, 1864.

John W. Reamy, transferred to Veteran Reserve Corps.

James M. Redfern, discharged January 6, 1863.

Thomas W. Roach, killed December 31, 1862, in battle of Stone River.

George W. Shepherd, transferred to Veteran Reserve Corps November 30, 1864.

John Shively, discharged August 6, 1863.

William Shuster, mustered out with the company.

James Smith, mustered out with the company.

David M. Snyder, died October 24, 1862, at Wild Cat, Ky.

Richard Steele, severely wounded September 20, 1863, in battle of Chickamauga, Ga.; discharged February 10, 1864.

Samuel H. Steele, transferred to Veteran Reserve Corps.

Samuel Stephenson, discharged February 10, 1863.

Columbus Strong, discharged December 1, 1862, to enlist in 4th U. S. Cavalry.

Mark Tinley, died August 16, 1864, in Andersonville prison.

John Towell, mustered out with the company.

Craven S. Turner, captured September 20, 1863, at battle of Chickamauga; exchanged; mustered out with the company.

Alonzo Vincent, mustered out with the company.

George Walters, mustered out with the company.

John Walters, mustered out with the company.

Francis Waugh, mustered out with the company.

Hamilton J. Willis, mustered out with the company.

John Wolford, transferred to Veteran Reserve Corps, September 19, 1864.

Jacob Zeigler, discharged October 25, 1862.

COMPANY C.

Captain Robert D. Caddy, killed September 20, 1863, in battle of Chickamauga, Ga.

Captain Augustus R. Keller, promoted from 1st Lieutenant Co. B, January 1, 1864; promoted to Captain and Assistant Quartermaster August 19, 1864.

Captain Samuel W. Stuckey, promoted to Sergeant Major from Sergeant, June 17, 1863; to 1st Lieutenant Co. E, January 1, 1864; to Captain December 30, 1864, mustered out with the company.

1st Lieutenant Alonzo W. Black, promoted to Captain Co. F, August 11, 1864; mustered out with the Company.

1st Lieutenant Henry F. Leib, promoted from Commissary Sergeant, August 11, 1864; appointed Adjutant February 22, 1865.

1st Lieutenant John C. Bateman, promoted from Sergeant Major May 18, 1865; mustered out with the Company.

2nd Lieutenant Jacob Bush, resigned October 23, 1863.

2nd Lieutenant Archibald M. Rodgers, promoted from 1st Sergeant, March 2, 1864; to 1st Lieutenant Co. B, August 11, 1864; mustered out with the Company.

1st Sergeant John W. Harper, appointed Sergeant from Corporal March 1, 1863; 1st Sergeant March 16, 1864; promoted to Sergeant Major May 25, 1865; mustered out with the Company.

1st Sergeant E. Burgess Watts, appointed Corporal September 28, 1862; Sergeant September 1, 1863; 1st Sergeant June 1, 1865; mustered out with the regiment.

Sergeant James P. Fent; mustered out with the Company.

Sergeant George P. Haskins; died January 20, 1863, at Nashville, Tenn.

Sergeant Charles Caddy; discharged March 11, 1863, at Cripple Creek, Tenn.

Sergeant Jacob S. Cockerill, appointed Corporal October 22, 1862; Color Sergeant March 11, 1864; mustered out with the Company.

Sergeant George W. Powell, appointed Corporal March 1, 1863; Sergeant August 23, 1864; mustered out with the Company.

Sergeant Martin L. Mock, appointed Corporal May 25, 1863; Sergeant June 1, 1865; mustered out with the Company.

Corporal Jacob Krebs, discharged April 25, 1863, at Nashville, Tenn.

Corporal William Beatty, died January 14, 1863, at Nashville Tenn.

Corporal John C. Fifer, discharged January 20, 1863, at Nashville, Tenn.

Corporal George Miller, appointed March 1, 1863; wounded September 19, 1863, at battle of Chickamauga, Ga.; mustered out with the Company.

Corporal Leroy Wilson, appointed November 21, 1863; marched every mile the regiment did, except from Nashville to Murfreesboro; mustered out with the Company.

Corporal Lewis Janes, appointed March 16, 1864; mustered out with the Company.

Corporal David Mock, appointed August 24, 1864; mustered out with the Company.

Corporal Daniel A. Janes, appointed August 24, 1864; mustered out with the Company.

Corporal William M. Boughn, appointed June 1, 1865; mustered out with the Company.

Corporal Isaac J. Dennon, appointed March 1, 1863; wounded September 19, 1863, in battle of Chickamauga, Ga., transferred to Vet. Reserve Corps.

Corporal James W. Horney, appointed June 1, 1865; mustered out October 3, 1865, at Victoria, Tex.

Corporal John C. Murphy, appointed June 1, 1865; mustered out October 3, 1865, at Victoria, Tex.

Alexander B. Creamer, Musician, captured September 19, 1863, at battle of Chickamauga, Ga.; exchanged; mustered out with the Company.

Louis F. Stolzenberg, Musician; discharged March 25, 1865, at Johnson's Island, O.

Cyrus B. Lakin, Musician; mustered out October 3, 1865, at Victoria, Tex.

Aaron Allen, died August 19, 1865, at Victoria, Tex.

Ephraim Allen, died July 30, 1864, at West Lancaster, O.

William H. Allen, mustered out with the Company.

William Allen, mustered out October 3, 1865, at Victoria, Tex.

Harvey S. Barney, died February 12, 1863, at Nashville, Tenn.

William C. Benson, mustered out October 3, 1865, at Victoria, Tex.

Albert Bonecutter, mustered out with the Company.

Ferdinand Bonecutter, mustered out October 3, 1865, at Victoria, Tex.

Martin Bonecutter, mustered out October 3, 1865, at Victoria, Tex.

William Bonecutter, mustered out with the Company.

John W. Boughn, died January 5, 1863, at Nashville.

Jooeph H. Boughn, killod Deoombor 15, 1864, in the battle of Nashville, Tenn.

Meredith Bowen, discharged April 19, 1863, at Nashville, Tenn.

Bigelow W. Brown, mustered out with the Company.

John Burton, wounded December 31, 1862, in the battle of Stone River, Tenn.; transferred Vet. Reserve Corps, October 31, 1863.

John W. Cahill, captured September 20, 1863, in the battle of Chickamauga; died August 6, 1864, in rebel prison at Andersonville, Ga.

David Calhoun, mustered out with the Company.

Samuel H. Carr, discharged September 20, 1864, at Columbus, O., for wounds received June 20, 1864, in action near Kenesaw Mountain, Ga.

David C. Conner, died January 11, 1865, at Jeffersonville, Ind., of wounds received July 2, 1864, in action near Nickajack Creek, Ga.

George W. Conner, discharged January 5, 1863, at Nashville, Tenn.

George H. Creamer, wounded at Resaca, Ga., May 14, 1864; mustered out with the Company.

John Creamer, killed December 31, 1862, in the battle of Stone River, Tenn.

Lewis Creamer, died November 18, 1863, at Bowling Green, Ky.

Wesley M. Creamer, mustered out May 18, 1865, at Camp Dennison, Ohio.

Jacob D. Doster, died February 10, 1863, at Murfreesboro, Tenn., of wounds received December 31, 1862, in the battle of Stone River.

John N. Doyle, mustered out with the Company.

Edward C. Duff, mustered out with the Company.

Hiram G. Duff, discharged March 29, 1863, at Columbus, O.

John J. Duff, mustered out with the Company.

John W. Ellis, mustered out with the Company.

John W. Engle, died January 14, 1863, at Nashville, Tenn.

Otho Engle, died January 23, 1863, at Nashville, Tenn.

James Feeney, discharged August 20, 1863, at Columbus, O.

Philip N. Fent, mustered out with the Company.

Samuel Flax, died September 4, 1864, at Chattanooga, Tenn., of wounds received July 4, 1864, in action near Nickajack Creek, Ga.

Daniel Gordon, died February 10, 1863, at Jeffersonville, O.

George M. Groves, died December 24, 1862, at Nashville, Tenn.

William Hammond, mustered out with the Company.

Lewis Hatfield, died June 24, 1863, at Cripple Creek, Tenn.

William Hidy, mustered out with the Company.

Robert J. Highland, wounded June 24, 1864, in action near Kenesaw Mountain, Ga.; mustered out with the Company.

Amzi Hire, died July 29, 1863, at Decherd, Tenn.

John C. Hogue, died July 4, 1864, at Chattanooga, Tenn., of wounds received in the battle of Kenesaw Mountain, Ga., June 27, 1864.

William A. Holston, died November 10, 1862, at Glasgow, Ky.

Forris Horney, mustered out with the Company.

George W. Horney, died October 7, 1865, in hospital in Central District of Texas.

Oliver E. Horney, discharged September 30, 1863, at Cincinnati, O.

Marshall Hosier, wounded June 21, 1864, in action near Kenesaw Mountain, Ga.; transferred to Co. D, 15th Regiment Vet. Reserve Corps, from which mustered out July 8, 1865, at Springfield, Ill.

William H. James, mustered out with the Company.

Oliver B. Jeffries, mustered out October 3, 1865, at Victoria, Tex.

Thomas A. Jenkins, discharged May 18, 1865, at Camp Dennison, Ohio, for wounds received June 16, 1864, in action near Kenesaw Mountain, Ga.

Moses C. King, discharged June 15, 1864, at Madison, Ind.

William A. Lynch, died May 31, 1864, at Nashville.

Newton McGinnes, discharged June 29, 1863, at Camp Dennison, O.

Harmon McIntyre, killed December 31, 1862, in the battle of Stone River.

William I. McVey, wounded December 15, 1864, in the battle of Nashville; mustered out June 13, 1865, at Louisville, Ky.

John H. Mahoy, died January 4, 1863, at Nashville.

Benjamin Miller, died December 11, 1863, at Cave City, Ky.

Marion Myers, died January 27, 1863, at Nashville.

James M. Parrett, died February 14, 1863, at Jeffersonville, O.

John S. Parrett, discharged March 21, 1865, at Camp Dennison, O.

George Richardson, discharged May 6, 1863, at Nashville, Tenn.

Paris Robinson, wounded December 31, 1862, in the battle of Stone River; transferred to Co. H, 8th Regiment Vet. Reserve Corps, from which mustered out July 2, 1865, at Chicago, Ill.

Daniel Rupert, died January 5, 1863, at Nashville.

Charles G. Sharrett, discharged July 18, 1863, at Louisville, Ky.

Jackson Smith, died October 12, 1863, at Chattanooga, Tenn., of wounds received September 20, 1863, in the battle of Chickamauga, Ga.

Solomon G. Snowden, discharged March 2, 1865, for wounds received September 1, 1864, in the battle of Jonesboro, Ga.

Jesse Sperlock, mustered out with the Company.

Milton Sperlock, mustered out with the Company.

George P. Straley, mustered out with the Company.

Wesley F. Straley, died August 22, 1863, at Nashville, Tenn.

From a photo taken at Huntsville, Ala., in 1865.

GROUP OF THE REGIMENTAL OFFICERS.

Leander W. Taylor, mustered out October 3, 1865, at Victoria, Tex.

John S. Tracy, discharged June 6, 1863, at Camp Dennison.

Elon Thornton, discharged August 29, 1863, at Nashville.

Joseph Tracy, mustered out with the Company.

Philip Tumblin, died August 21, 1865, near Victoria, Tex.

Andrew Ulmer, mustered out with the Company.

Gideon Vesey, mustered out with the Company.

Thomas C. Williams, mustered out with the Company.

Henry Wiley, transferred to Vet. Reserve Corps.

Samuel W. Williams, mustered out October 3, 1865, at Victoria, Tex.

Eli Wood, discharged August 31, 1863, at Manchester, Tenn.

William Wood, discharged March 13, 1863, at Cripple Creek, Tenn.

Benjamin Woolley, mustered out June 30, 1865, at Nashville, Tenn.

William Wybright, discharged May 6, 1863, at Columbus, O.

### COMPANY D.

Captain Alvah Perry, promoted to Major, April 14, 1863, resigned October 23, 1863.

Captain John M. Sutphen, promoted from First Lieutenant January 1, 1864; mustered out with the company.

First Lieutenant John D. Nicely, promoted to Second Lieutenant from First Sergeant, to date February 1, 1863; to First Lieutenant, January 1st. 1864; Captain, May 30, 1865, but not mustered. Mustered out with the company.

Second Lieutenant George W. Welsh promoted to First Lientenant, February 1, 1863, but not mustered. Resigned December 19, 1863.

First Sergeant John A. Arehart, appointed from Sergeant, November 24, 1863; promoted to First Lieutenant and R. Q. M., April 8, 1865. Mustered out with the regiment.

First Sergeant Stephen A. Parsons, appointed from Corporal February 14, 1863; First Sergeant May 1st, 1865; promoted to Second Lieutenant May 30, 1865, but not mustered. Mustered out with the company.

Sergeant John T. Williams, died December 19, 1862, at Nashville, Tenn.

Sergeant Sebastian C. Goss, appointed from Corporal March 1, 1863; wounded in the battle of Chickamauga, Ga., discharged for disability, April 18, 1864.

Sergeant William H. Strode, appointed from Corporal March 1, 1863. severely wounded June 27, 1864, in battle of Kenesaw Mountain, Ga.; mustered out with the company.

Sergeant Martin K. Thomen, appointed Corporal March 1, 1863; Sergeant April 18, 1864; died December 30, 1864, at Nashville, Tenn., of wounds received December 15, 1864, in the battle of Nashville, Tenn.

Sergeant Robert P. Ewing, appointed from Corporal April 14, 1864; died November 1, 1864, at Camp Dennison, Ohio.

Sergeant Charles Myers, appointed Corporal December 16, 1862; Sergeant, November 1, 1864; mustered out with the company.

Sergeant William Beecher, appointed Corporal

April 1, 1863; Sergeant, February 1, 1865; mustered out with his company.

Sergeant John Cross, appointed Corporal December 18, 1863; Sergeant, May 1, 1865; wounded in the battle of Stone river, December 31, 1862; mustered out with the company.

Corporal Charles E. Reck, transferred to Co. G, March 22, 1863, as Orderly Sergeant.

Corporal Samuel B. Holderman, appointed October 5, 1862; discharged March 13, 1863, for wounds received December 31, 1862 in battle of Stone River, Tenn.

Corporal William Springer, appointed December 18, 1863; died July 12, 1864, of wounds received June 20, 1864, in action near Kenesaw Mountain, Ga.

Corporal James W. Damude, appointed December 18, 1863; mustered out with the company.

Corporal Solomon D. Soliday, appointed March 22, 1864; mustered out with the company.

Corporal Henry C. Williamson, appointed March 22, 1864; shot through the elbow of right arm by a musket ball, December 14, 1864, in the battle of Nashville, and three weeks later the arm was amputated four inches below the shoulder; discharged June 12, 1865, at Covington, Ky.

Corporal James Rittenhouse, appointed July 18, 1864; mustered out with the company.

Corporal Wesley Pugh, appointed February 6. 1864; mustered out with the company.

Corporal Percival Stuter, appointed February 6, 1864; mustered out with the company.

Corporal Thomas S. Williamson, appointed February 6th, 1864; mustered out with the company.

Corporal Valentine Cupp, appointed May 1, 1865; wounded June 16, 1864, in action near Kenesaw Mountain, Ga., mustered out with the company.

Francis G. Philbrick, Musician, promoted to Principal Musician July 1, 1863.

William L. Armentrout, Musician, mustered out at Victoria, Tex., October 3, 1865.

Edward Griffin, Musician, mustered out at Victoria, Tex., October 3, 1865.

Henry G. Allen, mustered out with the company.

John Andregg, discharged April 5, 1863, for wounds received in battle of Stone River, December 31, 1862.

John S. Beck, promoted to Quarter Master Sergeant, July 18, 1863.

Adam Benadum, discharged October 1, 1862, at Louisville, Ky.

John Berger, discharged March 30, 1863, for wounds received December 31, 1862, in battle of Stone River.

Jacob Bibler, mustered out with the company.

Samuel S. Bibler, mustered out October 3, 1865, at Victoria, Tex.

Frederick Blosser, discharged December 26, 1862.

Israel Bolenbaugh, discharged July 21, 1863.

George Clark, mustered out with the company.

John C. Clark, discharged December 31, 1863.

George W. Combs, discharged April 1, 1863, at Camp Chase.

Adam Courtright, died February 12, 1863, at Danville, Ky.

David Cowden, mustered out June 7, 1865, at Columbus, Ohio.

James Davis, on muster roll as "John Davis"; discharged December 24, 1863.

Downs William, died December 28, 1862, at Nashville, Tenn.

Aaron Dum, transferred to Co. F, First Regiment, U. S. Vet. Vol. Engineers Corps, November 25, 1862, from which mustered out June 27, 1865.

Pulaski H. Ebright, mustered out with the company.

John H. Emrick, wounded September 19, 1863, at the battle of Chickamauga, Ga.; killed December 15; 1864, in battle of Nashville.

Levi England, mustered out with the company.

William Felton, promoted to Commissary Sergeant August 29, 1862.

Samuel Ferry, discharged August 18, 1863.

John Gallagher, wounded June 27, 1864, in the battle of Kenesaw Mountain, Ga.; discharged on account of wounds, October 25, 1864.

Henry Gray, transferred to 149th Co., Second Battalion, Vet. Res. Corps, April 1, 1864, from which mustered out June 30, 1865, at Nashville, Tenn.

John H. Haines, died March 27, 1863, at Cripple Creek, Tenn.

Isaac E. Hall, mustered out with the company.

Mahlon S. Harps, severely wounded May 14, 1864, in battle of Reseca, Ga.; mustered out with the company.

Wilson Hickle, captured December 31, 1862, at the battle of Stone River; died February 28, 1863, at Annapolis, Md.

Elijah Howard, wounded September 19, 1863, in the battle of Chickamauga, Ga.; transferred to Co. H,

19th Regiment, Vet. Res. Corps, April 1, 1864, from which mustered out July 13, 1865, at Elmira, N. Y.

Amos Kemp, died December 20, 1862, at Danville, Kentucky.

Samuel T. Law, mustered out with the company.

Henry F. Leib, promoted to Commissary Sergeant, June 17, 1863.

Ira Lines, mustered out with the company.

Noah Lutz, discharged February 29, 1864, at Louisville, Ky.

Jacob McDaniel, wounded December 15, 1864, in the battle of Nashville; mustered out June 13, 1865, at Louisville, Ky.

Thomas McDaniel, mustered out with the company.

James Moravy, died Jan. 14, 1864, at Bridgeport, Alabama.

Moses Mattox, discharged March 9, 1863.

Amos Mumaugh, discharged August 20, 1863, at Murfreesboro, Tenn.

Jackson Myers, transferred to 60th Co., Second Battalion, Vet. Res. Corps, May 1, 1864, from which mustered out June 28, 1865, at Cincinnati, Ohio.

John Patison, mustered out with the company.

Joseph D. Payne, mustered out with the company.

Amos Reed, mustered out with the company.

Abraham Smith, wounded December 31, 1862, in the battle of Stone River; mustered out with the company.

George Spangler, mustered out October 3, 1865, at Victoria, Tex.

John C. Strayer, died December 16, 1863, in hospital at Nashville, Tenn., of wounds received September 19, 1863, in the battle of Chickamauga, Ga.

Samuel Swope, wounded June 27, 1864, in the battle of Kenesaw Mountain, Ga.; mustered out with the company.

Abraham K. Thomen, captured at Antioch, Tenn., while guarding a railroad construction company, January 25, 1863. Exchanged October 1863. Mustered out with the company.

John P. Urbin, mustered out with the company.

Alexander Warren, died October 24, 1863, of wounds received in action at Chattanooga, Tenn.

Daniel Welsh, died December 30, 1864, at Louisville, Ky., of wounds received November 30, 1864, in the battle of Franklin, Tenn.

Henry Welsh, discharged June 23, 1863, at Cripple Creek, Tenn.

David Williamson, captured December 31, 1862, in the battle of Stone River; exchanged and returned to the company June 7, 1863; captured in the battle of Chickamauga, September 20, 1863; died July 12, 1864, in Rebel Prison at Andersonville, Ga.

Joseph Wilson, discharged May 12, 1865, for wounds received June 21, 1864, in action near Kenesaw Mountain, Ga.

William A. Wright, mustered out October 3, 1865, at Victoria, Tex.

#### COMPANY E.

Captain George Angle, promoted to Major November 23, 1863.

Captain Samuel T. Widener, promoted from First Lieutenant, Co. I, November 27, 1863; mustered out with the company.

First Lieutenant Daniel J. Nunnemaker, resigned October 18, 1863.

First Lieutenant Samuel W. Stucky, promoted from Sergeant Major January 1, 1864; to Captain Co. C, December 30, 1864.

First Lieutenant Charles E. Reck, promoted from First Sergeant, Co. G, October 12, 1864; mustered out with the company.

Second Lieutenant William J. Webb, promoted to First Lieutenant, Co. H, May 15, 1863.

First Sergeant William I. Bowers, discharged February 21, 1863.

First Sergeant Aaron W. Mosure, appointed from Sergeant February 22, 1863; promoted to First Lieutenant, Co. G, September 24, 1864.

First Sergeant Abraham Trout, appointed Sergeant from Corporal February 21, 1863; First Sergeant October 10, 1864; promoted to Second Lieutenant May 30, 1865, but not mustered; mustered out with the company.

Sergeant David Angle, died March 11, 1865, at Camp Dennison, Ohio.

Sergeant Barrah Moore, mustered out with the company.

Sergeant John W. Webb, mustered out with the company.

Sergeant James H. Johnson, appointed Corporal June 1, 1863; wounded July 4, 1864, in the battle of Nickajack Creek, Ga.; appointed Sergeant January 1, 1865; mustered out with the company.

Sergeant Thomas Meldrim, appointed from Corporal June 1, 1865; mustered out with the company.

Corporal James W. Wright, mustered out with the company.

Corporal John Mauk, discharged October 21, 1862.

Lee & Gordon's Mills, on the Chickamauga River, Ga.

Corporal Wilson Huggins, died November 28, 1862, at Louisville.

Corporal Sylvester I. Rogers, mustered out with the company.

Corporal David C. Goodwin, Color Bearer, severely wounded September 19, 1863, by a piece of shell; mustered out with the company.

Corporal Samuel W. Poland, appointed June 1, 1865, mustered out with the company.

Corporal Jason Guess, appointed October 12, 1862; wounded September 20, 1863, in the battle of Chickamauga, Ga.; mustered out with the company.

Corporal William G. Mauk, wounded May 14, 1864, in the battle of Resaca, Ga.; appointed Corporal January 1, 1865; mustered out with the company.

Corporal Joseph Marshall, appointed June 1, 1865; mustered out with the company.

Corporal Sylvester J. Smith, appointed July 20, 1864; killed December 15, 1864, in battle of Nashville, Tenn.

Corporal Philip Bainter, appointed June 1, 1863; died August 14, 1864, at Nashville, Tenn., of wounds received June 21, 1864, in action near Kenesaw Mountain, Ga.

Corporal James Z. Wilson, appointed June 1, 1865; mustered out October 3, 1865, at Victoria, Texas.

Cromwell Randall, Musician, discharged June 2, 1863, at Cripple Creek, Tenn.

William Wimer, Wagoner; mustered out with the company.

Andrew J. Amerine, discharged November 25, 1863.

Leander Amerine, discharged November 25, 1863.

Benjamin Aplin, captured September 11, 1863, in action near Ringgold, Ga.; mustered out June 19, 1865, at Camp Chase, Ohio.

John F. Armstrong, died November 16, 1864, at Chattanooga, Tenn.

David E. Avey, discharged December 25, 1862.

William Baird, mustered out with the company.

Charles Beagle, died April 19, 1864, at Logan, O.

Joseph C. Beery, captured September 11, 1863, in action at Ringgold, Ga.; died June 19, 1864, in rebel prison at Andersonville, Ga.

Lucius C. Black, discharged January 10, 1863.

William Blosser, transferred to Veteran Reserve Corps, from which mustered out July 5, 1865.

Thomas D. Book, mustered out with the company.

Benjamin Boucher, wounded September 19, 1863, in the battle of Chickamauga; mustered out with the company.

George Bowden, wounded September 19, 1863, in the battle of Chickamauga; transferred to Veteran Reserve Corps; mustered out June 28, 1865.

Abednego Bowers, mustered out with the company.

Hiram S. Brown, wounded September 19, 1863, in right leg in the battle of Chickamauga; wounded in the right arm at Resaca, Ga.; mustered out with the company.

William M. Bryan, captured December 31, 1862, in the battle of Stone River; died February 15, 1863, in rebel prison at Knoxville, Tenn.

Hiram Buck, died January 31, 1863, at Nashville.

William D. Buckingham, wounded December 31, 1862, in battle of Stone River; discharged October 3, 1863.

John R. Cage, mustered out with the Company.

John Call, died January 28, 1863, at Nashville, Tenn.

Nicholas M. Call, severely wounded June 23, 1864, in action near Kenesaw Mountain, Ga.; mustered out with the Company.

Isaac Carpenter, killed December 31, 1862, in the battle of Stone River.

Joseph Collins, mustered out with the Company.

Thomas D. Collins, mustered out with the Company.

John Crawford, severely wounded May 10, 1864, in action near Resaca, Ga.; mustered out with the Company.

Samuel B. Crow, mustered out with the Company.

Samuel L. Davis, discharged March 9, 1863, at Nashville.

Horace Donelson, discharged January 14, 1863.

Alexander Frankfother, mustered out with the Company.

James S. Freeborne, died January 24, 1863, at Nashville.

James Good, died February 15, 1863, at Nashville, Tenn., of wounds received in the battle of Stone River, December 31, 1862.

James V. Griffin, transferred to Veteran Reserve Corps.

Shelton Guess, wounded June 27, 1864, in the battle of Kenesaw Mountain, Ga.; mustered out with the Company.

Handley Hillver, wounded December 15, 1864, in the battle of Nashville; mustered out with the Company.

George Hooper, discharged November 25, 1863.

Daniel A. Horn, died June 14, 1863, at Nashville.

George Kull, wounded September 19, 1863. in the battle of Chickamauga, Ga.; mustered out with the Company.

Abraham Lane, mustered out with the Company.

Thomas Lee, mustered out with the Company.

Andrew Leohman, died January 8, 1863, at Nashville.

Lewis Leohman, captured September 20, 1863, in the battle of Chickamauga, Ga.; died February 1, 1864, in rebel prison at Richmond, Va.

Stephen Lent, mustered out with the Company.

David Luker, discharged December 25, 1862.

Josiah Luker, killed December 15, 1864, in the battle of Nashville.

Jacob Lutz, mustered out with the Company.

Robert Marshall, discharged December 14, 1863, at Murfreesboro, Tenn.

William J. Mason, mustered out with the Company.

Samuel S. Mauk, wounded in the battle of Chickamauga, Ga., September 20, 1863; captured and held a prisoner for nine days; his leg was amputated on the battlefield; discharged May 14, 1864, at Columbus, Ohio.

James H. Mitchell, mustered out with the Company.

Albert Morris, died February 15, 1863, at Nashville, from wounds received December 31, 1862, in the battle of Stone River.

Noah Nunnemaker, wounded September 19, 1863, in the battle of Chickamauga; mustered out with the Company.

John W. O'Hare, mustered out with the Company.

Thomas J. Passmore, transferred to U. V. V. Engineer Corps, August 7, 1864; mustered out June 30, 1865.

Samuel J. Price, discharged March 24, 1863, at Cripple Creek, Tenn.

Frederick Saumenig, mustered out with the Company.

Jonathan Shaw, mustered out with the Company.

Joseph Sherlock, mustered out with the Company.

Henry S. Sherrick, died October 25, 1863, at Chattanooga, Tenn., of wounds received September 19, 1863, in the battle of Chickamauga, Ga.

John S. Shore, mustered out with the Company.

Edward K. Slay, discharged January 31, 1863, to enlist in Mississippi Marine Brigade.

Daniel Smith, died January 11, 1863, at Nashville, from wounds received December 31, 1862, in the battle of Stone River.

Henry Smith, discharged January 30, 1863, to enlist in Mississippi Marine Brigade.

James Steel, discharged November 25, 1863.

Thomas Stewart, died August 11, 1863, at Nashville.

William Strite, died April 14, 1864, at Ooltewah, Tenn.

Parces Sweet, wounded April 6, 1865, at Asheville, N . C.; mustered out with the Company.

Josiah Tannahill, discharged April 26, 1864.

Edward Terry, discharged June 22, 1863, at Nashville.

George S. Thompson, captured at Antioch, near Nashville, Tenn.; mustered out with the Company.

Calvin Thornton, died January 17, 1863, at Nashville.

John N. Thornton, died January 5, 1863, at Nashville.

John W. Tritsch, mustered out with the Company.

Benjamin Vannatta, died November 14, 1862, at Danville, Ky.

Ward N. Woodard, mustered out with the Company.

Brazilla Warthman, mustered out with the Company.

COMPANY F.

Captain Thomas J. Watkins, resigned February 1, 1863.

Captain Thomas Raines, promoted from First Lieutenant February 1, 1863; wounded June 20, 1864, in action near Kenesaw Mountains, Ga.; killed August 19, 1864, in action near Atlanta, Ga.

Captain Alonzo W. Black, promoted from First Lieutenant Co. C, August 11, 1864, mustered out with the Company.

First Lieutenant George R. Crow, promoted from Second Lieutenant December 2, 1862, promoted to Captain Co. G, September 24, 1864.

First Lieutenant Hugh L. Ferguson, promoted from First Sergeant Co. H, September 24, 1864; mustered out with the company.

Second Lieutenant Nelson A. Patterson, appointed First Sergeant from sergeant January 14, 1863; promoted to Second Lieutenant November 8, 1862; died October 10, 1863, at Chatanooga Tenn. from wounds received in the battle of Chickamauga, September 19, 1863.

First Sergeant Amos S. Leist, appointed from Sergeant May 18, 1863; killed June 27, 1864, in the battle of Kenesaw Mountains, Ga.

First Sergeant Martin L. Stollard, appointed Corporal November 17, 1862; Sergeant January 14, 1863; First Sergeant July 1, 1864; promoted to Second Lieutenant May 30, 1865, but not mustered; mustered out with the company.

Sergeant Andrew J. Cochran, died January 24, 1863.

Sergeant John H. Rife, appointed from private January 14, 1863; mustered out with the company.

Sergeant James M. Griffith, appointed Sergeant from private May 18, 1863; mustered out with the Company.

Sergeant James C. Todd, appointed Corporal May 1, 1863; Sergeant December 4, 1864; mustered out with the Company.

Sergeant Noble M. Cochran, appointed from Corporal February 15, 1865; mustered out with the ompany.

Corporal Charles H. Allen, wounded September 20, 1863, in the battle of Chickamauga, Ga.; mustered out with the Company.

Corporal William Hendricks, captured December 31, 1862, in the battle of Stone River; exchanged, and mustered out with the Company.

Corporal Joseph M. Thurston, captured September 20, 1863, in the battle of Chickamauga; exchanged, and mustered out at Annapolis, Md., June 26, 1865.

Corporal John W. Heloising, appointed November 17, 1862, died January 13, 1864, in Pickaway County, Ohio.

Corporal James W. Loyd, appointed November 17, 1862; died December 26, 1862, at Nashville, Tenn.

Corporal Benjamin F. Skinner, appointed January 20, 1863; mustered out with the Company.

Corporal Joseph B. Rife, appointed February 15, 1865; never missed a day's service with the regiment; mustered out with the Company.

Corporal Joseph B. Schrawger, appointed February 15, 1865; mustered out with the Company.

Corporal Samuel H. Tilford, appointed February 15, 1865; mustered out with the Company.

Corporal David R. Porter, appointed February 15, 1865; mustered out with the Company.

Corporal Mahlon G. Groce, appointed January 20, 1863; wounded September 19, 1863, in the battle of Chickamauga; discharged April 25, 1864.

Smith A. Allen, mustered out with the Company.

John Archa, captured January 17, 1865, near Huntsville, Ala.; exchanged and discharged May 27, 1865.

Thomas C. Bennet, mustered out with the Company.

Walter Betts, mustered out with the Company.

Solomon B. Betz, wounded January 1, 1863, in the battle of Stone River; mustered out with the Company.

William H. Blasser, mustered out May 18, 1865.

George Borden, mustered out with the Company.

Ashton Briggs, wounded September 19, 1863, in the battle of Chickamauga; mustered out with the Company.

James Briggs, died January 22, 1863, at Nashville.

Alfred Britton, mustered out June 13, 1865.

Harvey Brooks, mustered out with the Company.

James D. Chaffon, mustered out with the Company.

Elbert Chittum, mustered out with the Company.

William Craybill, died January 25, 1863, at Nashville.

The Camp of the Army of the Cumberland, near Chattanooga, Tenn., after the battle of Chickamauga. Lookout Mountain is seen in the background.

Alexander Crooks, wounded September 19, 1863, at battle of Chickamauga; mustered out with the Company.

Lewis K. David, captured December 31, 1862, in the battle of Stone River; exchanged; mustered out with the Company.

John A. DeLong, wounded December 31, 1862, in the battle of Stone River; mustered out with the Company.

William Eby, killed June 21, 1864, in action near Kenesaw Mountain, Ga.

Aaron H. Ecord, captured August 29, 1864, in action near Atlanta, Ga., exchanged; perished by the explosion on the Steamer Sultana, on the Mississippi River, April 27, 1865.

Peter W. Ecord, discharged August 3, 1863.

Samuel B. Erskins, died December 14, 1862, at Nashville.

John N. Flowers, died August 20, 1863, at Nashville.

Israel Funk, transferred to Vet. Res. Corps, from which he was mustered out June 27, 1865, at Washington, D. C.

James N. Funk, mustered out at Nashville, May 13, 1865.

Philip M. Garrison, mustered out with the Company.

Isaac George, mustered out with the Company.

Nation Gooley, discharged February 5, 1863, at Columbus, O.

Michael Goss, captured September 20, 1863, in the battle of Chickamauga; exchanged; mustered out at Columbus, O., June 27, 1865.

Abraham M. Guseman, captured August 29, 1864, in action near Atlanta, Ga.; exchanged; mustered out at Columbus, O., June 30, 1865.

William M. Haigler, died January 3, 1863, at Nashville, Tenn.

James Henderson, discharged December 14, 1862, at Nashville.

Henry Hooper, severly wounded June 21, 1864, in action near Kenesaw Mountain, Ga., mustered out with the Company.

John Hoskins, killed June 10, 1864, in action near Pine Mountain, Ga.

David Lindsay, died March 27, 1863, at Cripple Creek, Tenn.

James R. Lindsay, mustered out with the Company.

John Lister, captured September 20, 1863, in the battle of Chickamauga; died December 17, 1863, in Rebel Prison at Danville Va.

Isaac Lindsay, discharged November 23, 1863, at Bridgeport, Alabama.

John McAllister, died June 26, 1863, at Nashville, Tenn.

Samuel W. McGath, severely wounded June 22, 1864, in action near Kenesaw Mountain, Ga., transferred to Vet. Res. Corps, from which mustered out at Chicago, Ill., July 12, 1865.

Emanuel Mangues, mustered out with the Company.

Benjamin F. Martin, transferred to Co. K, First Regiment U. S. Vol. Engineer Corps, August 7, 1864; from which mustered out June 30, 1865.

John Martin, mustered out with the Company.

John C. Moffitt, killed September 19, 1863, in the battle of Chickamauga, Ga.

Richard A. Patton, detailed as Hospital Steward from Sergeant, February 11, 1863; mustered out with the Company.

George W. Poland, mustered out with the Company.

Almer Porter, killed December 31, 1862, in the battle of Stone River.

James W. Ramey, mustered out with the Company.

Frank Rector, died January 5, 1863, at Nashville, from wounds received in the battle of Stone River.

Henry Rector, discharged January 15, 1863, at Columbus, O.

John P. Rector, died November 22, 1862, at Bowling Green, Ky.

Gideon W. Rife, mustered out with the Company.

John Rife, transferred to First Regiment U. S. Veteran Volunteer Engineer Corps, August 7, 1864, from which mustered out June 30, 1865.

Joseph E. Riggin, mustered out with he Company.

Lorenzo D. Rigin, discharged December 20, 1862.

Willian J. Sapp, mustered out with the Company.

James Shafer, mustered out with the Company.

Joshua Skinner, wounded September 19, 1863, in the battle of Chickamauga, transferred to Veteran Reserve Corps, from which mustered out June 29, 1865.

Lemuel Skinner, mustered out with the Company.

Isaiah Smith, died January 7, 1863, at Nashville, Tenn.

Isaac J. Snyder, discharged March 5, 1863, at Gallatin, Tenn.

John Snyder, discharged December 11, 1862, at Bowling Green, Ky.

Jonathan Stultz, mustered out with the Company.

William Tarbill, missing December 31, 1862, in the battle of Stone River; never heard from.

William Taylor, died February 9, 1863, at Murfreesboro, Tenn.

John Taylor, discharged April 27, 1863.

Cornelius Thomas, wounded September 15, 1864; in the battle of Nashville , Tenn.; mustered out June 19, 1865, at Camp Chase, O.

George R. Tilford, transferred to Co. G, Fifth Regiment, Veteran Reserve Corps, January 10, 1865, from which mustered out July 5, 1865, at Indianapolis, Ind.

Andrew J. Timmons captured December 31, 1862, in the battle of Stone River; died February 16, 1863, at Annapolis, Md.

Purnell Timmons, died December 8, 1862, at Danville, Ky.

John Tully, died January 16, 1863, at Nashville, Tenn.

Stephen Tully, mustered out with the Company.

Jacob Ulm, discharged January 14, 1863, at Camp Dennison, O.

Abram Vlerebome, promoted to Principal Musician, January 11, 1864; mustered out with the Company.

John Wolf, discharged November 5, 1863, at Bridgeport, Ala.

John E. Wolfley, discharged May 8, 1863, at Nashville.

DAYTON, O., DECEMBER 13, 1901.

*H. O. Harden:*

DEAR SIR — I want to mention the fact that the husband of my youth, Maxwell Gaddis Clarke, enlisted in the 90th O. V. I., and was largely instrumental in recruiting Company F, the company that went from New Holland, Ohio. While they were in camp at Circleville, O., his father, who was a noted Methodist minister, was taken suddenly ill in his pulpit, and died in a few hours, committing, in his dying moments, the care of a helples family into his son's hands. As Max was not strong, and the Surgeons averse to passing him, any way, he secured a discharge and assumed the care of his mother's family. It is now many years since his death — only living six years after he and I were married.

I do not know whether his name will appear in your history or not, but I would like very much it should. He was a brilliant young man — had no superior among the whole number in intelligence and heart qualities. He was a special friend of Adjutant Kingery, who was killed at Chickamauga. It was a bitter disappointment to him that he could not go to the front.

Very truly yours,

( MRS. ) CLARA CHAFFIN CLARKE-CLEMANS.

COMPANY G.

Captain Thomas W. Gardner, resigned May 17, 1863.

Captain Thomas E. Baker, promoted to 1st Lieutenant from 2nd Lieutenant July 30, 1862; to Captain May 15, 1863; wounded December 31, 1862 in the battle of Stone River; resigned September 21, 1864.

Captain George R. Crow, promoted from 1st Lieutenant Co. F, September 24, 1864; mustered out with Company.

1st Lieutenant James K. Jones, promoted to 2nd Lieutenant from Sergeant Co. B, April 10, 1863; to 1st Lieutenant Co. G, January 1, 1864; to Captain Co. H, September 24, 1864.

1st Lieutenant Aaron W. Mosure, promoted from 1st Sergeant Co. E, September 24, 1864; mustered out with the Company.

2nd Lieutenant Josiah J. Bragg, resigned May 17, 1863.

1st Sergeant William K. Martin, promoted to 2nd Lieutenant February 1, 1863, but not mustered; died February 7, 1863, at Nashville, Tenn.

1st Sergeant Charles E. Reck, transferred from Co. D; appointed 1st Sergeant April 1, 1863; promoted to 1st Lieutenant Co. E, October 12, 1864.

1st Sergeant John L. Maxwell, appointed Sergeant from Corporal February 21, 1863; 1st Sergeant January —, 1865; promoted to 2nd Lieutenant May 30, 1865, but not mustered; mustered out with the Company.

Sergeant William J. Sims, transferred to Vet. Res. Corps.

Sergeant Samuel Creighton, discharged January 19, 1863, at Nashville, Tenn.

Sergeant Presley O. Wright, discharged August 5, 1863, at Camp Dennison, O.

Sergeant James Peddycourt, appointed Corporal October 1, 1862; Sergeant July 23, 1863; mustered out with the Company.

Sergeant James Dobbins, wounded at battle of Chickamauga; appointed from Corporal November 1, 1862; mustered out with the Company.

Sergeant Isaac Barron, appointed from private November 20, 1863; mustered out with the Company.

Sergeant Samuel C. Dorman, appointed Corporal October 31, 1862; Sergeant June 1, 1865; mustered out with the Company.

Corporal Benjamin Coffland, discharged August 11, 1863, at Camp Dennison, O., for wounds received December 31, 1862, at battle of Stone River.

Corporal Thomas J. Allison, transferred to 1st Regiment, U. S. Veteran Volunteer Engineer Corps, August 7, 1864, from which mustered out June 30, 1865.

Corporal Isaac N. Hood, killed September 19, 1863, in the battle of Chickamauga, Ga.

Corporal Alva D. Eveland, died June 7, 1863, at Camp Dennison, O.

Corporal George P. Kelch, died September 12, 1865, at Camp Stanley, Tex.

Corporal Elbridge G. Williams, appointed August 20, 1863; mustered out with the Company.

Corporal James Harden, appointed September 1, 1864; mustered out with the Company.

Corporal Salem Herron, appointed September 1, 1864; mustered out with the Company.

Corporal William Johnston, appointed May 1, 1864; mustered out with the Company.

Corporal John Patterson, appointed January 1, 1865; mustered out with the Company.

Corporal William Switzer, appointed June 1, 1865; wounded in ankle at Stone River; wounded in right leg in battle of Chickamauga; mustered out with the Company

Corporal John Switzer, appointed June 1, 1865; wounded and captured in the battle of Chickamauga, Ga., September 20, 1863; exchanged after 8 months; mustered out with the Company.

William Ankrum, killed December 31, 1862, in the battle of Stone River.

David Baird, discharged January 17, 1863, at Nashville.

John W. Baird, mustered out with the Company.

Joseph T. Barron, mustered out with the Company.

William Barron, mustered out with the Company.

John W. Beatty, mustered out with the Company.

David Black., discharged December 4, 1862, at Louisville.

William Bowers, died February 10, 1863, at Nashville.

Edwin Brooks, discharged August 24, 1863, at Nashville.

Charles C. Brown, died June 22, 1863, at Louisville.

Harrison Burley, died August 28, 1863, at Nashville.

Andrew Carpenter, discharged January 24, 1863, at Nashville.

Robert Chilcoat, mustered out with the Company.

Abraham Devault, mustered out with the Company.

From a photo by H. O. Harden, 1900.

Gen. Bragg's headquarters on Mission Ridge, 1863. Two of the guns are the "Lady Buckner," and "Lady Breckinridge." The Monument was erected by the State of Illinois.

John English, died January 21, 1863, at Murfreesboro, Tenn., of wounds received in the battle of Stone River, December 31, 1862.

Byerly Eveland, transferred to 1st Regiment U. S. Veteran Volunteer Engineer Corps, July 20, 1864; mustered out September 26, 1865, at Nashville.

John A. Eveland, mustered out with the Company.

Shadrach A. Fairman, mustered out with the Company.

Harvey W. Fairman, mustered out October 3, 1865, at Victoria, Tex.

Bruce F. Green, discharged April 1, 1863, at Columbus, O.

Edwin R. M. Green, died October 22, 1862, at Louisville, Ky.

Alexander Harden, mustered out with the Company.

Henry O. Harden, mustered out with the Company.

James W. Harden, mustered out with the Company.

George Harkless, killed December 31, 1862, in the battle of Stone River.

James W. Harkless, mustered out with the Company.

Philip Harkless, died August 2, 1864, at Nashville, of wounds received June 27, 1864, in the battle of Kenesaw Mountain, Ga.

Josiah Hart, died August 24, 1863, at Louisville, Ky.

Seeley Hart, discharged July 26, 1863, at Manchester, Tenn.

John W. Heinlein, died January 10, 1863, at Nashville, Tenn.

John T. Hiles, died March 10, 1863, on steamer, en route from Louisville to Cincinnati.

Simon Hoffman, died January 20, 1863, at Murfreesboro, Tenn., of wounds received in battle of Stone River, December 31, 1862.

Jacob Jadwin, died February 1, 1863, at his home in Erie County, O.

. William Jadwin, killed September 19, 1863, in the battle of Chickamauga, Ga.

Finley Johnston, discharged February 26, 1863, at Nashville.

William B. Kelch, mustered out May 18, 1865, at Camp Dennison, O.

Henry A. Kimble, died December 21, 1862, at Louisville, Ky.

·Wilson Kitchen, discharged November 28, 1863, at New Albany, Ind.

George Lane, mustered out with the Company.

Elijah F. Lattimer, discharged August 25, 1863.

James McKitrick, wounded December 16, 1864, in the battle of Nashville; mustered out with the Company.

John Mann, died January 18, 1863, at Nashville.

Aaron Mattox, mustered out with the Company.

Robert Mattox, mustered out with the Company.

Jacob Miller, discharged September 7, 1863, at Louisville.

Addison Nihart, wounded at Rocky Face Ridge, Ga., and Spring Hill, Tenn.; captured at Spring Hill and taken to Andersonville prison; exchanged March 26, 1865, and was on the Sultana when it blew up April 26, 1865; discharged May 20, 1865.

Allen W. Oldfield, discharged January 20, 1865, at Camp Dennison, O.

Alfred Parish, mustered out with the Company.

Jesse Parks, died November 20, 1862, at Louisville, Ky.

Thomas Payne, discharged June 22, 1863, at Cripple Creek, Tenn.

Washington Pence, wounded December 15, 1864, in the battle of Nashville; mustered out with the Company.

Nathan Pence, mustered out with the Company.

Joseph Pettit, mustered out with the Company.

Joseph Phillips, mustered out with the Company.

Washington Poling, discharged May 12, 1863, at Nashville.

Lyman Potter, died January 6, 1863, at Nashville.

George Ramey, discharged August 3, 1863, at Nashville.

Frederick Reynolds, died January 9, 1863, at Murfreesboro, Tenn., of wounds received December 31, 1862, in the battle of Stone River.

John Rhodes, transferred to Vet. Res. Corps, January 15, 1864; died February 2, 1865, at Chicago, Ill.

George Russell, discharged February 15, 1865, at Camp Dennison, O.

John Russell, mustered out with the Company.

John Sharron, mustered out with the Company.

Joseph Sharron, discharged October 22, 1862, at Louisville, Ky.

John C. Shaw, shot across the abdomen December 31, 1862, at Stone River; wounded in hip and captured September 20, 1863, at the battle of Chickamauga, Ga.; exchanged February 26, 1865; mustered out June 29, 1865, at Camp Chase, O.

Thomas Siniff, discharged January 31, 1863, to enlist in the Mississippi Marine Brigade.

Benjamin F. Smith, mustered out with the Company.

Joseph Speelman, died January 18, 1863, at Nashville.

Samuel Tedrick, killed December 31, 1863, in the battle of Stone River.

Samuel Timberlake, mustered out June 14, 1865, at Louisville, Ky.

Henry J. Vicroy, died December 29, 1862, at Nashville.

Thomas B. Vorhees, transferred to Co. C, 15th Regiment, Vet. Res. Corps, January 31, 1865; mustered out July 13, 1865, at Cairo, Ill.

John Westenhaver, mustered out with the Company.

James A. Willemine, died November 9, 1862, at Danville, Ky.

Henry Williams, discharged March 1, 1863, at Nashville.

John C. Wolf, discharged March 16, 1863, at Louisville, Ky.

James Woods, transferred to 43d Co., 2d Battalion, Vet. Res. Corps, September 1, 1863.

### COMPANY H.

Captain Nicholas F. Hitchcock promoted to Major, September 8, 1864.

Captain James K. Jones, promoted from First Lieutenant, Co. G, September 24, 1864; mustered out with the company.

First Lieutenant Jacob Feeman, resigned December 21, 1862.

First Lieutenant William J. Webb, promoted from

Second Lieutenant, Co. E, May 15, 1863: R. Q. M., April 18, 1865; mustered out with the regiment.

Second Lieutenant John N. Selby, resigned January 27, 1863, on account of wounds received in the battle of Stone River, December 31, 1862.

Second Lieutenant George Ritchey, promoted from First Sergeant December 2, 1862; to First Lieutenant to date November 8, 1862, but not mustered; resigned July 20, 1863

First Sergeant Hugh L. Ferguson, appointed from Sergeant; promoted to First Lieutenant, Co. F, September 24, 1864.

First Sergeant Thomas Turner, appointed from Corporal Jan 14, 1863; First Sergeant, October 12, 1864; Second Lieutenant, May 30, 1865, but not mustered; mustered out with the company.

Sergeant Robert Ashbaugh, discharged January 6, 1863, at Camp Dennison, Ohio.

Sergeant Thomas S. Mains, mustered out with the company.

Sergeant William J. Smith, appointed from private June 10, 1863; mustered out with the company.

Sergeant Samuel Harris, appointed from private January 14, 1863; died December 16, 1864, at Nashville, of wounds received in the battle of Nashville, December 15, 1864.

Sergeant David A. Tharp, appointed corporal February 15, 1863; sergeant, January 1, 1865; mustered out with the company.

Sergeant John M. Wells, appointed from Corporal, January 1, 1865; mustered out with the company.

Coporal Perry A. Edington, discharged December 22, 1862, at Nashville, Tenn.

Corporal John C. Bateman, promoted to Sergeant Major, February 3, 1864.

Corporal Henry Adcock, wounded and captured December 31, 1862, in battle of Stone River, discharged April 10, 1863, at Camp Chase, Ohio.

Corporal' John W. Smittley, appointed Corporal May 1, 1865, wounded and captured in the battle of Stone River; mustered out with the company.

Corporal James Strait, appointed Corporal February 28, 1865; mustered out with the company.

Corporal Caleb Barnes, died January 27, 1863, at Nashville, Tenn.

Corporal William J. Dishong, appointed Corporal February 28, 1865; wounded at Jonesboro, Ga., and Nashville, Tenn.; mustered out with the company.

Corporal James J. Holliday, discharged February 22, 1865, at Chicago, Ill.

Corporal Basil Gordon, mustered out with the company.

Corporal Ovid A. Coleman, mustered out May 23, 1865, at Knoxville, Tenn.

Corporal Thomas W. Lyons, mustered out with the company.

Corporal Bradford Lott, appointed Corporal February 28, 1864; mustered out with the company.

Corporal Jacob Brown, appointed Corporal February 28, 1865; mustered out with the company.

Robert F. Price, Musician, promoted to Principal Musician, January 5, 1865.

Charles Brashears, Musician, mustered out with the company.

Jacob Ansel, mustered out with the company.

David Ashbaugh, mustered out with the company.

Solomon Axline, died April 9, 1863, at Somerset, Ohio.

Samuel M. Baird, died December 27, 1862, at Nashville.

Osias H. Black, discharged February 12, 1863.

William Black, mustered out with the company.

Henry Bowlby, drowned September 5, 1863, in the Tennessee River, at Shellmound, Tenn.

Philip M. Brunner, captured September 20, 1863, in the battle of Chickamauga; exchanged March 30, 1865; mustered out June 19, 1865, at Camp Chase, O.

Bernard Bugh, discharged December 12, 1862.

John M. Bumcrots, mustered out with the company.

William Bumcrots, mustered out with the company.

Josiah Chaney, captured December 31, 1862, in battle of Stone River; exchanged February 1, 1863, died February 8, 1863, at Annapolis, Md.

Jonas S. Chenoweth, mustered out with the company.

Henry C. Chilcote, died December 12, 1862, at Nashville, Tenn.

John W. Chilcote, mustered out with the company.

William H. Chilcote, died January 27, 1863, at Nashville.

Andrew Coons, (or Kuhns), mustered out with the company.

Erasmus M. Cooper, captured December 31, 1862, in battle of Stone River, discharged November 21, 1863.

John H. Damude, discharged September 5, 1863, at Camp Dennison, Ohio.

William C. Dundon, mustered out with the company.

James Eckenrode, transferred to First Regiment, U. S. Vet. Vol. Engineers Corps, Aug. 7, 1864, from which mustered out June 30, 1865.

Perry Edwards, wounded December 15, 1864, in the battle of Nashville, Tenn.; discharged May 30, 1865, at Camp Dennison, Ohio.

Henry Emrine, wounded May 10, 1864, in action near Dallas, Ga.; mustered out with the company.

William T. Fickel, discharged March 10, 1863, at Louisville, Ky.

Patrick N. Flowers, discharged March 27, 1863, at Camp Dennison, Ohio.

John H. Ford, mustered out with the company.

Josephus D. Fry, mustered out with the company.

Adam Gettman, mustered out with the company.

James W. Graves, wounded December 31, 1862, in the battle of Stone River; transferred to Co. E, Second Regiment, Vet. Res. Corps, from which mustered out July 5, 1865, at Detroit, Mich.

Daniel Grim, mustered out with the company.

Eli Guffey, died January 31, 1863, at Nashville.

Henry Hadley, dischrged January 20, 1863, at Nashville. Received a commission as Captain of U. S. Colored Troops, and rose to the rank of brevet Colonel.

Daniel Henderson, mustered out with the company.

John Hitchcock, discharged April 21, 1863, at Nashville.

Alexander Hook, on muster-in-roll as "Abraham Hook," died April 9, 1863, at Gallatin, Tenn.

Samuel Hook, mustered out with the company.

George W. Iles, mustered out with the company.

Absalom Jniper, died February 2, 1863, at Nashville.

From a photo by H. O. Harden, 1900.

Confederate Battery on Battery Rock, Lookout Mountain. The lady is Mrs. Flo Crites, daughter of H. O. Harden.

John Kinnon, captured December 31, 1862, in battle of Stone River, mustered out with the company.

Robert Kissick, mustered out with the company.

Samuel J. Krumlaugh, wounded June 20, 1864, in action near Kenesaw Mountain, Ga., mustered out May 16, 1865, at Nashville.

Michael Kulp, captured December 31, 1862, in battle of Stone River; discharged April 23, 1864.

Henry C. Laughman, mustered out with the company.

William Lutz, discharged February 1865, at Nashville.

William McClerg, mustered out with the company.

Lyman Melick, died November 18, 1862, at Danville, Ky.

Andrew J. Minor, died August 2, 1864, at Vining Station, Ga.

Thomas M. Minor, captured December 31, 1862, in battle of Stone River, discharged December 31, 1863, at Bridgeport, Ala.

Adam Mohler, mustered out with the company.

John W. Moore, captured by "Bushwhackers," in Tennessee in 1864; escaped; mustererd out with the company.

John T. Ormick, discharged November 25, 1863.

Isaiah J Potts, died January 13, 1863, at Nashville.

Jesse Reelhorn, died December 27, 1862, at Danville, Ky.

Ezra E. Rickett, wounded at Stone River, and Kenesaw Mountain; mustered out with the company.

William T. Roberts, mustered out with the company.

Daniel S. Snyder, promoted to Commissary Sergeant, August 23, 1864.

George Sowsley, transferred to Co. F, First Regiment, Vet. Vol. Engineer Corps, July 16, 1864, from which mustered out September 26, 1865, at Nashville.

James F. Speaks, died November 27, 1862, at Danville, Ky.

Thomas Spicer, wounded December 15, 1864, in the battle of Nashville; mustered out with the company.

William H. Spicer, discharged January 6, 1863.

William Strait, wounded and captured at Stone River; was a prisoner 29 days, 9 of which were in Libby, mustered out with the company.

Abraham Tracy, captured December 31, 1862, in battle of Stone River, discharged March 3, 1863, at Nashville.

John W. Tracy, died December 16, 1862, at Nashville.

Samuel Van Horn, died Jan. 11, 1864, at Vicksburg, Miss.

James R. Vansickle, mustered out with the company.

Stephen Vansickle, discharged April 21, 1863, at Nashville.

Richard H. Vertz, discharged February 10, 1863, at Camp Dennison, Ohio.

Robert Walker, died December 17, 1864, at Nashville, Tenn., of wounds received December 15, 1864, in the battle of Nashville.

William H. Walker, wounded and captured December 31, 1862, in the battle of Stone River; exchanged at City Point, January 1863; joined the regiment at Cripple Creek, Tenn.; discharged November 22, 1863, at Bridgeport, Ala.

Henry Whitmore, died December 21, 1862, at Nashville.

Isaac Williams, discharged November 22, 1863, at Bridgeport, Ala.

Aaron Yauger, tranferred to Vet. Res. Corps, February 5, 1864.

COMPANY I.

Captain Lewis R. Carpenter, resigned December 27, 1862.

Captain John S. Witherspoon, promoted from First Lieutenant, Co. B, April 14, 1863; severely wounded June 23, 1864, in action near Kenesaw Mountain, Ga.; resigned February 14, 1865.

Captain Jacob B. Orman, promoted from First Lieutenant and R. Q. M., March 18, 1865; mustered out with the Company.

First Lieutenant Augustus R. Keller, transferred to Co. B July 18, 1863.

First Lieutenant Samuel B. Widener, promoted from Second Lieutenant February 1, 1863; to Captain Co. E, November 27, 1863.

First Lieutenant William D. Hudson, promoted from First Sergeant, Co. A, July 13, 1864; mustered out with the company.

First Sergeant John L. Elder, promoted to First Lieutenant, Co. K, September 24, 1864.

First Sergeant Robert R. Pierce, appointed from Sergeant October 11, 1864; promoted to Second Lieutenant May 30, 1865, but not mustered; mustered out with the Company.

Sergeant John W. Strentz, wounded in the battle of Stone River; transferred to Co. G, 1st Regiment, Veteran Reserve Corps, January 1, 1864; from which mustered out June 28, 1865, at Washington, D. C.

Sergeant John Searles, discharged March 18, 1863.

Sergeant David H. Hufford, discharged May 30, 1863.

Sergeant Henry L. Layman, appointed from Corporal September 1, 1863; mustered out with the Company.

Sergeant Jacob Shutt, appointed Corporal September 28, 1862; Sergeant January 1, 1864; mustered out with the Company.

Sergeant Sylvester Rader, appointed Corporal November 18, 1862; Sergeant January 1, 1864; mustered out with the Company.

Sergeant Charles L. Smith, appointed Corporal December 20, 1862; wounded May 20, 1864, in action near Dallas, Ga.; appointed Sergeant October 11, 1864; mustered out with the Company.

Corporal William Mason, killed December 31, 1862, in the battle of Stone River.

Corporal Benjamin F. Carpenter, discharged September 20, 1863.

Corporal George W. Crumley, appointed October 17, 1862; discharged February 6, 1863; afterward served in 129th O. V. I., near Cumberland Gap, Tenn.; enlisted in the 178th O. V. I.; was Color Bearer, and while carrying the colors in the second battle of Stone River, December, 1864, was severely wounded in the leg by a shell.

Corporal Philomen B. Wilcox, appointed January 1, 1865; mustered out with the Company.

Corporal Homer Anderson, discharged December 26, 1862.

Corporal John H. Berry, appointed November 1, 1863; mustered out with the Company.

Corporal John Seaman, appointed January 1, 1865; wounded at Stone River, Chickamauga and Atlanta; never was sick, and was with the regiment every day, at the front.

Corporal James H. Foster, appointed November 1, 1863; mustered out with the Company.

Corporal Nathaniel Knotts, appointed November 1, 1863; mustered out with the Company.

Corporal Samuel M. Shaefer, appointed January 1, 1864; mustered out with the Company.

Corporal William H. Smith, appointed September 20, 1863; mustered out with the Company.

Corporal Paul Westenberger, appointed November 1, 1863; wounded June 27, 1864, in the battle of Kenesaw Mountain, Ga.; mustered out with the Company.

John Homerickhouse, Musician, captured September 20, 1863, in the battle of Chickamauga; died in Libby prison, at Richmond, Va., December 6, 1863.

John A. Clark, Musician, promoted to Principal Musician May 1, 1865.

Thomas Anderson, died July 14, 1864, at Chattanooga, Tenn.

Martin V. Andrews, wounded May 14, 1864, in the battle of Resaca, Ga.; mustered out June 22, 1865, at Camp Chase, Ohio.

Martin H. Berry, transferred to 1st Regiment, U. S. Vet. Vol. Engineer Corps, August 7, 1864, from which mustered out June 30, 1865.

Alvin D. Betz, died February 18, 1863, at Nashville, Tenn.

Silas Brennan, discharged December 13, 1862.

Andrew Buren, discharged November 21, 1863.

Christian Buren, discharged August 29, 1862.

David Campbell, mustered out October 3, 1865, at Victoria, Texas.

James S. Church, severely wounded June 20, 1864, in action near Kenesaw Mountain, Ga.; died July 12, 1864, at Bremen, Ohio.

Abraham O. Conner, discharged February 13, 1863.

Henry Conrad, wounded December 31, 1862, in the battle of Stone River; discharged April 5, 1863, on account of said wounds; afterward served in the 159th O. V. I.

Reuben D. Conrad, discharged February 10, 1863.

Wesley Conrad, transferred to 1st Regiment, U. S. Vet. Vol. Engineer Corps, August 7, 1864, from which mustered out June 30, 1865.

David Crist, died November 17, 1862, near Nashville.

Jacob T. Crites, mustered out with the Company.

George W. Danforth, transferred to Veteran Reserve Corps November 14, 1864, from which mustered out.

George Davis, mustered out May 18, 1865, at Camp Dennison, Ohio.

Richard S. Elzy, mustered out with the Company.

Josiah Evans, died February 26, 1863, at Nashville.

Joseph Friesner, died November 28, 1862, at Danville, Ky.

Peter Fricker, mustered out with the Company.

John T. Gibbony, mustered out with the Company.

David Hamilton, died December 5, 1862, at Nashville.

Joseph Heft, discharged June 14, 1863.

Charles Heller, died May 25, 1863, at Murfreesboro, Tenn.

Lorenzo D. Hiles, mustered out June 13, 1865, at Columbus, Ohio.

Enoch Hilyard, died July 6, 1864, at Chattanooga, Tenn.

David Hutchinson, mustered out October 3, 1865, at Victoria, Texas.

James L. Jackson, transferred to Veteran Reserve Corps December 17, 1863, from which mustered out.

James Kerns, discharged December 22, 1862.

John L. Keller, wounded December 15, 1864, in the battle of Nashville; mustered out May 23, 1865, at Louisville, Ky.

George W. Lamott, discharged December 22, 1862.

Clay Leist, killed December 31, 1862, in the battle of Stone River, Tenn.

Isaac E. Long, accidentally wounded May 25, 1864; transferred to Veteran Reserve Corps December 22, 1864, from which mustered out.

William F. Lytle, missing in a skirmish November 10, 1864; never heard from.

David McCrillis, died February 25, 1863, at Cripple Creek, Tenn.

Samuel McLaughlan, died November 22, 1862, at Nashville, Tenn.

John B. Mason, transferred to Veteran Reserve Corps December 17, 1863, from which mustered out.

William Moneger, died August 20, 1863, at Nashville.

William Monlux, discharged January 7, 1863.

Edward Musser, died November 28, 1862, at Danville, Ky.

Michael Nedro, discharged December 22, 1862.

Noah Neibling, died Feberuary 24, 1863, at Nashville.

Elza Nichols, transferred to Veteran Reserve Corps August 1, 1863, from which mustered out.

Samuel S. Platner, promoted to Hospital Steward April 22, 1864.

John W. Powell, wounded December 31, 1862, in the battle of Stone River; transferred to Co. K, 5th Regiment, Veteran Reserve Corps, December 30, 1863; mustered out July 5, 1865.

William B. Reed, mustered out October 3, 1865, at Victoria, Texas.

Isaac N. Rinehart, mustered out October 3, 1865, at Victoria, Texas.

William F. Rudolph, mustered out with the Company.

Emanuel Seitz, discharged January 19, 1863, for wounds received December 31, 1862, in the battle of Stone River.

Columbus C. Shaefer, mustered out with the Company.

William Sherwood, died July 14, 1864, at Chattanooga, Tenn.

Aaron Thomas, killed June 27, 1864, in the battle of Kenesaw Mountain, Ga.

Samuel J. Thomas, mustered out with the Company.

Henry R. Thompson, mustered out with the Company.

John H. Thompson, transferred to Co. F, 7th Regiment, Reserve Corps, December 17, 1863, from which mustered out at Washington, D. C., June 28, 1865.

Charles W. Vandemark, mustered out with the Company.

Lawrence Waters, mustered out October 3, 1865, at Victoria, Texas.

Andrew J. Westenberger, wounded September 20, 1863, in the battle of Chickamauga; died March 4, 1864, at Nashville, Tenn.

Alexander L. Westenberger, mustered out October 3, 1865, at Victoria, Texas.

David Westenberger, died February 26, 1863, at Nashville.

Jacob D. Westenberger, transferred to Co. K, 6th Regiment, Veteran Reserve Corps, February 11, 1865; mustered out July 5, 1865, at Cincinnati, Ohio.

James T. Westenberger, transferred to 124th Co., 2nd Battalion Veteran Reserve Corps, December 9, 1864, from which discharged February 1, 1865, at Columbus, Ohio.

John Westenberger, died January 1, 1863, at Nashville.

Andrew Whitehurst, discharged March 3, 1863.

Samuel H. Worm, mustered out with the Company.

Charles L. Wright, wounded May 15, 1864, in the battle of Resaca, Ga.; also December 15, 1864, in the battle of Nashville; mustered out June 26, 1865, at Louisville, Ky.

John Wright, mustered out October 3, 1865, at Victoria, Texas.

Stephen E. Wright, wounded May 15, 1864, in the battle of Resaca, Ga.; mustered out with the Company.

Thomas Wright, mustered out with the Company.

Captain Morris B. Rowe, wounded December 31, 1862, in the battle of Stone River; resigned December 19, 1863.

Captain James F. Cook, promoted to Captain from 1st Lieutenant, January 1, 1864; to Major May 30, 1865, but not mustered; mustered out with the Company.

1st Lieutenant John L. Elder, promoted from 1st Sergeant Co. I, September 24, 1864; mustered out with the Company.

2nd Lieutenant Lewis W. Reahard, wounded December 31, 1862, in the battle of Stone River; resigned April 11, 1863.

1st Sergeant Edward A. Elliott, appointed from Sergeant November 1, 1862; promoted to 2nd Lieutenant December 10, 1863, but not mustered; to 1st Lieutenant Co. A, August 11, 1864.

1st Sergeant Jonathan Ellis, appointed Sergeant from Corporal January 1, 1863; wounded September 19, 1863, in the battle of Chickamauga; also severly wounded July 4, 1864, in the battle of Nickajack Creek, Ga.; appointed 1st Sergeant August 23, 1864; promoted to 1st Lieutenant Co. A, May 30, 1865.

1st Sergeant John M. Gibson, appointed Sergeant from private, March 1, 1863; 1st Sergeant June 4, 1865; mustered out with the Company.

Sergeant David Cameron, transferred to 1st Regiment U. S. Vet. Vol. Engineer Corps, August 7, 1864; from which mustered out June 30, 1865.

Sergeant Harvey Culberson, captured December 31, 1862, in the battle of Stone River; exchanged; returned to Company August 13, 1863; appointed from private July 1, 1864; mustered out with the Company.

Sergeant John W. Silcott, appointed Corporal January 1, 1863; Sergeant January 1, 1865; mustered out with the Company.

Sergeant Henry C. Larimer, appointed from Corporal; mustered out with the Company.

Sergeant Thomas Finnegan, appointed Corporal December 1, 1864; Sergeant June 1, 1865; mustered out October 3, 1865, at Victoria, Tex.

Corporal Henry Harper, died January 27, 1863, of wounds received December 31, 1862, in the battle of Stone River.

Corporal John W. Kinney, discharged December 24, 1862.

Corporal John R. Core, killed January 1, 1863, in the battle of Stone River.

Corporal George B. Carle, appointed July 1, 1864; mustered out with the Company.

Corporal Jonathan Richardson, appointed July 1, 1864; mustered out May 15, 1865, at Nashville.

Corporal Samuel S. Stover, appointed Color Corporal January 1, 1865, and was with the colors until mustered out. Brought the colors to Washington, C. H., O., and has looked after them ever since, by request of Col. Yeoman.

Corporal William H. Weller, appointed June 1, 1865; mustered out with the Company.

Corporal Michael Klever, appointed June 1, 1865; mustered out with the Company.

Corporal David Defenbaugh, appointed June 1, 1865; mustered out with the Company.

Corporal James P. Mills, captured December 31, 1862, in the battle of Stone River; returned to Company June 7, 1863; appointed Corporal June 1, 1865; mustered out with the Company.

Corporal William A. Miller, appointed June 1, 1865; mustered out with the Company.

Corporal Benjamin E. Orr, appointed June 1, 1865; mustered out October 3, 1865, at Victoria, Tex.

John R. Craig, Musician, discharged October 8, 1862.

David Throckmorton, Musician; also served as orderly for General Stanley; mustered out October 3, 1865; at Victoria, Tex.

John Foster, Wagoner, discharged August 28, 1863.

William Adams, mustered out with the Company.

Henry Albert, died January 27, 1863, at Louisville, Ky.

George Anderson, discharged January 23, 1863.

Thomas E. Armstrong, mustered out with the Company.

Charles E. Barnes, mustered out May 12, 1865, at Columbus, O.

William Bennett, mustered out with the Company.

William Bogenwright, mustered out with the Company.

Jesse Bunker, died December 10, 1863, at Murfreesboro, Tenn., of wounds received in the battle of Chickamauga, September 19, 1863.

John T Burke, mustered out with the Company.

Robert M. Christy, discharged May 3, 1863.

William Clabaugh, mustered out with the Company.

Anthony W. Clarridge, mustered out October 3, 1865, at Victoria, Tex.

Lewis O. Cline, mustered out with the Company.

James Culberson, mustered out with the Company.

George W. Downey, discharged June 5, 1865.

Benjamin F. Elliott, died April 20, 1863, at Cripple Creek, Tenn.

Solomon W. Ely, mustered out October 3, 1865, at Victoria, Tex.

James W. Fichthorn, mustered out with the Company.

James Gibson, wounded December 31, 1862, in the battle of Stone River; discharged March 26, 1863.

James Gifford, wounded June 27, 1864, in the battle of Kenesaw Mountain, Ga.; mustered out with the Company.

John W. Godin, captured December 31, 1862, in the battle of Stone River; died February 9, 1863.

William A. Goings, captured August 28, 1864, in action near Jonesboro, Ga.; mustered out June 19, 1865, at Camp Chase, O.

Randolph Green, mustered out June 6, 1865, at Madison, Ind.

Elijah H. Griffith, mustered out with the Company.

Albert Grim, mustered out October 3, 1865, at Victoria, Tex.

John C. Grim, mustered out May 25, 1865, at Chattanooga, Tenn.

William Grim, mustered out July 5, 1865, at Camp Dennison, O.

Henry Grub, transferred to 1st Regiment U. S. Vet. Vol. Engineer Corps, August 7, 1864, from which mustered out June 30, 1865.

George M. Hampton, captured December 31, 1862, in the battle of Stone River; returned to Company June 7, 1863; mustered out with the Company.

John Hemphill, mustered out with the Company.

Andrew Henline, mustered out with the Company.

Frederick Horning, mustered out May 12, 1865, at Knoxville, Tenn.

Daniel Johnson, discharged January 31, 1865.

Elijah Johnson, killed June 22, 1864, in action near Kenesaw Mountain, Ga.

John W. Johnson, wounded September 19, 1863, in the battle of Chickamauga; transferred to Co. B, 15th Regiment Vet. Res. Corps; mustered out July 7, 1865, at Springfield, Ill.

Bazil Jones, mustered out with the Company.

William Keyser, mustered out October 3, 1865, at Victoria, Tex.

Henry S. Klever, wounded at Bald Knob, Ga., by a spent shell; mustered out with the company.

Smith R. Lambert, discharged September 14, 1863.

David Lively, killed December 31, 1862, in the battle of Stone River.

Charles Long, mustered out with the Company.

Benjamin D. McArthur, discharged June 20, 1863.

Thomas S. McDonald, mustered out with the Company.

Isaac McKeene, died February 16, 1863, of wounds received December 31, 1862, in the battle of Stone River.

James D. McMahan, died July 13, 1864, of wounds received in the battle of Resaca, Ga., May 14, 1864.

Henry Mitchell, missing September 19, 1863, in the battle of Chickamauga; never heard from.

James Morgan, discharged April 23, 1863.

Samuel Moyer, died December 23, 1862, at Nashville, Tenn.

Patrick Murphy, died January 3, 1863, of wounds received December 31, 1862, in the battle of Stone River.

Edmund R. Ott, mustered out with the Company.

Joseph H. Ott, mustered out with the Company.

Douglass Owens, mustered out October 3, 1865, at Victoria, Tex.

Richard Parker, died December 2, 1862.

James H. Parris, killed December 31, 1862, in the battle of Stone River.

Nathan Pearson, mustered out May 28, 1865, at Chattanooga, Tenn.

Jonathan Powless, discharged May 15, 1863.

Ami Propst, died December 29, 1862, at Nashville.

George Propst, discharged February 20, 1863.

John Propst, died August 20, 1863, at Nashville.

John G. Reif, wounded and missing September 19, 1863, in the battle of Chickamauga; never heard from.

Benjamin Robey, mustered out with the Company.

George W. Rowe, mustered out with the Company.

Solomon Solmor, mustered out with the Company.

Harrison Shiflet, discharged January 28, 1863.

Simeon Shiflet, mustered out with the Company.

William Smith, captured December 31, 1862, in the battle of Stone River; returned to Company June 14, 1863; mustered out with the Company.

George Streets, mustered out with the Company.

Lafayette Strope, discharged May 13, 1863.

John Stumbaugh, mustered out October 3, 1865, at Victoria, Tex.

Thomas Summers, mustered out with the Company.

Isaac Thompson, mustered out with the Company.

Hugh Tomlinson, discharged December 18, 1862.

Frederick Turner, mustered out with the Company.

Richard Venemon, mustered out with the Company.

William H. Warrenburg, died July 1, 1863, at New Albany, Ind.

Jonathan D. Williams, captured December 31, 1862, in the battle of Stone River; returned to Company June 7, 1863; died September 10, 1864, of wounds received September 1, 1864, in the battle of Jonesboro, Ga.

Howard Wimer, died January 17, 1863, of wounds received December 31, 1862, in battle of Stone River.

Shadrach C. Wroten, died November 14, 1863, at Murfreesboro, Tenn.

# POSTOFFICE ADDRESS OF LIVING MEMBERS.

## FIELD AND STAFF.

Colonel Charles H. Rippey, San Diego, Cal.
Surgeon Henry W. Carpenter, Lancaster, Ohio.
Adjutant Henry F. Leib, Oberlin, Kan.
Chaplain William C. Holliday, Columbus, Ohio.
R. Q. M. John S. Beck, Dayton, Ohio.
Commissary Sergeant David S. Snyder, Ellsworth, Kansas.
Musician Robert F. Price, Logan, Ohio.
Musician Abraham Vlerebome, Dayton, Ohio.
Musician John A. Clark, Augusta, Ga.

## COMPANY A.

Captain William Felton, Columbus, Ohio.
Captain W. A. Denny, Chicago, Ill.
Lieutenant Andrew J. Willoughby, Dayton, Ohio.
George Ater, Carey, Ohio.
Henry Shannon, Ashville, Ohio.
John H. Huffman, Reeseville, Ohio.
Martin E. Neff, Era, Ohio.
John I. Radcliff, Darbyville, Ohio.
William Adkins, Sandusky, Ohio.
William Ater, Clarksburg, Ohio.
William Bateman, Circleville, Ohio.
Seymour Bolin, Derby, Ohio.
Simeon Garrett, Owens, Ohio.
Johnson Guseman, South Bloomfield, Ohio.
Stanley Gray, Columbus, Ohio.
Elias F. Hines, Peoria, Ill.

John W. Hook, Sandusky, Ohio.
John McDonald, Commercial Point, Ohio.
Jonathan Minton, Derby, Ohio.
John W. Miller, Lovington, Ill.
George S. W. Neff, Palestine, Ohio.
Nathaniel P. Neff, Pherson, Ohio.
Frederick Owen, Mt. Sterling, Ohio.
James R. Patterson, Darbyville, Ohio.
Jonas Ross, Williamsport, Ohio.
Robert B. Rice, Glen Roy, Ohio.
Levi Septer, Springfield, Ill.
Joseph Tatman, Piatt, Ill.
Henry Vanvickle, Deland, Ill.
Thomas B. Whitehead, Lockbourne, Ohio.
Benj. F. T. Yoakum, Monticello, Ill.
John F. Williams, Terre Haute, Ind.
George W. Dennis, Pleasant Green, Kan.
John W. Sheets, Derby, Ohio.
John W. McGuire, Derby, Ohio.
John H. Wilson, South Bloomfield, Ohio.
Samuel Graham, Filmore, Ill.

### COMPANY B.

Captain Edward A. Elliott, Windsor, Ohio.
Lieutenant Archibald M. Rodgers, Independence, Missouri.
Lieutenant John L. Hatfield, Indianola, Iowa.
James Jones, Fredonia, Kan.
Lee Ogan, Pleasantville, Iowa.
Wilson H. Claypool, Caledonia, Ohio.
Richard Steele, Logan, Ohio.
Willis Parcels, Marquette, Michigan.
Henry Dozer, Taylorsville, Ohio.
Emery F. Redfern, South Perry, Ohio.

Benjamin P. Ansel, Zaleski, Ohio.
James R. Boyles, Logan, Ohio.
Orison Champlin, Hamden Junction, Ohio.
John B. Claypool, Hamden Junction, Ohio.
Samuel Dearth, Chillicothe, Ohio.
Joseph L. Devault, Wilksville, Ohio.
John H. Derry, Wilksville, Ohio.
Joseph W. Ewan, Frazeysburg, Ohio.
John R. Gardner, Allensville, Ohio.
Lewis Gardner, Allensville, Ohio.
Lafayette Gaston, Kerr, Ohio.
Benjamin Jadwin, Logan, Ohio.
David A. Kreibble, Fandon, Ill.
Abner C. Linn, Pursell, Ohio.
Jacob G. Miller, Wilksville, Ohio.
John North, South Bloomingville, Ohio.
Thomas Parrish, Stella, Ohio.
Jasper Pennell, Zaleski, Ohio.
John Shively, Stella, Ohio.
William Shuster, Shickley, Neb.
John Towell, Zaleski, Ohio.
George Walters, Murray, Ohio.
Hamilton J. Willis, Marquette, Kan.
Francis Waugh, McArthur, Ohio.
Sylvester Wyckoff, Wichita, Kan.
George R. Dickerson, Geneva, Ind.
Andrew W. Karnes, Columbus, Ohio.

### COMPANY C.

Lieutenant Jacob Bush, Parrotts, Ohio.
Lieutenant John C. Bateman, Soldiers' Home, Dayton, Ohio.
David Calhoun, Mansfield, Ark.
John C. Murphy, Pink Hill, Mo.

William Allen, Springfield, Ohio.
John W. Ellis, Jamestown, Ohio.
Oliver E. Harney, Jamestown, Ohio.
Farris Harney, West Lancaster, Ohio.
William Hidey, Milledgeville, Ohio.
Marshall Hosier, Oceola, Iowa.
William H. James, Chickasaw, Ohio.
Oliver B. Jeffries, Lexington, Ill.
Thomas H. Jenkins, Parrotts, Ohio.
Parris Robinson, Shiloh, Ill.
Jesse Sperlock, Roundhead, Ohio.
Milton Sperlock, Roundhead, Ohio.
Charles G. Sharrett, West Lancaster, Ohio.
George P. Straley, Kansas City, Mo.
Elon Thornton, Washington C. H., Ohio.
Joseph Tracy, Sedalia, Ohio.
John S. Tracy, Kenton, Ohio.
Andrew Ullmer, Bluffton, Ind.
William Wood, Jeffersonville, Ohio.
Thomas C. Williams, Jeffersonville, Ohio.
Samuel W. Williams, Grove Hill, Ohio.
Leroy Wilson, La Jara, Colorado.
Louis F. Stoltzenberg, Washington C. H., Ohio.
E. Burgess Watts, Atlanta, Ga.
Martin L. Mock, Guthrie, O. T.
Jacob S. Cockerill, New Martinsburg, Ohio.
E. Lewis Janes, Jeffersonville, Ohio.
David Mock, Jeffersonville, Ohio.
William M. Boughn, Washington C. H., Ohio
Daniel A. Janes, Shanes Crossing, Ohio.
Alexander B. Creamer, Mechanicsburg, Ohio.
Albert Bonecutter, Staunton, Ohio.
Meredith Bowen, Lamar, Mo.
John Burton, Ashville, Ohio.

Bigelow W. Brown, West Mansfield, Ohio.
William Bonecutter, Xenia, Ohio.
Samuel H. Carr, South Charleston, Ohio.
George W. Conner, Xenia, Ohio.
George H. Creamer, Jeffersonville, Ohio.
Wesley M. Creamer, Salem, Mo.
John N. Doyle, Roundhead, Ohio.
John J. Duff, Jeffersonville, Ohio.
Edward C. Duff, Sedalia, Ohio.
John W. Harper, Lapara, Texas.

## COMPANY D.

Captain John M. Sutphen, Lancaster, Ohio.
Lieutenant George W. Welsh, Lancaster, Ohio.
Lieutenant John N. Arehart, Zanesville, Ohio.
S. A. Parsons, Columbus, Ohio.
Sebastian C. Goss, Tiffin, Ohio.
William H. Strode, Lancaster, Ohio.
John Cross, Commercial Point, Ohio.
Samuel B. Holderman, Lancaster, Ohio.
Solomon D. Soliday, Fort Wayne, Ind.
Henry C. Williamson, Lancaster, Ohio.
James Rittenhouse, Follett, Ind.
James W. Daymude, Yates Center, Kan.
William L. Armentrout, Terre Haute, Ind.
John Andregg, Basil, Ohio.
John Berger, Basil, Ohio.
Israel Bolenbaugh, Royalton, Ohio.
Frederick Blosser, Carbon Hill, Ohio.
George W. Combs, Rushville, Ohio.
Pulaski H. Ebright, Science Hill, Ky.
Levi England, Jerome, Ind.
Edward F. Griffin, Staunton, Ind.
Henry B. Gray, Lancaster, Ohio.

Ira Lines, Etna, Ohio.
Elijah Howard, Royalton, Ohio.
Noah Lutz, Bremen, Ohio.
Thomas J. McDaniel, Basil, Ohio.
Jacob McDaniel, Basil, Ohio.
Jackson Myers, Lima, Ohio.
Joseph D. Payne, Columbus, Ohio.
Abraham Smith, Amanda, Ohio.
George W. Spangler, Lancaster, Ohio.
Samuel Swope, Stony Ridge, Ohio.
Abraham K. Thomen, Thurston, Ohio.
John P. Urbin, Kewanna, Ind.
Joseph Wilson, Hooker, Ohio.
William Bechtel, Cowdin, Ill.
John S. Beck, Dayton, Ohio.
Percival Stuter, Amalie, Cal.
George Clark, Soldiers' Home, Sandusky, Ohio.
John Gallagher, Meredin, Conn.
Thomas S. Williamson, Lancaster, Ohio.

### COMPANY E.

Lieutenant Daniel J. Nunnemaker, Radcliffs, Ohio.
Lieutenant Aaron W. Mosure, Columbus, Ohio.
David E. Avery, Newark, Ohio.
Hiram S. Brown, Starr, Ohio.
William J. Mason, Hope, Mich.
Alexander Frankfother, Struthers, Ohio.
William I. Bowers, Logan, Ohio.
Abraham Trout, Ord, Kan.
Barrah Moore, Union Furnace, Ohio.
Thomas S. Meldrim, Ilesboro, Ohio.
John R. Mauk, Cambridge City, Ind.
David C. Goodwin, Columbus Grove, Ohio.
Samuel W. Poland, Columbus, Ohio.

Joseph Marshall, Sugar Grove, Ohio.
Benjamin Aplin, DesMoines, Iowa.
Thomas D. Book, Luhrig, Ohio.
John R. Cage, Union Furnace, Ohio.
Nicholas M. Call, Mt. Sterling, Ohio.
Joseph Collins, Logan, Ohio.
Samuel B. Crow, Logan, Ohio.
Shelton Guess, Logan, Ohio.
Samuel L. Davis, Magnetic Springs, Ohio.
Handley Hillyer, Nelsonville, Ohio.
Abraham Lane, Athens, Ohio.
Thomas Lee, Washington, Kan.
Samuel Mauk, Logan, Ohio.
James H. Mitchell, Starr, Ohio.
Jonathan S. Shaw, Logan, Ohio.
Parces Sweet, Junction City, Ohio.
John W. Tritsch, Logan, Ohio.
William Wimer, Cold Water, Mich.
Ward N. Woodard, Nelsonville, Ohio.
Joseph Sherlock, Kansas City, Mo.
George S. Thompson, Wichita, Kan.
James H. Johnson, Smith Center, Kan.
John W. O'Hare, Lebanon, Kan.
John W. Webb, Soldiers' Home, Dayton, Ohio.
William Baird, Fulton, Kan.
Noah Nunnemaker, Carroll, Ohio.
Frederick Saumering, New York City.
Thomas J. Passmore, Buffalo, Mo.
James Z. Wilson, Circleville, Ohio.
Sylvester I. Rogers, Columbus, Ohio.

## COMPANY F.

Captain Alonzo W. Black, Cleveland, Ohio.
Captain George R. Crow, Los Angeles, Cal.
Lieutenant Charles E. Reck, Kansas City, Mo.
M. L. Stollard, Tarlton, Ohio.
James C. Todd, Jeffersonville, Ohio.
William Hendricks, Paola, Kan.
Benjamin F. Skinner, Columbus Grove, Ohio.
Joseph B. Rife, Stockton, Ill.
Joseph B. Schrawger, West Jefferson, Ohio.
David R. Porter, New Holland, Ohio.
John Archa, Lima, Iowa.
William H. Blosser, Shawnee, Ohio.
George Borden, Columbus, Ohio.
Harvey Brooks, Atlanta, Ohio.
James D. Chaffin, New Holland, Ohio.
Elbert Chittum, Pancoastburg, Ohio.
Alexander Crooks, Greenland, Ill.
Lewis K. Davis, Baltimore, Ohio.
James Funk, New Holland, Ohio.
Israel Funk, Big Plains, Ohio.
Isaac George, Lancaster, Ohio.
James Hudson, Portland, Ind.
Isaac Ludwig, Circleville, Ohio.
Samuel McGath, New Holland, Ohio.
Emanuel Mangus, Ashville, Ohio.
Benjamin F. Martin, Ogden, Kan.
John Martin, Ogden, Kan.
George W. Poland, Derby, Ohio.
John Rife, East Ringgold, Ohio.
Lorenzo D. Riggin, Circleville, Ohio.
Joshua Skinner, Wymore, Neb.
Cornelius Thomas, Tarlton, Ohio.

Jacob Ulm, Circleville, Ohio.
Noble M. Cochran, Exline, Ill.
Ashton Briggs, Columbus, Ohio.
Philip M. Garrison, Garnett, Kan.
Stephen Tully, Los Banos, Cal.
Henry Hooper, Lincoln, Neb.
Abram M. Guseman, Lancaster, Ohio.
Samuel Tilford, Waverly, Kan.
George R. Tilford, Waverly, Kan.

### COMPANY G.

Captain Thomas W. Gardner, Sedalia, Mo.
Captain Thomas E. Baker, Logan, Ohio.
John L. Maxwell, Gallipolis, Ohio.
James Peddycourt, South Perry, Ohio.
James Dobbins, Jeffersonville, Ohio.
Samuel C. Dorman, Delaware, Ohio.
Thomas J. Allison, South Bloomingville, Ohio.
John Switzer, Crossenville, Ohio.
William Switzer, Mendon, Mo.
John W. Baird, Columbus, Ohio.
Joseph T. Barron, Rockbridge, Ohio.
John W. Beatty, Lamar, Kan.
Andrew J. Carpenter, Delphos, Kan.
Abraham Devault, Nancy, Ohio.
Byerly Eveland, Eagleport, Ohio.
John A. Eveland, South Bloomingville, Ohio.
Bruce Green, Washington C. H., Ohio.
James Harden, Orland, Ohio.
Henry O. Harden, Stoutsville, Ohio.
Finley Johnson, Haynes, Ohio.
George Lane, Logan, Ohio.
Robert Mattox, Eagleport, Ohio.
Addison Nihart, Bolivar, Mo.

Washington Poling, New Lexington, Ohio.
James Harkless, Monroe, Ind.
Allen W. Oldfield, Logan, Ohio.
Joseph Pettitt, South Bloomingville, Ohio.
George Russell, South Bloomingville, Ohio.
John C. Shaw, Circleville, Ohio.
Samuel Timberlake, Haynes, Ohio.
John C. Wolf, Logan, Ohio.
James Woods, Nelsonville, Ohio.
Presley O. Wright, Corning, Iowa.
William Johnson, Kidder, Mo.
Salem Herron, Pape, Mo.
Thomas B. Vorhees, Gibisonville, Ohio.

## COMPANY H.

Captain James K. Jones, Sheridan, Mo.
Lieutenant Hugh L. Ferguson, Westerville, Ohio.
Lieutenant Thomas N. Turner, Cincinnati, Ohio.
Thomas S. Mains, New Lexington, Ohio.
David C. Ashbaugh, Logan, Ohio.
David A. Tharp, Hemlock, Ohio.
John M. Wells, Harveysburg, Ohio.
John W. Smittley, Troy, Ohio.
James Strait, Amoret, Mo.
William J. Dishong, Morley, Mich.
Thomas W. Lyons, Ehler, Iowa.
Bradford Lott, Yellow Springs, Ohio.
Jacob L. Brown, Pawnee, Neb.
Jacob Ansel, Zanesville, Ohio.
John M. Bumcrots, Sego, Ohio.
Jonas S. Chenoweth, Stoutsville, Ohio.
Erasmus M. Cooper, Somerset, Ohio.
Ovid A. Coleman, Soldiers' Home, Sandusky, Ohio.
John W. Chilcote, Sego, Ohio.

William C. Dundon, New Holland, Ohio.
John H. Damude, Columbus, Ohio.
James Ecenrode, Leipsic, Ohio.
Perry Edwards, Emporia, Kan.
Josephus D. Fry, Springfield, Ohio.
John Ford, Mt. Perry, Ohio.
Daniel Grim, Napoleon, Ohio.
James W. Graves, Somerset, Ohio.
Henry H. Hadley, New York City.
Daniel Henderson, Casstown, Ohio.
Robert Kissick, Gratiot, Ohio.
Michael Kulp, Somerset, Ohio.
Samuel J. Krumlauf, Somerset, Ohio.
Henry C. Laughman, Cerro Gordo, Ill.
William McClerg, Casstown, Ohio.
Adam Mohler, Somerset, Ohio.
John W. Moore, Sego, Ohio.
Thomas Minor, McCluney, Ohio.
Ezra E. Rickett, Moxahala, Ohio.
William Strait, Shawnee, Ohio.
James R. Vansickle, Chalfants, Ohio.
William H. Walker, Somerset, Ohio.
Andrew Kuhns, Portsmouth, Ohio.

### COMPANY I.

Captain John S. Witherspoon, Creola, Ohio.
Captain Lewis R. Carpenter, Independence, Mo.
Captain Jacob B. Orman, Lancaster, Ohio.
John W. Strentz, Logan, Ohio.
Emanuel Seits, St. Louisville, Ohio.
Henry L. Layman, Lake City, Ill.
Jacob Shutt, Lancaster, Ohio.
John Searles, Columbus, Ohio.
Sylvester Rader, Allis, Mich.

Charles L. Smith, Logan, Ohio.
Benjamin F. Carpenter, Magnetic Springs, Ohio.
George W. Crumley, Amanda, Ohio.
Homer Anderson, Peekskill, N. Y.
John H. Berry, Omaha, Neb.
John Seman, Columbus, Ohio.
James H. Foster, Sugar Grove, Ohio.
Martin H. Berry, Springfield, Ohio.
Silas Brennan, Sugar Grove, Ohio.
Henry Conrad, Amanda, Ohio.
Richard D. Conrad, Amanda, Ohio.
Wesley Conrad, Oxford, Kan.
Richard S. Elzy, Decatur, Ind.
Peter Fricker, Newark, Ohio.
John T. Gibbony, Lancaster, Ohio.
David Hutchinson, Columbus, Ohio.
Samuel T. Law, Somerset, Ohio.
Isaac E. Long, Revenge, Ohio.
Samuel J. Thomas, Marion, Ill.
John H. Thompson, New Hampshire, Ohio.
Henry R. Thompson, Haydenville, Ohio.
Charles W. Vandermark, Clearcreek, Ohio.
James T. Westenberger, Lancaster, Ohio.
Charles L. Wright, Flint, Mich.
Thomas Wright, Yellow Springs, Ohio.
Stephen E. Wright, Lancaster, Ohio.
Jacob D. Westenberger, Fort Jennings, Ohio.
John L. Keller, Mt. Vernon, Ohio.
Isaac N. Rinehart, Grant City, Mo.
Thomas Wright, Columbus, Ohio.
Lawrence Waters, Revenge, Ohio.
John W. Powell, Bowling Green, Ohio.

COMPANY K.

Captain James F. Cook, Washington C. H., Ohio.
Lieutenant Lewis W. Reahard, Pittsburg, Pa.
Harvey Culberson, Sabina, Ohio.
George B. Carle, Windsor, Kan.
Samuel S. Stover, Milledgeville, Ohio.
Michael Klever, Sedalia, Mo.
David Defenbaugh, Crescent, O. T.
William A. Miller, Milledgeville, Ohio.
John R. Craig, Staunton, Ohio.
Charles E. Barnes, Washington C. H., Ohio.
William Bogenrife, Mt. Sterling, Ohio.
James W. Fichthorn, Milledgeville, Ohio.
Rudolph Green, Washington C. H., Ohio.
George M. Hampton, Williamsport, Ohio.
Andrew Henline, Hillsboro, Ohio.
Bazil James, Bolens Mills, Ohio.
Daniel Johnson, Milledgeville, Ohio.
John W. Johnson, Milledgeville, Ohio.
Henry S. Klever, London, Ohio.
Joseph H. Ott, Cooks, Ohio.
Douglass Owen, Flora, Ind.
Benjamin Robey, Era, Ohio.
Solomon Solmar, Bloomingburg, Ohio.
Harrison Shiflet, Meadeville, Mo.
Simeon Shiflet, New Holland, Ohio.
Jonathan Richardson, Yatesville, Ill.
James Culberson, Sabina, Ohio.
John T. Burke, Mt. Sterling, Ohio.
David C. Throckmorton, Circleville, Ohio.
Lafayette Strope, New Holland, Ohio.
Thomas Summers, New Holland, Ohio.
George Streets, Mt. Sterling, Ohio.

John Stumbaugh, South Charleston, Ohio.
John Silcott, Pleasantville, Iowa.

The above list is as nearly correct as we can make it at this time. Some may be dead whose names appear, and, no doubt, some are living whose address is unknown. — Ed.

# PRESIDENT WILLIAM McKINLEY.

MEMORIAL SERVICES HELD AT THE 90TH REUNION,
SEPTEMBER 18, 1901, AT STOUTSVILLE, OHIO.

As had been announced a memorial service was held for one hour, in memory of comrade and President William McKinley. Rev. J. D. Neff read from the Scriptures, Rev. J. M. Weinreich offered prayer, and Rev. H. C. Schluter offered the following resolutions, which were adopted.

As residents of Stoutsville and citizens of this great state and nation, we are assembled on a mournful occasion to pay tribute to the memory of our late great President William McKinley. We deplore his untimely death caused by the bullets of a treacherous assassin. We bow in sorrow before God under this great loss, and feel humiliated that our country should contain one, who under the mask of friendliness and esteem is able to shoot down our chief magistrate.

Resolved, That irrespective of parties, we hereby express the regard we feel for our late President; that we thank God for his pure life as a husband, citizen and Christian, and that we this day enshrine him in the "Hall of Martyrs," in the midst of Lincoln and Garfield.

Resolved, That we extend our sympathies and prayers to Mrs. McKinley in this hour of her deep grief, and that we pray to God for the removal of the spirit of anarchy and all evil from our fair land.

The band then played a dirge, after which Capt. J. S. Witherspoon and J. B. Rife spoke feelingly and sympathetically of the tragic end of the head of the greatest nation on the globe. During this service all stores and business houses in the town were closed, and the people assembled.

RESOLUTION ON THE DEATH OF PRESIDENT MCKINLEY.

The 90th O. V. I., in Reunion assembled, at Stoutsville, Ohio, this 18th day of September, 1901, adopt the following resolutions on the death of our Comrade, President Wm. McKinley.

Whereas, Our illustrious and beloved President, friend and comrade, Wm. McKinley, has been murdered by the hand of an assassin, and,

Whereas, In his death this country has lost a brilliant statesman, a patriotic citizen, a brave soldier, and his wife a loving husband; therefore, be it

Resolved, that this Association condemn in the strongest terms the inhuman act of assassinating our President, and favor the enactment of such laws as will prevent the importation and provide for the deportation from this country of true liberty all persons imbued with anarchism.

Resolved, That we extend to the devoted and beloved wife of our late President, our sincere and heartfelt sympathy in her great bereavement, and that a copy be sent to Mrs. McKinley, and that they be placed on the records of the Association.

D. C. GOODWIN,
S. H. TILFORD,
GEO. WALTERS,
T. J. ALLISON,
J. S. COCKERRILL.
*Committee.*

# ROLL OF HONOR, 90TH O. V. I.

Following is given the names of the 90th, who were killed, died of disease or wounds, while in the service of their country.

Our feelings have been sad, indeed, as we went over the muster rolls, saw the signatures of the young men and boys, many, who then actually signed their own death warrants. Little did these boys think, when they signed their names, that they would have to give up their lives in a very short time—some in less than three months. They did not live to see the glorious results of their sacrifice, but let us, the survivors, and those who come after us, look over the long list, and then remember it was for us and them they gave up their lives; and may they ever be held in sacred remembrance by future generations. Their names and sacrifices are sacred things. Young men, just entering on the duties of life; young husbands and fathers leaving their families, never more to meet them on earth. Theirs was a most glorious and heroic death.

### FIELD OFFICERS.

Major George Angle, killed near Marietta, Ga., July 2, 1864.

Adjutant Daniel N. Kingery, killed at Chickamauga, September 20, 1863.

### COMPANY A.

Henry R. Markley, died January 18, 1863, of wounds received in battle of Stone River.

David Pritchard, died March 8, 1864, at Ooltewah, Tennessee.

John E. Ashbrook, died at Murfreesboro, Tenn., January 28, 1863.

William S. Williams, died December 19, 1864, at Bowling Green, Ky., of wounds received in the battle of Nashville.

Isaac H. Gray, died at Camp Chase, O.,May 12, 1863.

James Hardesty, died at Nashville, Tenn., February 1, 1863.

William McKinley, died in Pickaway county, O., May 21, 1865.

Thornton Ater, died at Bowling Green, Ky., November 27, 1862.

Lewis C. Bower, died at Nashville, Tenn., January 15, 1863.

Joseph Briggs, died at Manchester, Tenn., July 23, 1863.

Joseph Brobeck, killed in battle of Nashville, Tenn., December 15, 1864.

William Brown, died at Nashville, Tenn., December 5, 1862.

Nelson D. Caddy, drowned in the Tennessee river, December 3, 1863, at Bridgeport, Ala.

Martin Crabill, died at Nashville, Tenn., December 12, 1862.

Daniel Gouchenour, died at Bowling Green, Ky., February 15, 1863.

Robert Hankinson, died at Tullahoma, Tenn., Sept. 2, 1863.

John M. Justus, died at Nashville, Tenn., December 24, 1862.

Elias Justus, died at Chattanooga, Tenn., August 13, 1864, of wounds received June 27, 1864, in battle of Kenesaw Mountains.

Isaac Lance, died at Nashville, Tenn., December 17, 1862.

Jacob Morris, died January 15, 1863, at Nashville, Tenn., of wounds received December 31, 1862, in battle of Stone River.

Jesse H. Pritchard, died at Nashville, Tenn., December 15, 1862.

John Smith, killed in battle of Chickamauga, September 19, 1863.

William H. Tilton, died at Nashville, Tenn., May 28, 1863.

John Weigand, died at Bowling Green, Ky., December 3, 1862.

George W. Wood, killed in battle of Stone River, December 31, 1862.

### COMPANY B.

John Schreckengaust, died at McArthur, O., December 18, 1862.

Nathan H. Curry, died at Louisville, Ky., August 22, 1863.

Richard W. Kennard, died at Covington, Ky., May 9, 1863.

Thomas W. Jefferson, killed in battle of Chickamauga, September 20, 1863.

Joseph Wyatt, died in Andersonville Prison, Ga., Aug. 31, 1864.

John Burns, missing in battle of Stone River, December 31, 1862, never heard of, and no further record found.

William Eidson, died January 18, 1863, at Nashville, Tenn.

Harvey Hawk, died at Nashville, Tenn., January 14, 1863.

Henry Johnson, died at Nashville, Tenn., January 25, 1863.

William H. Ledlie, died at Cripple Creek, Tenn., April 20, 1863.

Thomas S. Miller, killed at battle of Stone River, December 31, 1862.

Lafayette Mollihan, died at Chattanooga, Tenn., May 31, 1864.

Thomas W. Roach, killed in battle of Stone River, December 31, 1862.

David M. Snyder, died at Wild Cat, Ky., October 24, 1862.

Mark Tinley, died in Andersonville Prison, Ga., August 16, 1864.

### COMPANY C.

Captain Robert D. Caddy, killed in battle of Chickamauga, September 20, 1863.

George P. Haskins, died at Nashville, Tenn., January 20, 1863.

William Beatty, died at Nashville, Tenn., January 14, 1863.

Aaron Allen, died at Victoria, Tex., August 19, 1865.

Ephraim Allen, died at West Lancaster, O., July 30, 1864.

Harvey S. Barney, died at Nashville, Tenn., February 12, 1863.

John W. Boughn, died at Nashville, Tenn., January 5, 1863.

Joseph H. Boughn, killed in battle of Nashville, Tenn., December 15, 1864.

John W. Cahill, died in Andersonville Prison, Ga., Aug. 6, 1864.

David C. Conner, died January 11, 1865, at Jeffersonville, Ind., of wounds received in the battle of Nickajack Creek, Ga., July 2, 1864.

John Creamer, killed in the battle of Stone River, December 31, 1862.

Lewis Creamer, died at Bowling Green, Ky., November 18, 1863.

Jacob T. Doster, died February 10, 1863, at Murfreesboro, Tenn., of wounds received in battle of Stone River, December 31, 1862.

John W. Engle, died at Nashville, Tenn., January 4, 1863.

Otto Engle, died at Nashville, Tenn., January 23, 1863.

Samuel Flax, died September 4, 1864, at Chattanooga, Tenn., of wounds received July 4, 1864, at Nickajack Creek, Ga.

Daniel Gordon, died at Jeffersonville, O., February 10, 1863.

George M. Groves, died at Nashville, Tenn., December 24, 1862.

Lewis Hatfield, died at Cripple Creek, Tenn., June 24, 1863.

Amzi Hire, died at Decherd, Tenn., July 29, 1863.

John C. Hogue, died at Chattanooga, Tenn., July 4, 1864, of wounds received in battle of Kenesaw Mountain, Ga., June 27, 1864.

William A. Holston, died at Glasgow Ky., November 10 1862.

George W. Horney, died Oct. 7, 1865, in Texas.

William A. Lynch, died at Nashville, Tenn., May 31, 1864.

Harmon McIntyre, killed in battle of Stone River, December 31, 1862.

John H. Mahoy, died January 4, 1863, at Nashville, Tenn.

Benjamin Miller, died at Cave City, Ky., December 11, 1863.

Marion Myers, died at Nashville, Tenn., January 27, 1863.

James M. Parrett, died February 14, 1863, at Jeffersonville, O.

Daniel Rupert, died at Nashville, Tenn., January 5, 1863.

Jackson Smith, died October 12, 1863, at Chattanooga, Tenn., of wounds received in the battle of Chickamauga, September 20, 1863.

Wesley F. Straley, died at Nashville, Tenn., August 22, 1863.

Philip Tumblin, died August 21, 1865, at Victoria, Texas.

### COMPANY D.

John F. Williams, died at Nashville, Tenn., December 19, 1862.

Martin K. Thomen, died December 30, 1864, at Nashville, Tenn., of wounds received in battle of Nashville, December 15, 1864.

Robert P. Ewing, died at Camp Dennison, O., November 1, 1864.

William Springer, died July 12, 1864, of wounds received June 20, 1864, in action near Kenesaw Mountain, Ga.

Adam Courtright, died February 12, 1863, at Danville, Ky.

William Downs, died at Nashville, Tenn., December 28, 1862.

John H. Emick, killed in the battle of Nashville, December 15, 1864.

John Haines, died at Cripple Creek, Tenn., March 27, 1863.

Wilson Hickle, captured at Stone River, died February 28, 1863, at Anapolis, Md.

Amos Kemp, died at Danville, Ky., December 20, 1862.

James Moravy, died at Bridgeport, Ala., January 14, 1864.

John C. Strayer, died December 16, 1863, at Chattanooga, Tenn., of wounds received in battle of Chickamauga, September 19, 1863.

Alexander Warren, died October 24, 1863, at Chattanooga, Ten.n, of wounds received at the battle of Chickamauga.

Daniel Welsh, died December 30, 1864, at Louisville, Ky., of wounds received in the battle of Franklin, Tenn., November 30, 1864.

David Williamson, did July 12, 1864, in Andersonville Prison, Ga., of wounds received September 20, 1863, at battle of Chickamauga.

### COMPANY E.

David Angle, died March 11, 1865, at Camp Dennison, O.

Wilson Huggins, died November 28, 1862, at Louisville, Ky.

Sylvester J. Smith, killed December 15, 1864, in the battle of Nashville.

Philip Bainter, died August 14, 1864, at Nashville, Tenn., of wounds received in the battle near Kenesaw Mountain, Ga., June 26, 1864.

John F. Armstrong, died at Chattanooga, Tenn., November 16, 1864.

Charles Beagle, died April 19, 1864, at Logan, O.

Joseph C. Beery, died June 19, 1864, in Andersonville Prison, Ga.

William M. Bryan, captured December 31, 1862, at battle of Stone River; died February 15, 1863, in Rebel Prison at Knoxville, Tenn.

Hiram Buck, died January 31, 1863, at Nashville, Tenn.

John Call, died June 28, 1863, at Nashville, Tenn.

Isaac Carpenter, killed in the battle of Stone River, December 31, 1862.

James S. Freeborne, died January 24, 1863, at Nashville, Tenn.

James Good, died February 15, 1863, at Nashville, Tenn., of wounds received December 31, 1862, in battle of Stone River.

Daniel A. Horn, died June 14, 1863, at Nashville, Tenn.

Andrew Leohman, died January 8, 1863, at Nashville, Tenn.

Josiah Luker, killed December 15, 1864, in the battle of Nashville.

Albert Morris, died February 15, 1863, at Nashville, Tenn., of wounds received December 31, 1862, in the battle of Stone River.

Henry S. Sherrick, died October 25, 1863, at Chattanooga, Tenn., of wounds received September 19, 1863, in the battle of Chickamauga.

Daniel Smith, died January 11, 1863, at Nashville, Tenn., of wounds received December 31, 1862, in battle of Stone River.

Thomas Stewart, died at Nashville, Tenn., August 11, 1863.

William Strite, died April 14, 1864, at Ooltewah, Tenn.

Calvan Thornton, died January 17, 1863, at Nashville, Tenn.

John N. Thornton, died January 5, 1863, at Nashville, Tenn.

Benjamin Vannatta, died November 14, 1862, at Danville, Ky.

Lewis Leohman, died February 1, 1864, in Rebel Prison, at Richmond, Va.

### COMPANY F.

Captain Thomas Rains, killed near Atlanta, Ga., August 19, 1864.

Nelson A. Patterson, died October 10, 1863, at Chattanooga, Tenn., of wounds received in battle of Chickamauga, September 19, 1863.

Amos S. Leist, killed June 27, 1864, in the battle of Kenesaw Mountain, Ga.

Andrew J. Cochran, died January 24, 1863, at Nashville, Tenn.

John W. Helvering, died January 13, 1864, in Pickaway County, O.

James W. Loyd, died December 26, 1862, at Nashville, Tenn.

James Briggs, died January 22, 1863, at Nashville, Tenn.

William Craybill, died January 25, 1863, at Nashville, Tenn.

William Eby, killed June 21, 1864, in action near Kenesaw Mountain, Ga.

Aaron H. Ecord, captured August 29, 1864, in action near Atlanta, Ga.; exchanged; perished by the explosion of Steamer Sultana, on the Mississippi River, near Memphis, Tenn., April 27, 1865.

Samuel B. Erskins, died December 14, 1862, at Nashville, Tenn.

John N. Flowers, died August 20, 1863, at Nashville, Tenn.

William M. Hagler, died January 3, 1863, at Nashville, Tenn.

John Haskins, killed June 10, 1864, in action near Pine Mountain, Ga.

David Lindsey, died at Cripple Creek, Tenn. March 27, 1863.

John Lister, captured September 20, 1863, at battle of Chickamauga; died in Rebel Prison at Danville, Va., December 17, 1863.

John McAllister, died June 26, 1863, at Nashville, Tenn.

John C. Moffitt, killed September 19, 1863, in battle of Chickamauga.

Almer Porter, killed December 31, 1862, in battle of Stone River.

Frank Rector, died January 5, 1863, at Nashville, Tenn., of wounds received in the battle of Stone River, December 31, 1862.

John P. Rector, died November 27, 1862, at Bowling Green, Ky.

Isaiah Smith, died January 7, 1863, at Nashville, Tenn.

William Tarbill, missing December 31, 1862, in the battle of Stone River. No further record.

William Taylor, died February 9, 1863, at Murfreesboro, Tenn.

Andrew J. Timmons, captured December 31, 1862, battle of Stone River; exchanged; died February 16, 1863, at Aanapolis, Md.

Purnell Timmons, died December 8, 1862, at Danville, Ky.

John Tully, died January 16, 1863, at Nashville, Tenn.

COMPANY G.

William K. Martin, died February 7, 1863, at Nashville, Tenn.

Isaac N. Hood, killed at the battle of Chickamauga, September 19, 1863.

Alva D. Eveland, died June 7, 1863, at Camp Dennison, O.

George P. Kelch, died September 12, 1865, at Camp Stanley, Tex.

William Ankrum, killed in the battle of Stone River, December 31, 1862.

William Bowers, died February 10, 1863, at Nashville, Tenn.

Charles C. Brown, died June 22, 1863, at Louisville, Ky.

Harrison Burley, died August 28, 1863, at Nashville, Tenn.

John English, died January 21, 1863, at Murfreesboro, Tenn., of wound received December 31, 1862, in battle of Stone River.

Edwin R. M. Green, died October 22, 1862, at Louisville, Ky.

George Harkless, killed December 31, 1862, at the battle of Stone River.

Philip Harkless, died August 2, 1864, at Nashville, Tenn., of wounds received June 27, 1864, at battle of Kenesaw Mountain.

Josiah Hart, died August 24, 1863, at Louisville, Ky.

John T. Hiles, died March 10, 1863, on steamer *en route* from Louisville to Cincinnati.

John W. Heinlein, died January 10, 1863, at Nashville, Tenn.

Simon Hoffman, died January 20, 1863, at Murfreesboro, Tenn., of wounds received in the battle of Stone River, December 31, 1862.

William Jadwin, killed in the battle of Chickaamauga, September 19, 1863.

Jacob Jadwin, died February 1, 1863, in Erie County, O.

Henry A. Kimball, died at Louisville, Ky., December 21, 1863.

John Mann, died January 18, 1863, at Nashville, Tenn.

Jesse Parks, died November 20, 1862, at Louisville, Ky.

Lyman Potter, died January 6, 1863, at Nashville, Tenn.

Frederick Reynolds, died January 9, 1863, at Murfreesboro, Tenn., of wounds received December 31, 1862, in battle of Stone River.

John Rhodes, died February 2, 1865, at Chicago, Ill.

Joseph Speelman, died January 18, 1863, at Nashville, Tenn.

Samuel Tedrick, killed December 31, 1862, in battle of Stone River.

Henry J. Vicroy, died December 29, 1862, at Nashville, Tenn.

James A. Willemine, died November 9, 1862, at Danville, Ky.

### COMPANY H.

Samuel Harris, died December 16, 1864, at Nashville, Tenn., of wounds received December 15, 1864, in battle of Nashville.

Caleb Barnes, died at Nashville, Tenn., January 27, 1863.

Solomon Axline, died at Somerset, O., April 9, 1863.

Samuel M. Baird, died December 27, 1862, at Nashville, Tenn.

Henry Bowlby, drowned in the Tennessee River at Shellmound, Tenn., September 5, 1863.

Jeriah Chaney, captured at Stone River; exchanged; died February 8, 1863, at Anapolis, Md.

Henry C. Chilcote, died December 12, 1862, at Nashville, Tenn.

William H. Chilcote, died January 27, 1863, at Nashville, Tenn.,

Eli Guffey, died January 31, 1863, at Nashville, Tenn.

Alexander Hook, died April 9, 1863, at Gallatin, Tenn.

Abraham Juniper, died February 2, 1863, at Nashville, Tenn.

Lyman Melick, died November 18, 1862, at Danville, Ky.

Andrew J. Minor, died August 2, 1864, at Vining Station, Ga.

Isaiah J. Potts, died January 13, 1863, at Nashville, Tenn.

Jesse Reelhorn, died December 27, 1862, at Danville, Ky.

James F. Speaks, died November 27, 1862, at Danville., Ky.

John W. Tracy, died December 16, 1862, at Nashville, Tenn.

Samuel Van Horn, died January 11, 1864, at Vicksburg, Miss.

Robert Walker, died December 17, 1864, at Nashville, Tenn., of wounds received December 15, 1864, in the battle of Nashville.

Henry Whitmore, died December 21, 1862, at Nashville, Tenn.

Osias H. Black, died February 20, 1863, at Nashville, Tenn.

COMPANY I.

William Mason, killed December 31, 1862, in the battle of Stone River.

John Homerickhouse, captured September 20, 1863, in the battle of Chickamauga; died December 6, 1863, in Libbey Prison, Richmond, Va.

Thomas Anderson, died at Chattanooga, Tenn., July 14, 1864.

Alvin D. Betz, died February 18, 1863, at Nashville, Tenn.

James S. Church, died at Bremen, O., July 12, 1864, of wounds received June 20, 1864, near Kenesaw Mountain, Ga.

David Crist, died November 17, 1862, near Nashville, Tenn.

Josiah Evans, died February 26, 1863, at Nashville, Tenn.

Joseph Friesner, died November 28, 1862, at Danville, Ky.

David Hamilton, died December 5, 1862, at Nashville, Tenn.

Charles Heller, died May 12, 1863, at Murfreesboro, Tenn.

Enoch Hilyard, died July 6, 1864, at Chattanooga, Tenn.

Clay Leist, killed at Stone River, December 31, 1862.

David McCrillis, died at Cripple Creek, Tenn., February 25, 1863.

Samuel McLaughlin, died November 22, 1862, near Nashville, Tenn.

William Monger, died August 20, 1863, at Nashville, Tenn.

Edward Musser, died November 28, 1862, at Danville, Ky.

Noah Neibling, died February 24, 1863, at Nashville, Tenn.

William Sherwood, died at Chattanooga, Tenn., July 14, 1864.

Aaron Thomas, killed June 27, 1864, in the battle of Kenesaw Mountain, Ga.

Andrew Westenberger, died March 4, 1864, at Nashville, Tenn., of wounds received in battle of Chickamauga, September 20, 1863.

David Westenberger, died February 26, 1863, at Nashville, Tenn.

John Westenberger, died Jan. 1, 1863, at Nashville, Tenn.

Andrew Whitehurst, died March 4, 1863, at Nashville, Tenn.

## COMPANY K.

Henry Harper, died January 27, 1863, of wounds received in the battle of Stone River, December 31, 1862.

John R. Core, killed January 1, 1863, in the battle of Stone River.

Henry Albert, died January 27, 1863, at Louisville, Ky.

Jesse Bunker, died December 10, 1863, at Murfreesboro, Tenn., of wounds received September 19, 1863, in battle of Chickamauga.

Benjamin F. Elliott, died at Cripple Creek, Tenn., April 20, 1863.

John W. Godin, captured at Stone River, December 31, 1862; died February 9, 1863, —.

Elijah Johnson, killed June 22, 1864, in the battle near Kenesaw Mountain, Ga.

David Lively, killed December 31, 1862, in battle of Stone River.

Isaac McKeene, died February 16, 1863, of wounds received at the battle of Stone River, December 31, 1862.

James D. McMahon, died July 13, 1864, of wounds received in battle of Resaca, Ga., May 14, 1864.

Henry Mitchell, missing in battle of Chickamauga. No further record.

Samuel Moyer, died December 23, 1862, at Nashville, Tenn.

Patrick Murphy, died January 3, 1863, of wounds received at the battle of Stone River, December 31, 1862.

Richard Parker, died December 2, 1862, in Fayette County, O.

James H. Parris, killed December 31, 1862, in the battle of Stone River.

Ami Propst, died December 29, 1862, at Nashville, Tenn.

John Propst, died August 20, 1863, at Nashville, Tenn.

John G. Reif, wounded and missing, September 19, 1863, at the battle of Chickamauga. No further record.

William H. Warenburg, died July 1, 1863, at New Albany, Ind.

Jonathan D. Williams, captured at Stone River, December 31, 1862; exchanged; died September 10, 1864, of wounds received September 1, 1864, in the battle of Jonesboro, Ga.

Howard Wimer, died January 7, 1863, of wounds received December 31, 1862, in the battle of Stone River.

Shadrach C. Wroten, died November 14, 1863, at Murfreesboro, Tenn.

Making a total of 234 who were killed or died of disease, and the two who were missing, no doubt died, making the total deaths 236.